W9-BEI-336

PSYCHOLOGICAL CONSULTATION IN PARENTAL RIGHTS CASES

Psychological Consultation in Parental Rights Cases

FRANK J. DYER

THE GUILFORD PRESS
New York London

A Division of Guilford Publications, Inc.
72 Spring Street, New York, NY 10012
http://www.guilford.com

Printed in the United States of America

This book is printed on acid-free paper.

Last digit is print number: 9 8 7 6 5 4 3 2 1

Library of Congress Cataloging-in-Publication Data

Dyer, Frank J.
Psychological consultation in parental rights cases / Frank J. Dyer.
p. cm.
Includes bibliographical references and index.
ISBN 1-57230-474-X (hardcover : acid-free paper)
1. Evidence, Expert—United States. 2. Psychology, Forensic—United States. 3. Parent and child (Law)—United States. 4. Custody of children—United States. I. Title.
KF8965.D94 1999
347.73′67—dc21 99-29101
CIP

In loving memory of my parents,
Frank J. and Frances W. Dyer

Acknowledgments

I wish to express my appreciation to Seymour Weingarten, Editor-in-Chief of The Guilford Press, for his initial acceptance of this project for publication and for his ongoing guidance in the development of the manuscript. The editorial contribution of Rochelle Serwator in improving the organization and clarity of the work and in addressing practical concerns regarding the treatment of clinical material is also gratefully acknowledged. I would like to thank two anonymous reviewers whose comments on several drafts of sections of the project improved the presentation of the research and legal material and led to the inclusion of many additional issues of concern to forensic practitioners. Special thanks are also due to Dr. Joseph T. McCann, whose incisive and scholarly critiques of several chapters provided invaluable guidance from both a psychological and legal perspective. Responsibility for any deficiencies in the present work, of course, rests solely with the author.

About the Author

Frank J. Dyer, PhD, ABPP, is a former member of the New Jersey Board of Psychological Examiners and served as Chair of the Board's committee to develop guidelines for psychological evaluation in child custody/visitation cases. He is currently in private practice in Montclair, New Jersey, and serves as a consultant to a number of state agencies and professional boards. He is coauthor, with Joseph T. McCann, of *Forensic Assessment with the Millon Inventories* (Guilford Press, 1996).

Contents

Introduction

The subject matter of this book goes to the core of what has been termed "family values" in the political rhetoric. Family values, it seems, is one of those terms that is capable of evoking a visceral response without actually having to be defined. This allows for the curious situation of diametrically opposed points of view being advanced under this banner. Up until recently, the notion that the government has the power to sever the sacred blood tie between parents and their children was viciously attacked by "family values" adherents who asserted that the biological family should remain inviolate, no matter what its problems. In fact, there is a great deal of historical support for that position.

Williams (1980) notes that under Roman law, the power of a father over his children was absolute and that even luminaries of the ancient world such as Aristotle and Seneca affirmed the chattel status of children. The Bible contains many passages that justify parents' regarding their offspring as mere objects to be controlled at all costs. Some of the more egregious passages include the following: "Withhold not correction from a child," "Thou shall beat him with a rod and deliver his soul from hell," and "If thou beatest the child with a rod, he shall not die, but shall be saved" (cited in Williams, 1980) This unquestioned right of parents to control their children at all costs, a reflection of the biblical injunction to break children of their evil impulses, led an opponent of a 19th-century British child labor bill to complain that passage of an act regulating child labor threatened the British birthright of parents regarding what the parents could do with their children (Williams, 1980).

Swan (1998) notes that Christian fundamentalist groups teach that the willfulness of children is a primary evil that needs to be extinguished by any means. Children should be hit until they "accept" their punishment, which variously means that the child must be made to cry or else be beaten until he or she stops crying. The child is then expected to express love for the abusing parent through physical affection. Swan cites another religiously oriented child discipline text that advises beating children with implements such as "rods" rather than the hand so that children will regard the hand as an instrument of love. I have heard this rationalization—the superiority of using objects rather than the hand for physical punishment—expressed by parents who categorically deny the abusive nature of their behavior.

DeMause (1980) states that the right of parents to do anything to their children in the interest of controlling the children was virtually unquestioned throughout history. DeMause writes:

> Century after century of battered children grew up and battered their own children in turn. John Milton's wife complained that she hated to hear the cries of his nephews as he beat them. . . . Even infants were often beaten. John Wesley's wife Susannah said of her babies, "when turned a year old (and some before), they were taught to fear the rod and cry softly." Rousseau reported that young babies were often beaten to keep them quiet. An early American mother wrote of her battle with her four-month-old infant: "I whipped him till he was actually black and blue, and until I could not whip him any more, and he never gave up a single inch." (p. 15)

The publicity given to child abuse and neglect over the past two decades, along with the intuitive recognition that abuse and family instability tend to produce extreme psychological problems in children, including delinquency and drug abuse that directly affect society, has resulted in a change of attitude toward termination of parental rights on the part of policy makers. Along with this change of attitude has come a redefinition of the "family values" spin on parental rights away from the sanctity of the blood tie and toward the notion that children have a right to grow up in a family where they can experience physical safety; nurturance; structure; adequate social, emotional, and cognitive stimulation; and positive parental role models.

The Adoption and Safe Families Act of 1997 (Public Law 105-89), signed by President Bill Clinton on November 19, 1997, gives legal support to this revised family values perspective on parental rights. It is now the will of Congress that children in foster care be protected from spending lengthy periods of their childhood in that limbo status and that they be moved toward adoption within a specified time after their initial placement rather than be left to languish in temporary care while state agencies attempt to rehabilitate the children's birth parents. This new act has teeth in the form of power to withhold federal funds from states that do not display an adequate track record for such adoptive placements. Thus, states are now mandated to pursue termination of parental rights much more speedily than was required or done in the past and are now faced with significant sanctions for failing to do so.

Perhaps another factor driving this ratcheting up of the child welfare enforcement standards is the enormous increase in the number of child placements and the extent to which children in the United States are neglected and maltreated. While many placements of children out of the home are occasioned by child abuse, which occurred in roughly 1,000,000 substantiated cases in 1988 (American Humane Association, 1989), and which tends to be the form of child maltreatment that receives the most attention in the media, most foster placements are necessitated by child neglect. In contrast to the situation prevailing even a couple of decades ago, when child neglect was associated primarily with parental alcoholism, mental illness, or physical incapacitation, it is my observation that, at least with inner-city populations, drugs are the primary culprit in most of these cases.

The country's pandemic drug problem has resulted in a noticeable change in case profiles over the past 10 years or so. The typical neglected child who requires placement outside the home is born to a mother who has had no prenatal care and whose drug abuse or dependency results in her spending her welfare grant on drugs rather than on food. In fact, during the last decade there has been an enormous increase in the practice by inner-city storekeepers of redeeming customers' food stamps for cash on a discounted basis, providing even more ready cash for the purchase of drugs. The children are frequently left with inappropriate caretakers or, in many instances, are simply left on their own, while the parents seek drugs in the streets. This explosion of the drug problem has resulted in a corresponding increase in the number of children who are placed out of the home.

Between 1980 and 1989 the number of children in the foster care system rose by 19%, to a total of 360,000 (North American Council on Adoptable Children, 1990). Of the children in placement in 1984, adoption was the planned case goal for 14%, with 11% actually adopted. However, long-term foster care was the planned goal for fully 16% of these children. This produces a combined 30% of children for whom the goal was either long-term or permanent separation from their birth parents, or slightly over 100,000 children. A more recent estimate (Carnegie Corporation of New York, 1994) lists a figure of 460,000 children who are currently in foster care, an increase of 100,000 in 4 years. According to the Child Welfare League of America (1997), there was a 21% increase in children in out-of-home care from 1990 to 1995, with a total of 483,629 children in such placements in 1995. It is obvious that the experience of the events leading to placement, the act of placement itself, and the subsequent forming of new attachments and mourning of lost attachments are all sources of extreme stress for a very significant number of children in the United States, especially for children whose personalities are in the formative stage.

Two things happen when the state takes the extreme action of removing a child from the care of a dysfunctional parent. First, the child is rescued from a situation of physical danger, or threat to its well-being. Second, the child is subjected to a separation from a caretaker with whom he/she may have bonded, even though the caretaker may have been extremely dysfunctional. In the case of children above the age of 6 months, this separation produces adverse psychological effects that are generally outweighed by the prospect of physical protection as a result of the removal. Judges and child care workers, then, have an exquisitely difficult task before them, namely, to protect the child's physical well-being while simultaneously respecting the rights of the birth parents and safeguarding the child's psychological welfare. This volume is intended to offer some guidelines as to the last consideration.

In contrast to the more academic studies of child development and attachment theory in the research literature, the focus of this volume is specifically geared to applications that involve assisting judges, attorneys, mental health professionals, and child protective service workers in making actual placement and permanency decisions about children in the foster care system. I have testified in more than 250 cases in which the termination of parental rights was at issue, a child had been in foster care for an extended period of time, and the state wished to pursue adoption. The courtroom, as may be imagined, is a quite different forum for the exploration of these ideas—quite different from the more dispassionate atmosphere of the psychological laboratory and the refereed psychological journal.

In forensic work one is confined to responding to questions posed by counsel, and occasionally by the judge. The answers depend to some extent upon the appropriateness and relevance of the questions, which roughly half the time are formulated by attorneys who are attempting to impeach the witness. The opinions expressed here about psychological bonding have been tested in the crucible of questioning by hostile counsel for the purpose of undermining their validity (or, failing that, at least their credibility) by boring pinholes into their minutiae and attempting to gouge these pinholes into gaping rents. Needless to say, even the expert who is the most well grounded in theory will on occasion be pushed by the constraints of a simple yes or no response into making apparently contradictory or irreconcilable statements in response to somewhat differently worded questions. The situation of the psychological expert in the termination of parental rights cases is made even more tortuous by the fact that many attorneys who are assigned by the courts to represent indigent birth parents have absolutely no experience whatsoever in this type of case and do not receive adequate training for this new role (Johnson, 1996). Such attorneys go about the business of cross-examining the expert as though they were litigating a property dispute, with the children in question cast in the role of chattel, which, ironically, is the parental view of the children that led in many cases to the children's long-term stay in placement.

The present work attempts to develop a set of ground rules or guidelines for the presentation of scientific evidence in termination cases by formulating specific questions and issues to be addressed in all such cases. This formulation is drawn from a set of concepts emerging from the present state of knowledge regarding the impact of foster care, loss of birth or foster parents, and related factors on the psychological development and mental health of children in placement. The intent is to highlight those issues that should be salient in the direct and cross-examination of expert witnesses and to alert counsel, judges, and experts to red herrings that only serve to obscure matters that are most directly relevant to the child's best interests. It is my conviction that in every case there are core factors that demand consideration and that omission of such factors in the presentation and examination of an expert's testimony deprives the child in question of justice.

In this type of situation in which an expert is attempting, under exceedingly adverse conditions, to apply conclusions that can be legitimately drawn from complex and in some respects recondite theory to a real-world decision, it is easy for attorneys and judges to misunderstand the expert's testimony. This misunderstanding may result from a failure on the expert's part to explain with sufficient clarity or to hide behind jargon or to be dragged into some untenable position through either subtle or sledgehammer cross-examination (in informal legal terminology, "blown out of the water"). It may also result from the fact that the psychological theory under consideration deals with internal mental processes that are not always readily observable in overt behavior. Or it may result from that fact that it may simply not be possible for a nonpsychologist to listen to up to three hours of an expert's citing general theoretical and experimental findings and then to put all that information into the proper perspective as applied to a specific set of facts.

Where there is such misunderstanding, it is certain that the overall impact of the expert's testimony becomes a hindrance rather than a help to judicial decision making and that the failure of communication ultimately works to the detriment of the child in question. On the other hand, expert testimony that covers all of the crucial issues, relates theory and empirical research results to the specifics of the case, and does not go beyond what we can legitimately infer from the existing base of knowledge in the field, as applied to children in placement, can greatly assist the trier of fact in deciding ultimate legal issues. This review of the clinical, empirical, and psycholegal issues pertaining to termination cases is intended to foster the latter sort of testimony, consistent with the standards articulated in *Daubert v. Merrell-Dow Pharmaceuticals, Inc.* (1993).

The present work, intended to serve as a manual for mental health professionals who consult in termination of parental rights cases, necessarily differs from many books in the field of psychology in that the approach is neither exclusively clinical nor exclusively academic/scientific in nature but rather is a hybrid of clinical and scientific perspectives. This approach reflects the unique demands placed upon the forensic psychologist or other mental health professional who consults in termination of parental rights litigation. Above all else, these matters should be considered as clinical cases involving the psychological welfare of one or more children who have typically undergone multiple traumatic experiences stemming from abuse, neglect, and separation or loss. At the same time, psychologists who testify in these cases are expected to provide opinions to the court that are based on something beyond their individual clinical judgment, especially when these witnesses are called upon to render predictions about the consequences of various outcomes for the child. Here, the appropriate standard is that of reasonable psychological certainty, which is, according to one definition, an opinion that is based on substantive clinical observations, well-accepted theory, empirical research results, or an integration of these, and which is clearly not speculative (New Jersey Board of Psychological Examiners, 1993).

Thus, a handbook for mental health consultants in these cases must necessarily address theoretical and empirical research matters, and should do so in a more detached and academic manner than would be characteristic of a purely clinical work. Still, there remain two additional dimensions to the task of preparing a comprehensive manual of practice for consultation in termination cases. First, termination cases are the result of events that take place within a state's child protective services system in interaction with the family court system. Witnesses must understand the workings of this system in order to have an adequate appreciation of the context in which their consultation takes place. Second, there are a number of rules or criteria that need to be absorbed by experts who offer services in this area. These include the ethical standards of the profession as applied to the particular circumstances of abused and neglected children and their birth parents, the rules governing expert testimony, and the statutory and case law relating to child welfare and parental rights issues.

The present work is organized in such a way as to provide an orientation to the social, institutional, ethical, and legal context before addressing theory, research, and clinical practice. First, there are some general remarks concerning the child welfare system: how intervention is triggered, what types of problems child welfare systems address, case management strategies, how the court monitors the adequacy of the social services agency's assistance to the birth parent and the birth parent's compliance with the case plan, and at what stage the state moves to terminate the rights of the birth parents. To provide an orientation for mental health professionals, with special consideration of various pitfalls that invalidate expert testimony, there follows a discussion of basic legal issues and of proposed model legislation relating to termination cases. It is especially important for mental health professionals to be knowledgeable about termination issues from the legal standpoint, as it is frequently the case that such professionals are engaged by attorneys who are inexperienced in these matters and who are representing birth parents on a pro bono basis. Given the circumstances of the involvement of these lawyers, it is not unusual for them to rely heavily on experts for guidance in preparing certain aspects of the case. The present work also analyzes recent federal legislation, signed into law in November 1997, that mandates facilitation of termination of parental rights based on factors such as the age of the child and the chronicity of the family's problems.

From the perspective of the requirements of the expert's own discipline, the present volume explores ethical issues in consultation, primarily drawn from psychologists' codes of ethics and other psychological guidelines. These cases tend to have their own particular issues of confidentiality, professional competence, informed consent, and other ethical considerations, apart from the purely legal aspects of the case. The ethical issues in termination cases are differentiated from those in divorce/custody matters, which, although similar in some respects, tend to be confused by both mental health experts and judges who lack experience in this area.

Discussed in detail are the requirements of the psychological examination of parties in termination cases, including individual assessments of birth parents and children as well as bonding assessments of the children with birth parents and with foster parents or other caretakers. Factors that differentiate these examinations from ordinary clinical examinations are the forensic psychological guidelines on the use of psychometric instruments in court and the recent changes in federal rules of evidence governing scientifically based expert testimony. Testing and interviewing techniques in termination evaluations are discussed in depth, as well as the question of whether specific measures of child abuse potential and parenting skills are more appropriate than are general psychological assessment instruments in this setting.

The principal theoretical issues in child welfare cases are discussed with specific reference to their application in termination cases. Particular attention is given to the controversy surrounding the work of Goldstein, Freud, and Solnit (1979), whose theoretical views, translated into model legislation to terminate rights, have informed professional practice for many years. Various theoretical views from the psychoanalytic camp are explored to provide a picture of the impact of traumatic separations, losses, and deprivation on personality development in young children. Attachment theory, which is perhaps the most widely cited theory in termination cases, is discussed in depth. Although cognitive theory is conspicuously silent on developmental issues, a perspective derived from that school of thought is offered regarding children's reactions to disruption and loss.

The empirical literature on the psychological consequences of children's separation and parental object loss is reviewed from the standpoint of the presentation of these findings in court. Proceeding from the most impressionistic set of findings, namely, those derived from intensive psychotherapy with adults who recalled their childhood experiences, the review moves toward the most scientifically rigorous studies that employed comparison groups and appropriate statistical techniques and that employed both retrospective and longitudinal methodology. The review provides research evidence in support of predictions regarding future vulnerability to psychopathology, disturbed capacity for emotional intimacy, and poor prognosis for parenting the next generation associated with the experience of loss and separation during childhood.

Standards for scientific evidence in court are discussed, with particular reference to the types of clinical and scientific issues that crop up in termination hearings. Addressed also is the unique status of the psychological or other mental health expert as one who typically presents a blend of rigorous scientific research findings and clinical impressions based upon specialized or technical knowledge. And the present work covers other expert witness topics, including credentialing (*voir dire*), expectations relating to the role of the expert witness, and coping with frequently asked cross-examination questions, especially relating to attachment issues.

In many termination cases there are special issues that provide additional dimensions of expert testimony and attack upon that testimony in the form of cross-examination. Concerns among African

American professional groups over the phenomenon of transracial adoption are not sufficiently appreciated by most professionals working in this area. Position statements by the National Association of Black Social Workers on this topic are discussed, along with current legislative changes and empirical research findings regarding transracial adoption. Gay and lesbian foster and adoptive parenting of children in the care of the state has recently come to receive legal recognition. This highly charged situation is explored, sometimes involving death threats from birth parents to gay foster parents and to the caseworkers who placed children with them. The state of the current empirical literature on gay and lesbian parenting capacity and the effects on children who are reared in same-sex relationship families are examined, particularly as these issues relate to termination actions.

The legal, ethical, clinical, and scientific topics treated in the text provide the focus for a series of case studies. These studies run the gamut from birth parents with various sorts of chronic impairments that disqualify them from rearing their children to cases of children who have formed an attachment to substitute caretakers and who resist any contact with birth parents, or who retain a strong emotional tie to the absent birth parent despite placement into foster care, or who have been so damaged by the foster care system that no new intimate attachment is possible. One highly publicized case involving abrupt removal of a preschool child from adoptive parents is analyzed in light of the above issues.

In general, termination of parental rights cases can be viewed along two major axes. The first of these is a parental fitness versus child's attachment profile dimension. In some termination cases the salient issue is that of the fitness of the birth parent, making considerations of the child's attachment pattern irrelevant. These birth parents present an extremely poor prognosis for fitness by virtue of (1) extended incarceration that precludes them from caring for a child until at least adolescence; (2) chronic, severe mental illness that is poorly controlled with medication; (3) intractable drug addiction; or (4) tendencies toward abuse or neglect that cannot be modified through any sort of social service, educational, or psychological intervention. The state's burden here is to demonstrate this clinical picture to the court and to relate it to predicted outcomes were the child reunified with such a caretaker.

At the other pole are cases in which the child's attachment profile is the salient issue. Here, the birth parents may be rehabilitated to the point where they could be expected to function at least marginally as a caretaker for the child, but the child has developed an attachment to the foster parents or other substitute caretakers. In the case of young children or children who have special needs that render them especially vulnerable to separation and loss, the removal from their attachment figures would inflict a devastatingly traumatic loss with profound implications for their future personality development and mental health. In such cases the state must demonstrate that the birth parents' rehabilitation has come too late, that the best interests of the child would be harmed by a return of custody, and that the only guarantee of the child's future psychological well-being is termination of parental rights in order to permit adoption by the child's attachment figures. At both poles of this axis the case turns on predictions by mental health experts.

The other major axis along which it is useful to view termination cases is that of the child's age. Cases involving children who are still in the preschool years present dramatically different issues from those involving children above 8 years of age, especially adolescents. Preschool children are still in the process of personality formation, and their day-to-day interactions with caretakers provide the raw material, as it were, for identifications, emotional connections, and attitudes that shape their sense of themselves, capacity for mood regulation, anxiety tolerance, impulse control, basic trust, self-confidence and optimism, and behavior in future intimate relationships. Further, young children lack the capacity for mature cognitive processing of events in their lives and are thus unable to understand circumstances such as their having two sets of mommies and daddies, one foster and one natural. They may not be able to comprehend interview questions pertaining to visitation and permanent living arrangements. With older children, there is a likelihood that the child has spent a significant portion of his or her childhood with the birth parent and has developed an attachment of some type (although this might be a trauma bond that is psychologically destructive to the child, as discussed in Chapter 8).

Bush and Goldman (1982) found that, in many instances, an older child will identify with a birth parent's family to such a degree that the older child will resist the idea of adoption as something that would rob him or her of this core component of personal identity. Frequently there are loyalty conflicts in older children who may feel guilty because they experience adoption as a rejection of a birth parent. Finally, older children's personalities are for the most part fully structured, and their cognitive capacities resemble those of mature adults, enabling them to evaluate their circumstances in a fairly realistic manner, with their perceptions of their situations in many cases being isomorphic with those of the adults who are involved with them (Bush & Goldman, 1982). Thus, the psychological interventions, including placement recommendations, that best safeguard the mental health of older children, especially adolescents in placement, are quite different from those that would apply to younger, especially preschool, children in substitute care.

The passage of the Adoption and Safe Families Act represents a sea change in the area of adoption and termination of parental rights. There is now a deemphasis on the child's biological ties as a criterion for deciding that child's future, and there is a turn toward an assessment of the birth parents' fitness and the child's attachment profile. The Adoption and Safe Families Act mandates permanent placement of children in foster care according to strict time guidelines, protecting such children from spending their childhood in an odyssey through temporary foster placements. The push toward adoption of foster children, however, entails coming to grips with the issue of terminating parental rights in order to free the child. The present work is intended to serve as a manual, to provide a framework for professional consultation in these cases. Its aim is to guide professionals toward a scientifically and ethically based practice in working toward termination in cases in which such action is warranted while at the same time guaranteeing birth parents due process and competent, objective assessment of their situation and that of their children. Although this is not intended as a legal text and although I make no claim to expertise in that area beyond the collateral knowledge of pertinent legal issues appropriate for a forensic psychologist, my book should provide an adequate orientation to the general legal issues for assigned attorneys who may not have had any experience with family court matters. The book will also serve to acquaint attorneys with the role of experts in termination cases and with the state of professional practice and science upon which the experts' testimony is based. For psychologists and other mental health professionals working in this area, this book is intended to serve as a *vade mecum* in the consultation room and on the witness stand, proceeding as it does, not from the heights of the ivory tower, but from the depths of the trenches. Additionally, it is my hope that by including both psychological and legal perspectives on a complex topic that at times demands Solomonic wisdom on the part of decision makers, this book will be able to contribute structure and direction to the debate on child welfare issues within the professions of law and psychology, with the unique insights of each permitting broader and more incisive analysis among practitioners and scholars of both disciplines.

CHAPTER 1

Background to a Termination Action

The filing of an action to terminate the rights of a birth parent to a child is the culmination of a lengthy process that is governed by statute, case law, and public policy considerations at every stage. The goal of child protective services involvement with families is not to separate birth parents from their children, but to intervene to protect a child in such a way as to produce the least disruption in the child's life and to preserve the family structure if possible. As noted in Chapter 3, the tide is turning away from an emphasis upon preservation of parental rights at all costs and toward the facilitation of adoption, with required termination of parental rights, in cases in which a child has been in placement for two years, and in some cases less than that, or in which a child in placement is an infant. Nevertheless, the filing of a termination action is an extreme step that must be preceded by a number of negative events signaling that a child's needs would best be served by a permanent placement outside the family. There are strong legal protections for the rights of birth parents, and it is only at the point where the birth parent has failed the child repeatedly or has placed the child in grave danger or has been convicted of inflicting a life-threatening injury that the case reaches the point where a termination action is filed.

This chapter reviews the events leading up to a termination of parental rights action, from the initial reporting to the final hearing. Issues in reporting suspected abuse and neglect are discussed, including confidentiality, duty to report, and national child abuse/neglect data banks. The scope of the problem of abuse and neglect is presented through statistics that cover incidence of various types of cases, rates of placement outside the home, and other recent data. The discussion turns to specific types of abuse and neglect, including some medical indications for differentiating abusive from accidental injuries. The long legal road to termination is examined, from the initial removal of the child and the show-cause hearing through adjudicative and review hearings, with the responsibilities of birth parents, social service agencies, and others defined. Due process issues are explored. The chapter concludes with an examination of aspects of the termination hearing.

CHILD-ABUSE-REPORTING STATUTES

The initial step in the legal process occurs when there is a report of harm to a child. This may take the form of a neighbor who reports the sounds of a child who is screaming, a school nurse who reports that bruises have been discovered on a child at school, police who report that very young children have been discovered alone in an apartment, or a hospital social worker who reports that a child has been born with cocaine in his or her system. State laws on reporting of suspected child abuse or neglect are typically very strict. Professionals including physicians, teachers, social workers, and licensed mental health professionals are required to report suspected cases of abuse or neglect within a specified period of time and can be held liable for subsequent harm to the child caused by their failure to make such a report.

Child-abuse-reporting laws typically supersede any confidentiality provisions of the laws and regulations governing the professions. In some jurisdictions laypersons also have a legal duty to report cases in which they have a good faith suspicion of child abuse or neglect, and failure to make such a report is a disorderly persons offense. Persons who file a child abuse report are usually protected against suit for reporting (Faller & Stone, 1981); however, state statutes cannot extend immunity against suits for deprivation of constitutional rights in suits filed in federal court under federal statutes and the United Sates Constitution (Duquette, 1981b). Persons who report suspected abuse (other than professionals who have mandated reporting responsibilities) can chose to have their identity remain confidential. Faller and Stone (1981) note, however, that this anonymity provision of reporting law proves to be a false safeguard if the case proceeds to court. In such a case, the reporting party may be compelled to testify under subpoena in a hearing where the birth parent or other alleged abuser is present.

Several writers on the topic of child abuse reporting stress the ambiguity of these situations and note that the fact that there is no uniform definition of abuse that differentiates it from overdiscipline creates many problems (Faller & Stone, 1981; Melton, Petrila, Poythress, & Slobogin, 1987; Myers, 1997; Duquette, 1981a).

INCIDENCE OF ABUSE, REPORTING, LEGAL ACTION

Faller and Stone (1981) note that less than half of the initial referrals received by state child protective services result in the opening of a case. Duquette (1981b) states that in approximately 10–15% of opened cases there is court action filed by the state either to protect the child from immediate danger or to ensure the cooperation of birth parents in efforts to rehabilitate them. As of this writing, the most recent information available (Child Welfare League of America [CWLA], 1997) shows a 27% increase in the number of children reported as abused and neglected per 1,000 children in the population, from 33 per 1,000 in 1986 to 42 per 1,000 in 1995. Of these, the numbers of children per 1,000 children in the population with *substantiated* reports of abuse or neglect in 1995 varied from 2.3 children per 1,000 in Pennsylvania to 37.9 children per 1,000 in Alaska, with a median of 12.6 children. (The study notes that the extremely low number for Pennsylvania is due to a major difference in reporting practices.) Myers (1997) cites a figure of 2½ million reports of child maltreatment annually, with half of these involving abuse and half involving neglect.

The CWLA (1997) study also notes that in some states, such as Texas, over half of the cases of children reported as being abused or neglected are not referred for a formal investigation. Further, a median of 2.3 children per 1,000 in the population were removed from their homes in 1995 because of abuse and neglect; and of every 1,000 children who were reported as being abused or neglected in 1995, only 49 children were removed on average. Thus, it appears that less than 5% of initial referrals of child abuse or neglect result in any type of legal action; and according to the most recent statistics, only about 5% of reported children were removed from their homes (CWLA, 1997). It should be noted, however, that there is a rather wide variation among states in the number of reported children who were subsequently removed, ranging from 6.8 per 1,000 in Alabama to 163.9 in Pennsylvania.

Although the actual numbers of children who are placed outside the home are low, even among children who are reported for abuse or neglect, the stakes are quite high in these cases. The CWLA (1997) study reports that in 1995 there was a median of 1.4 deaths per 1,000 children in the population due to maltreatment, as compared to a median of maltreatment-related fatalities of 1.8 children per 1,000 in the population in 1990. A survey by the National Committee to Prevent Child Abuse (1997, cited in CWLA, 1997) found that of children who died between 1994 and 1996, 41% had contact with child protective services. Myers (1997) reports that in 1990 approximately 1,211 children died from abuse or neglect, and that from 1985 to 1990 reported fatalities increased by 38% nationwide. Myers also notes that official reports probably underestimate the number of fatalities and that the true statistic is probably closer to 5,000 deaths each year, or one every 2 hours. Ninety percent of abuse fatalities involve children below age 5 years (Myers, 1997).

According to the CWLA, there was a 21% increase in children in out-of-home care from 1990 to 1995, with a total of 483,629 children in such placements in 1995. Of the children who left care in 1995, the median number of months spent in foster care was 11. Of the children who remained in care in 1995, the median number of months spent in foster care was 22.1. Thus, the typical foster child who leaves care in any one year has spent somewhat under a year in placement, and the typical foster child who remains in care in any one year has spent somewhat under 2 years in placement. Most foster care placements are short term. Further, those children who eventually end up adopted represent a small fraction of the population. There has been absolutely no change in this statistic from 1987 to 1995, with 1.9 out of every 1,000 children in the population adopted in each of those years.

Termination of parental rights to permit adoption of a child therefore represents the end of a very long road on which an extremely small fraction of birth parents are forced by circumstances to travel.

TYPES OF CHILD ABUSE AND NEGLECT

Duquette (1981a) notes that the definition of child abuse for reporting purposes is different from and much broader than legal standards that empower a court to take coercive action regarding the child in question. Duquette states that in many cases, the interpretation of child abuse actually requires an outright value judgment on the part of the judge, who must decide whether the behaviors alleged against the parents violate the community's minimum standard of child care. In such cases there is a two-pronged test: not only must the facts of the case be proven true, but the facts as proven must violate normative community standards of child rearing. Duquette cites the examples of a parent's leaving an 8-year-old girl alone for 4 hours and a parent's administering a spanking that leaves bruises on the child's buttocks as falling within this indeterminate area of abuse and as being subject to local child-rearing norms that designate abuse or neglect.

In many states, such as New York, the abuse standard is one of inflicting physical injury by other than accidental means, and in Utah an abused child is one who has suffered or has been threatened with nonaccidental physical or mental harm (Myers, 1997). Courts generally consider the child's age, type of discipline inflicted, the means used, and the degree of bodily injury or pain inflicted in deciding whether corporal punishment exceeds "reasonable" limits. Myers also notes that in some states, such as Washington, the law provides that the juvenile court shall not interfere with reasonable discipline, including corporal punishment and that in several states "reasonable discipline" is actually a defense against criminal prosecution in these matters. Swan (1998) states that 41 states have religious exemptions from civil child abuse or neglect charges and that 31 states have religious exemptions from one or more types of criminal charges. Swan notes that Iowa and Ohio offer a religious defense for manslaughter. Both Delaware and West Virginia have religious defenses for the murder of a child, and Oregon has a religious defense for homicide by abuse.

There are many types of abuse or neglect that can result in the referral of a child to the local child protective services authorities. These types broadly fall into four distinct categories: physical abuse, sexual abuse, emotional abuse, and neglect. Faller, Bowden, Jones, and Hildebrandt (1981) catalog the various types of physical abuse about which there is no need for judicial deliberation as to whether prevailing community standards have been violated. Most common evidences of physical abuse are bruises, abrasions, lacerations, and scars. Myers notes that the most common site for accidental bruises is skin overlying bony prominences, such as knees and shins. Bruises of the forehead are also common, especially in young children. There are several types of injuries that arouse the suspicion of child abuse. For example, it is uncommon for children to have accidental bruises on the buttocks, back of the legs, or back. Also bruises of the mouth, cheeks, vulva, and rectal area should be considered as nonaccidental. Bruises around the mouth and injuries inside the mouth in infants are likely to be nonaccidental, as well as bruises behind the ear (Faller et al., 1981). Myers (1997) also notes that bruises on the abdomen and other soft tissue areas, particularly the inner thighs, are suspicious. Genital or inner thigh bruises are sometimes inflicted as punishment for toileting accidents (Myers, 1997).

Faller et al. (1981) also note that objects used to inflict injuries on children leave telltale signs, such as loop marks from cords used to administer beatings, hand prints from slaps, parallel linear marks from belts, and grasp marks from forcibly holding children down. Human bites leave crescent or oval shapes. Myers (1997) states that in cases where the caretaker alleges that a bite mark was inflicted by another child, it is possible for physicians or dentists to distinguish a child-inflicted bite from one inflicted by an adult. If the distance between the canines is greater than 3 centimeters, then the bite is that of an adult (Kessler & Hyden, 1991, cited in Myers, 1997).

Faller et al. (1981) state that linear, parallel, or crescent-shaped marks along the back, thighs, or buttocks may be found several days after a whipping with a belt, switch, or cord. Scars, marks, and blemishes of various sorts are found in all children; however, those that are inflicted as a result of child abuse have certain distinctive characteristics. Round scars may signal cigarette burns (Faller et al., 1981). Myers (1997) notes that adults often have cigarettes in hand during times of stress and may inflict deep, circular cigarette burns on their children, most often on the hands and arms, and usually multiple. The injury that results when a child brushes against a lighted cigarette held by an adult is usually single, shallow, and not circular. Myers states that burns are commonly inflicted as punishment, particularly in children under 3 years of age. Toilet training mishaps may be punished by immersion of the child in scalding water, which serves the purpose of both a cleaning and a punishment. Myers notes that, in contrast to a situation in which an unrestrained child accidentally enters a tub of scalding water and naturally thrashes around, creating splash burns with blurred margins, a restrained child's tub burns will have clear margins. Myers also states that accidental contact burns, such as glancing contact with a stove or iron, may be differentiated from deliberately inflicted burns, as the latter result in steady contact that causes deep symmetrical imprints with crisp margins. Crescent-shaped scars along the flank or buttocks may be the result of beatings with a belt. Also, large scars signaling major injuries that were never treated should arouse concern. Myers notes that diagnosis of abuse is often made on the basis of cumulative suspicious injuries, as normal healthy children are unlikely to suffer one suspicious injury after another.

Faller et al. (1981) state that there are certain types of fractures that are abuse related as opposed to accidentally incurred. They note that babies under a year of age seldom sustain accidental fractures, as they are not active enough to do things that would cause a fracture. Also, in contrast to many reports of abusive parents to the effect that the parents did not notice their infant's fracture because the child showed no signs of discomfort, it is extremely uncommon for an infant with a fracture not to register discomfort. Such parents not only deny any knowledge of their child's injuries but also delay seeking medical treatment for the child until the condition becomes frightening.

The most common type of fracture that occurs in toddlers is the greenstick variety, in which one side of a bone is broken and the other bent. This type of fracture may occur when a child is jerked with considerable force or when a limb is twisted (Faller et al., 1981). Myers (1997) notes that a hallmark of the battered child syndrome is multiple fractures at different stages of healing. Myers (1997) also states that fractures are most often caused by direct blows, twisting, shaking, and squeezing, often with a discrepancy between the parent's explanation of the injury and the mechanism required for its production. Both Faller et al. (1981) and Myers (1997) note that spiral fractures, in which the bone is twisted until it breaks, are commonly encountered nonaccidental fractures.

Head and brain injuries may result from (1) skull fracture, (2) depressed fracture where bone fragments have been pressed down into the bone cavity (requiring a severe blow such as might result from a blunt instrument or automobile accident or fall from an upper story), (3) concussion resulting from a violent jar or whiplash, or (4) epidural and subdural hematomas in which blood collects either between the skull and the dura or between the dura and the brain following a severe jolt or shaking that causes veins to rupture. Faller et al. (1981) note that subdural hematomas are a common result of shaking an infant, especially an infant who does not yet have head control. There is usually increased head circumference in an infant whose skull bones have not yet fused. Retinal hemorrhages are a common result of shaking an infant. Myers (1997) notes that shaken baby syndrome is an accepted medical diagnosis and is so well recognized that it should not be subjected to either the *Frye* (*Frye v. United States*, 1923) test or *Daubert* (*Daubert v. Merrell-Dow Pharmaceuticals*, 1993) standards for admissibility of scientific evidence.

The validity of shaken baby syndrome was recently challenged in the case of *Commonwealth v. Woodward* (1997), involving a British nanny who was convicted of second-degree murder in the death of the 8-month-old boy for whom she was caring. The defense argument was that the defendant had merely been rough with the victim and had not shaken him violently. The judge, in reducing the conviction from second-degree murder to involuntary manslaughter, wrote in his decision that the defendant had become rough with the baby and that "the roughness was sufficient to start (or restart) a bleeding that escalated fatally." One pediatrician, Dr. Randell Alexander, quoted in a *New York Times* article (Goldberg, 1997), stated that it is not bleeding that kills a shaken baby but rather the swelling of its brain tissue that puts pressure on regions of the brain that control vital functions. This type of massive swelling can only result from a massive injury, according to Dr. Alexander.

Goldberg (1997) states that shaken baby syndrome is estimated to result in 300 deaths per year as well as in hundreds of nonfatal injuries per year among children under 2 years of age. Faller et al. (1981) and Myers (1997) state that injury to the brain and head is the most common cause of death from child abuse.

Myers (1997) notes that skull and brain injuries are often caused by a hitting a child with a blunt instrument, such as a fist, or by throwing a child against the wall or floor. Myers states that in many cases of serious head injury the caretaker will state that the injury was caused by an accidental fall from a bed, couch, or crib. He cites a study by Helfer, Slovis, and Black (1977) who demonstrated that none of a sample of 246 young children who accidentally fell from cribs and beds had a serious injury and that only 1% had a skull fracture and another 1% had a fracture at some other site. Eighty percent of these children were completely uninjured. Myers (1997) cites another study (Chadwick, Chin, Salerno, Landsverk, & Kitchen, 1991) that found that a life-threatening head injury requires at least a 15-foot fall.

Faller et al. (1981) note that such internal injuries as crushing injuries to the chest that damage the heart and lungs are usually accompanied by fractured ribs. A blow to the abdomen, however, may not cause any superficial bruising of the skin. In fact, bruises over the abdomen are not common even with major abdominal injury (Kessler & Hyden, 1991, quoted in Myers, 1992). In such cases, however, the liver or spleen may be damaged or bleeding or an obstruction may be created in the intestinal tract. Such injuries typically occur when an adult hits or kicks a child or infant in the chest or abdomen. Kessler and Hyden (1991) report that a blow-out rupture of a hollow organ such as the stomach or intestine is the most common abdominal injury and that children with such injuries, usually under the age of 2 years, are typically treated later than are victims of accidental abdominal injuries. Myers (1992) states that rib fractures commonly result when a young child is grabbed around the chest and shaken. Myers (1992) also states that the amount of force to rupture an internal organ or to compress an organ against the spinal column is considerable, sometimes equating it to the type of force that would result from a 50- or 60-mile-per-hour head-on collision if sustained in an automobile accident. Chest and abdominal injuries are a particularly alarming child abuse phenomenon, as the morbidity rate is quite high. Myers (1992) reports that 50% of children with such injuries do not survive them.

Myers (1992) states that neglect can involve the failure to provide a child with the basic necessities, including food, clothing, shelter, education, and medical care, as well as a failure to protect the child from maltreatment inflicted by others. In the case of medical neglect, religious belief is often the central factor underlying the parental behavior. Myers (1992) quotes an Arizona case, *Matter of Appeal in Cochise County Juvenile Action* (1982), regarding the conflict between child welfare and religious belief: "If there is a direct collision of a child's right to good health and a parent's religious beliefs, the parent's rights must give way." Myers (1992) notes that courts have permitted child protective services to intervene in cases in which parents attempt to prevent a child from receiving a blood transfusion or other essential medical care.

The failure to provide an abused child with medical care for the abuse-related injuries constitutes an additional element of intentional neglect, according to Myers (1997). Citing the case of *People v. Steinberg* (1992), Myers notes that the defendant, an attorney acting as the child's father, failed to obtain medical care for the 6-year-old-female victim who was unconscious as a result of severe head injuries that she sustained while in the defendant's care. The defendant argued that only a person with medical knowledge could intentionally cause serious injury to a child by failing to obtain medical care. The New York Court of Appeals rejected this argument, noting that there are situations in which the need for immediate medical care would be obvious to anyone, situations such as a 6-year-old girl who was lying unconscious after a blunt head trauma. It is noted that this decision was in connection with homicide charges against the defendant and was not related to any termination of parental rights action.

Nonorganic failure to thrive is a condition caused by extreme parental neglect of an infant (Myers, 1992). It is related to a diagnosis of reactive attachment disorder of infancy or early childhood according to the criteria of the fourth edition of the *Diagnostic and Statistical Manual of Mental Disorders* (DSM-IV), and has also been described in the literature as psychosocial dwarfism. As the basis for a termination of parental rights action, Myers (1992) cites several cases relating to an infant's nonorganic failure to thrive.

Another frequent cause for intervention of child protective services is the administration of drugs to children by adults. Myers (1992), citing Schwartz (1989), states:

> When crack cocaine or marijuana is being smoked by adults in confined spaces such as closed rooms or cars, children may inhale the smoke and be harmed. . . . When irresponsible adolescents or young adults are intoxicated, they may, as a kind of sadistic "amusement," deliberately blow puffs of marijuana smoke into the noses or open mouths of crying irritable infants to sedate them. (p. 185)

Myers (1997) notes that the failure to protect a child from maltreatment by others can constitute neglect. Beyond that, Myers (1997) also states, "A parent who knows his or her child is being abused by another adult, but who does nothing to protect the child, can be prosecuted under statutes expressly criminalizing such behavior, or under general principles of accomplice liability" (p. 363).

Citing *West Virginia Department of Health v. Doris S.* (1996), Myers (1997) notes that parental rights can be terminated where it is shown that severe physical abuse of a child has occurred and the parents, even in the face of knowledge of the abuse, have taken no action to identify the abuser. In my practice, the State of New Jersey pursued a termination action against birth parents whose 6-month-old infant presented at a hospital emergency room with 22 fractures in various stages of healing. The birth mother fled the hospital upon learning that the physician intended to contact child protective services. Neither parent offered any theory as to the cause of the child's injuries, and the parents expressed skepticism at the diagnosis of multiple fractures, declaring it to be impossible. In another case, a schizoid, depressed woman was present when, according to the testimony of the older children in the family, her paramour threw one of the younger children onto the floor and abused the child in other ways on multiple occasions. This birth mother did not intervene in any manner when witnessing these brutal assaults and was therefore found guilty of child endangerment.

Conte (1991) asserts that sexual abuse of children is quite common and that sexual abuse is underreported. Conte cites one study that found that only 2% of incestuous abuse in a random sample of San Francisco households had ever been reported to the authorities. The widespread incidence of child sexual abuse is corroborated indirectly by a study of offenders performed by Abel et al. (1987), who report that a sample of 158 incestuous pedophiles who targeted female children had a total of 286 victims and that 44 incestuous pedophiles who targeted male children had a total of 75 victims. While less relevant to the present discussion, the Abel et al. statistics on nonincestuous pedophiles are of considerable interest. The sample of 224 nonincestuous pedophiles studied in that research who targeted female children had a total of 4,435 victims, while the comparable figure for a sample of 155 nonincestuous pedophiles who targeted males was an astounding 29,981 victims.

Conte (1991) lists a number of the most common forms of child sexual abuse. These include not only the perpetrator's exhibiting himself or herself in front of the victim, fondling the victim, having heterosexual or homosexual intercourse with the victim, performing oral sex on the victim, masturbating in front of the victim, and photographing the victim nude or in a sexual act, but also inducing or forcing the victim to engage in a sexual act, or to perform oral sex on the perpetrator, to engage in prostitution, or to watch pornography. Conte (1991) notes that children in one study were exposed to an average of 3.5 sexual behaviors and that only 20% of the victims experienced one type of sexual behavior. Conte (1991) also includes the nonsexual elements of sexual abuse as important factors that have additional adverse effects on the child. These elements include coercion, intimidation, manipulation, force and violence, ambivalence, secrecy, lack of control, isolation, blame, betrayal, and loss.

Faller et al. (1981) note that child sexual abuse is often accompanied by physical trauma such as lacerations, bruises, contusions, or bite or sucking marks on the inner thighs, genitals, or anal region. Whether there are any physical and behavioral symptoms specific to child sexual abuse is the subject of great controversy within the profession. This topic is treated in detail in Myers (1997). Finkelhor and Browne (1985) detail the traumatic sequelae of child sexual abuse as it affects children's psychological functioning.

LEGAL ACTION SUBSEQUENT TO OPENING A CASE

If social services personnel feel that a child requires some immediate intervention beyond merely monitoring the home, the usual practice is to initiate litigation against the birth parents or other caretakers. The initial step in the litigation process is the drafting of a petition by the state that asks the court to exercise its power over a certain child (Duquette, 1981a). The petition must state what facts and what legal authority permit the court to take action. Family or juvenile court action to intervene in alleged child abuse or neglect cases is governed by due process, which requires that the defendant be apprised of the specific charges with sufficient notice and that the charges are stated with sufficient clarity to enable the person charged to prepare a defense. Additional elements that are brought up subsequent to the filing of the petition cannot be introduced at trial except by an amended petition.

Duquette (1981b) notes that at all stages of the litigation process a negotiated settlement is highly preferable to a litigated decision. Duquette (1981b) states that attorneys who represent birth parents should encourage clients to enter into negotiated resolutions of the problem. There is also a conflicting role element for such attorneys, as they are required to provide zealous representation to their clients, even though others may view the child in question as being at risk if the birth parents resist complying with the interventions proposed by the state. As Duquette (1981b) states: "Responsibility of the parent for injuries to or possible neglect of a child may be a contested issue. The lawyer has a duty to defend this client with the utmost vigor and resourcefulness. The lawyer in juvenile court, no less than in any other court, must stand as the ardent protector of his [*sic*] client's constitutional and personal rights" (p. 192).

In some exceptional situations, a child may be removed from the home in the absence of any court order. Each state's child welfare laws contain a provision that gives emergency removal power to police officers and to child protective services workers and that is to be employed in cases in which there is imminent danger to the child's physical safety. Some states also allow physicians to hold children in a hospital setting rather than release them to parents suspected of abuse or neglect. Duquette (1981a) notes that as far as the infringement of parents' constitutional rights are concerned the potential consequences of such emergency removal laws is formidable and that such laws should be applied only under grave and urgent circumstances.

One means for the placement of a child out of the home is the voluntary placement agreement. This is a document in which the birth parent or other caretaker agrees to the placement of the child, often for a specified period of time or under specified conditions. While in theory this procedure is less adversarial and more respectful of parents' rights than going to court to secure an order for the removal of the child, in practice there are drawbacks. Duquette (1981a) states that because the threat of court action is present in every child welfare case, birth parents may be intimidated into "voluntarily" signing placement agreements out of a fear that they will lose their children; when added to the fact that these clients are typically poor and powerless, there is a real danger of infringement of personal freedom. It has been my experience that this is a very frequent complaint among birth parents, who say that if they had known from the outset that the document that they were signing for temporary placement of their children into foster care gave the state such enormous power over them, they would have refused to sign and would have sought to resist the placement legally. Johnson

(1996) notes that reports of child abuse and neglect lead to a situation in which there is a disproportionate adverse impact on poor parents whose parental rights are not protected in the same way as are the rights of more economically advantaged birth parents who can afford private legal representation.

THE PRELIMINARY HEARING

In less-than-emergency situations, the placement of a child into foster care or other intervention (such as mandatory counseling), the transfer of the child to the care of a relative, or the initiation of in-home services for the family is often accomplished by means of legal proceedings, the first of which is usually termed a preliminary hearing. Duquette (1981a) states that the purposes of such hearings include (1) advising parents of the allegations in the petition; (2) advising parents of their legal rights, including the right to counsel and appointment of counsel if the parents cannot afford private representation; and (3) addressing the question of probable cause. Probable cause refers to the burden on the state to demonstrate to the court that there is probable cause to believe that the facts in the petition are true and that those facts constitute legal abuse or neglect. This is the basis for the court's authority to intervene in the case. If there is a preliminary finding of abuse or neglect, then the court must decide upon the appropriate level of intervention, pending a full trial. At this stage the court may issue a set of preliminary orders concerning placement of the child, visitation, medical care for the child, and psychological or psychiatric examinations of the child and birth parents before the trial date.

THE TRIAL

At this stage there is still no question regarding the parental rights of the birth parents; the issue immediately before the court is whether the child is an abused or neglected child under state statute. Should the court reach such a finding, then a further question of disposition arises. At disposition, the court issues a set of orders mandating interventions to protect the child and to rehabilitate the family, if that is deemed feasible. Typically dispositional orders are scheduled for review after a specified period of time. The court typically has broad powers in issuing such orders, including the power to mandate visitation between children and incarcerated birth parents at the expense of the state, with child protective services providing transportation. In the case of birth parents who have left the state or foster parents who have relocated out of state, the court may direct state child protective service agencies to provide transportation of either the child or the parents by air so that parents may continue to have contact with their children in placement.

The judicial review process may extend over a period of months or years. One purpose is to monitor the progress of the birth parents and the child and the parents' compliance with court-mandated interventions such as counseling, parent skills training, employment, adequate housing, or drug and alcohol rehabilitation. Another purpose of the court's review of the orders in a case is to monitor the extent to which child protective services are assisting the birth parents with mandated services. There have been instances in which caseworkers have actually been jailed by judges because of laxness in providing essential services for a family under a court order. Activist family court judges who view themselves as advocates for the rights of economically disadvantaged defendants may routinely apply significant pressure upon child protective agencies to insure that defendants receive mandated services in a timely fashion. Duquette (1981a) notes that casework personnel should thoroughly document the social treatment plan in anticipation of the court's holding the agency and other professionals accountable. Such plans should be shared with the parents, all attorneys, and all helping professionals involved with the family and should specify what the parents are to do and when and what is expected of the other professionals involved and by what dates (Duquette, 1981a).

As part of its current efforts at judicial reform, the Essex County, New Jersey, courts have instituted a program that reflects the elements of good case supervision as stated by Duquette. This procedure, known as G.A.T.E. (Goals and Time Entry), is aimed at facilitating the progress of child abuse and neglect cases through the system. Under the terms of the new procedure, when an initial protective order is issued, the judge will automatically issue an order appointing either a private or pool attorney to represent the birth parents. The initial order also includes a listing of the child protective services worker assigned to the case, along with that worker's telephone number and extension, as well as the number of the worker's supervisor. The fact that this appears as the second item of the court order reflects the heightened concern that courts and child protective services workers in New Jersey have over clients' access to their caseworkers. The K. L. F. case, reviewed in Chapter 3, is an egregious example of (1) the problems that result from parents' assertions that they have been unable to contact their caseworker for an extended period of time and (2) the impact of this entire issue upon the litigation if the case proceeds to a termination petition.

Also written into the G.A.T.E. order is the date by which the agency is to develop a case plan for the family. This insures that there is a clear direction from the outset as to the needs that the family presents and the opinion of casework personnel as to the appropriate interventions to address those needs. G.A.T.E. orders also call for the development of a list of relatives who might be willing to take custody of the children in question within a specified period of time. The most recent CWLA (1997) statistics indicate that kinship care is becoming an increasingly popular method of protecting children who have been removed from their homes; and although there does not at present exist any legal presumption for kinship care as the preferred placement for such children, agencies increasingly look to relatives as potential caregivers.

Other elements of the G.A.T.E. procedure include virtually automatic referrals for psychiatric and drug/alcohol assessments of the birth parents within 30 days of the date of the order and referrals of birth parents to parenting skills classes, with the New Jersey Division of Youth and Family Services named in the order as the party charged with the responsibility of coordinating the referrals. G.A.T.E. also mandates the establishment of a visitation schedule, allowing the caseworker to modify that schedule at his or her discretion.

Taking into account the due process issues in the court involvement of parents accused of abuse or neglect, the order mandates that any case-update material be served upon all parties by affidavit or certification no later that 5 days prior to the next court review and that any change in the placement of the children be brought to court for review within 20 days of the transfer. The G.A.T.E. order also sets a date for the next judicial review of the matter and orders that, in the event of a finding of abuse or neglect, a disposition hearing be held to determine the placement of the child. Finally, the G.A.T.E. procedure requires that separate orders be given to each defendant.

TERMINATION OF PARENTAL RIGHTS

In some states the child protective agency system is divided into (1) casework units that handle investigation, emergency intervention, monitoring, and ongoing services in cases in which the goal is family reunification and (2) adoption units that handle cases in which the goal has changed to a permanent placement with parties other than the birth parents. As noted in Chapter 3, state and federal laws concerning child welfare explicitly recognize the principle of permanency that requires professionals to devise a plan for the child's permanent placement, whether with the birth parents or with relatives or adoptive parents, within a specified period of time after the initial placement outside the home.

Once a decision to pursue adoption for the child is made within the child protective agency, parents are offered an opportunity to sign a surrender document, by means of which they voluntarily give over their rights to the child. Surrenders must be appropriately witnessed, and there must be a record that the terms of the document have been explained to the birth parents and that the parents are aware of the finality of the act and that the signing of the surrender is not the result of undue coercion but represents the parents' voluntary choice. As in the case of voluntary placement agreements, there is often an element of subtle pressure or a misunderstanding on the part of the parents that they would face some sort of legal sanction if they refuse to sign. A fair number of surrenders are contested on the grounds that the surrenders were not truly voluntary.

Some states have as an option what is termed a "directed surrender," meaning that the birth parent relinquishes rights under certain conditions. For example, a 17-year-old birth mother signed a surrender of rights with the understanding that her 3-year-old daughter would be adopted by the foster mother who had been the birth mother's caretaker while she was pregnant with this child and who had raised the child from birth. None of the individuals whom the birth mother had named as possible biological fathers of her child were confirmed via DNA testing. When the child was a little more than 2 years of age, the birth mother offered the name of another adolescent sex partner of hers as a possible biological father. Upon being confirmed as the child's father by DNA testing, this 19-year-old man and his parents requested and were granted visitation with the child. They petitioned the court for custody, and the child protective agency, noting that the birth father had previously been precluded from making any efforts on the part of the child because he had not been informed of her existence, changed the case goal from foster home adoption to placement with this birth father. The birth mother promptly withdrew her surrender of parental rights, as the birth father planned to take the child out of state, whereas the foster mother to whom she thought she had assigned her parental rights had informally promised her continued contact with the child after adoption.

When the parent either refuses to sign a surrender of rights or contests a signed surrender of rights, the child protective agency files a petition for guardianship of the child. The guardianship complaint has as its purpose the severing of the parent's rights to the child, for whom the state then becomes the guardian. This frees the child for adoption. The guardianship petition gives the official name and title of the complaining agency and its address. It identifies the attorney representing the agency, usually named as the state attorney general, and a specific deputy attorney general assigned to the case. The complaint also identifies all of the children and adults involved and presents a history of pertinent developments in the case, including details of the initial referral, subsequent referrals, and findings of abuse, neglect, or abandonment; attempted interventions to assist the family, the results of psychological, psychiatric, medical, and drug/alcohol assessments, and any significant incidents that demonstrate a birth parent's incorrigibility. Also included in the guardianship petition are the results of any assessment of the attachment profiles of the children, particularly in the case of younger children who have been in placement for a considerable length of time and who have had minimal contact with their birth parents.

Of particular importance in many cases is a listing in the petition of the numbers of scheduled visits between birth parents and their children in placement and how many of these visits were actually attended by the birth parents. The complaint documents the adjustment of the children to their caretakers, as well as the stated interest of foster parents in adopting them; if selected home adoption is the goal rather than foster home adoption, the complaint documents the efforts on the part of the agency in arranging for such an adoption. The petition ends with a summary of the reasons for the state's seeking termination of the parents' rights and a formal request to the court to terminate rights. The petition is typically supported by affidavits from casework personnel who attest to the truth of the allegations contained in the petition, birth certificates of the children, and a brief case summary listing the major problems of the children and their placement histories.

At the termination hearing, the state presents social casework witnesses who have documented efforts to work with the family and expert witnesses who testify in regard to evaluations of the birth parents, children, and, in some instances, the foster parents. Birth parents are granted the opportunity to present their own experts, who may be paid at the state's expense. Birth parents' experts may contradict the opinions of the state's experts regarding parental fitness and the degree of the child's attachment to the foster or preadoptive caretakers as opposed to the child's attachment to the birth parents. As noted in Chapter 2, parents have the right of appeal in the event of a decision to terminate their rights. Indeed, there have been cases in which children freed for adoption by termination of parental rights and subsequently legally adopted were returned to the birth parents as a result of a reversal of the termination decision by a higher court.

CHAPTER 2

Legal Issues in Termination of Parental Rights

It is crucial for mental health experts who consult in termination of parental rights cases to have an adequate appreciation of the legal issues that provide context for their testimony. Transition from a clinical to a forensic role in such matters entails a revision of one's perspective on the specifics of report writing and on the general scope and nature of assessments. This chapter will address the bases for terminating parental rights under the law, the types of referral questions posed to experts, the role of diagnosis and its relation to specific psycholegal questions, and the role of experts in assisting the court in these cases. These issues are illustrated by case summaries, comments of psychological and legal authorities, reviews of state termination of parental rights statutes, and two examples of model legislation in this area.

The law in the area of termination of parental rights has followed a seesaw course from (1) virtually reflexive severing of parental rights based on psychiatric diagnosis and a lenient standard of proof of unfitness to (2) a focus on protecting the birth parents' rights at the expense of children's psychological welfare to (3) recent federal legislation that facilitates adoption and fast-tracking in cases of egregious maltreatment or manifest parental unfitness. There is still a trend among some state courts to continue to stress the importance of preserving the blood tie by lowering the bar to a successful defense by birth parents who have abandoned their children until served with guardianship complaint. However, the overall legal climate in all likelihood will shift dramatically toward a more child-focused approach in the foreseeable future, influenced by recent federal legislation and continuing research in child development that demonstrates the crucial importance of stable attachments for future mental health.

Grisso (1986), in reviewing state statutes governing termination of parental rights, lists five criteria that are universally found in such laws: (1) abandonment of the child; (2) severe neglect and/or abuse; (3) parental incapacity through mental retardation or mental illness; (4) moral unfitness, including parental characteristics such as drug addiction, alcoholism, and unstable lifestyle; and (5) parental unavailability through civil commitment or incarceration. Grisso points out that until comparatively recently the rights of birth parents were largely ignored in termination actions and that as late as the 1960s or 1970s the presence of any of the above conditions was construed by many courts as sufficient grounds for termination of parental rights. Grisso notes that current thinking in this area requires a specific demonstration of a nexus between the birth parent's mental disability and specific deficiencies in that individual's capacity to raise the child in an acceptable manner. Further, many states require a demonstration that the birth parent's mental condition that allegedly impairs parenting capacity is either permanent or cannot be cured within a reasonable period of time.

The five criteria cited by Grisso translate into a number of specific referral questions that may be addressed by psychological and psychiatric evaluators within the parameters of acceptable forensic practice. The first criterion, abandonment of the child, raises issues pertaining to the psychological health of the child. One issue is that of the impact on the child of the act of parental abandonment. This relates to the legal issue of defining the harm that the birth parent has committed upon the child. The second issue is that of the consequences to the child's mental health resulting from a return of custody to the birth parent. This question is most appropriately addressed through evaluations of both the child and the birth parent. The child's evaluation is to determine the attachment profile and any specific relationship issues that may exist due to facts unique to the case. The assessment of the birth parent is necessary in order to determine the latter's sensitivity to the child's emotional problems, acknowledgment of past harm, and probable responses to the child's expressing positive feelings toward foster caretakers upon being returned to the birth parent.

The criterion of parental unavailability raises questions concerning the child's developmental needs, which may be addressed by a combination of examination results and the expert's knowledge of child development research and theory. Typical questions relating to this criterion center around the issue of how long a child can be expected to wait for the release of an absent birth parent without suffering psychological damage and of what nature, if any, this damage may be. Here the expert must weave current findings and observations together with valid prediction based on theory in order to assist the court in giving appropriate weight to the time factor. In cases in which the birth parent is unavailable for examination because of psychiatric confinement or incarceration, a further complication arises. In cases in which there is a comprehensive psychiatric history with a number of independent diagnoses available, the expert may still provide valuable information for the court relating to the birth parent in spite of the fact that there has been no direct examination of the parent. Canter, Bennett, Jones, and Nagy (1994) state that, although the ethical code of the American Psychological Association prohibits statements concerning individuals who have not been personally examined, experts may testify on the basis of a record review if the record is used as the basis for responding to hypothetical questions.

Grisso (1986) notes that evidentiary standards in termination cases vary among states. He cites several cases that point to a very low standard of proof, "preponderance of evidence," thus permitting courts excessive latitude in terminating birth parents' rights on the basis of parents' lifestyle, poverty, or lack of available services. He cites cases in which courts found birth parents unfit because of conditions such as "personal weakness," "neurosis," and "personality disorder."

Grisso (1986) draws a distinction between legal concepts of parental fitness in the case of termination proceedings and parenting capacity in divorce custody cases. This is an essential difference that evaluators in termination matters need to be aware of, as a confusion of the two situations may lead to testimony in which an extremely heavy sanction, complete severance of a birth parent's rights, is urged on the basis of relatively minor failings (e.g., a birth parent's losing the "parenting contest" with foster caretakers even though the former may actually be fit to parent the child in question). The issue before the court in a termination case is not merely who would be able to provide a relatively better environment for the child, as in a divorce case in which the noncustodial parent may nonetheless be awarded visitation privileges. Rather, the burden on the state is to demonstrate that the birth parent is so egregiously flawed that there are compelling reasons to end that parent's legal right to any involvement with the child. Melton et al. (1987) note that termination of parental rights is one of the most severe sanctions that can be meted out by a court, as most terms of imprisonment are finite, whereas termination of rights is permanent. In *M. L. B. v. S. L. J.* (1996), Justice Ginsburg's majority opinion, guaranteeing the right of appeal of termination actions to indigent defendants, states, "She [the birth parent appellant M. L. B.] is endeavoring to defend against the State's destruction of her family bonds, and to resist the brand associated with a parental unfitness adjudication. Like a defendant resisting criminal conviction, she seeks to be spared from the state's devastatingly adverse action" ("Needy Who Lose Parental Rights," 1996, p. A22).

THE SIGNIFICANCE OF PSYCHIATRIC DIAGNOSIS AS PROOF OF PARENTAL UNFITNESS

Courts have consistently found that even a severe psychiatric diagnosis is not in and of itself a sufficient cause for termination of parental rights. The state has the burden of demonstrating a nexus between the diagnosed psychiatric disorder in the parent and specific defects in that individual's parenting capacity. Ackerman and Kane (1990) cite two cases in which mentally disturbed parents were found not to be adjudicated as unfit solely on the basis of their disorder. In *In re J. M.* (1982) the court ruled not only that mental illness is per se not sufficient grounds for termination but that the confinement of both birth parents to a mental institution does not establish that they are unfit. In *In re C. P. B. and K. A. B.* (1982) the court ruled that termination of parental rights due to mental illness is justifiable only when there is a clear showing that the parental relationship is harmful to the children or would be harmful in the future. Several state appellate and supreme court cases point out the need to demonstrate a nexus between the diagnosed condition and specific aspects of parental unfitness as well as the inability of the birth parent to profit from rehabilitative services. Shapiro (1984) notes that a Massachusetts court ruled in *In re The Custody of a Minor* (1979) that a mere finding of a mental disorder is insufficient to terminate parental rights.

There must be a further showing of specified symptoms or dysfunction that would pose a risk to the child. *Colorado ex rel. S. J. C.* (1989, cited in Ackerman & Kane, 1990) found that the trial court had properly terminated the parental rights of a birth father on the ground of unfitness due to emotional illness. The court cited statutory language indicating that the alleged illness must render the birth parent incapable of caring for the child and that testimony from psychologist and social work expert witnesses had demonstrated specific deficiencies and a poor prognosis for positive change. In *In re Waggoner* (1979) the court held that a mentally disabled parent, by virtue of her disability, lacked the ability to cope with the special challenges presented by her child, who had low frustration tolerance, engaged in self-injurious behavior, and required constant attention. The court in *In re C. C.* (1987) upheld the termination of parental rights of a birth father who had multiple severe problems, including drug abuse, violent urges, impulsivity, and aggressiveness, and refused to participate in therapy. Under a standard of clear and convincing evidence (a more difficult standard to meet than preponderance of evidence), the court found that there had been a sufficient showing of parental unfitness.

In *In re Kelly* (1992, cited in Ackerman & Kane, 1996) a state appeals court found that the trial court had erred in removing a child, absent specific proof of parental harm to the child or an absence of an ongoing parental relationship. The trial court had relied solely on the birth mother's history of mental illness, including psychiatric hospitalizations, and permitted placement of the child directly from the hospital after birth. The birth mother suffered from hallucinations, angry aggressive behavior, and two different personalities. Her hygiene was poor, and she lived in homeless shelters. The child required specialized care due to medical problems and developmental delays. When the child was 1 year of age, the trial court simultaneously terminated the birth mother's rights and gave custody to state child protective services. The appeals court reversed the termination, stating that there was no proof that the mother's behavior had injured the child and that potential harm from the mother was mere speculation. The court stated that termination requires evidence of parental acts or omissions that deny the child necessary care and cause serious harm to the child.

A Nebraska case relates specifically to predictions relating to the factor of time. In *Nebraska v. D. S.* (1990) the Nebraska Supreme Court found that expert testimony had competently demonstrated that a birth mother who had a lengthy history of drug abuse and suicide attempts was incapable of parenting her 7-year-old son and 6-year-old daughter and that the birth mother did not present a realistic prognosis for rehabilitation before these children had achieved the age of majority.

In *In re Guynn* (1993, cited in Ackerman & Kane, 1996) a state appeals court found that the birth mother's mental illness constituted sufficient evidence to terminate the parental rights of the couple. The court found clear and convincing evidence that the birth mother's diagnosed depression, suicidal tendencies, and borderline personality disorder prevented her from properly caring for her daughter. The borderline personality disorder manifested itself in mood swings, inappropriate and intense uncontrolled anger, and other typical borderline phenomena.

In contrast to this case, *In re Scott* (1989) found that the trial court had inappropriately terminated the rights of a birth mother who had been diagnosed as suffering from a personality disorder. The court noted that the state's psychiatric witness admitted on cross-examination that the mother's disorder did not preclude her from caring for her children. The court also cited the fact that there had been no showing that the birth parent's condition would continue throughout the children's minority.

In *In re Joshua O.* (1996, cited in Ackerman & Kane, 1997) the state appellate court ruled on criteria for terminating parental rights on the grounds of mental illness. The court stated that child protective services must meet a standard of clear and convincing evidence to demonstrate that the birth parent is currently, and will remain into the foreseeable future, incapable of caring for his or her children by virtue of mental illness. In this case it was found that there was clear and convincing evidence from an examining psychologist that the mother, who had numerous mental problems and was mildly mentally retarded, had difficulty in controlling her emotional outbursts and was unable to understand the complex needs of a child or to plan for the future.

Also cited in Ackerman and Kane (1997) is a 1995 California appeals court case, *In re Elizabeth R.*, in which the birth mother of three daughters was diagnosed with bipolar disorder during her midteens and underwent frequent psychiatric hospitalizations thereafter. Although the birth mother complied with nearly all aspects of a reunification plan that included parenting classes, learning nurturing skills, and taking her medications, her parental rights were terminated. The appeals court reasoned that, although family reunification should be the first priority in these cases, children's need for stability and security within a given time frame is paramount. The court decided that the birth mother's continuing psychiatric hospitalizations were of such concern that her compliance with the reunification plan was insufficient to prevent termination.

In another case cited in Ackerman and Kane (1997), *In re Donald L. L.* (1992), a birth mother's rights were terminated on the basis of testimony by a psychiatrist who never met with her but who reviewed hospital and clinical records. The psychiatrist, with whom the respondent refused to meet for an examination, testified that she suffered from borderline personality disorder and from schizophrenia, paranoid type, and that these conditions prevented her from being able to care for her children appropriately.

There is another class of cases in which the effects of the parent's psychiatric disorder are so extreme that a demonstration of links to specific parenting deficiencies becomes superfluous. Myers (1997), for example, cites *K. N. v. State* (1993) in which it was found that mental illness alone is not enough to terminate rights but that the effects of a parent's mental illness on a child may be sufficient to warrant termination. He states, "When mental illness impairs a parent's ability to provide for a child's basic needs . . . or otherwise endangers a child, intervention is appropriate, as is termination of parental rights" (p. 352). Myers (1997) cites *In re Andrea*, a 1990 California appeals court case, in which a birth mother diagnosed with schizotypal personality disorder forced her daughter to eat frozen vomit covered with chocolate syrup, pricked her skin to draw blood, and performed other acts that led the court to conclude that long-term foster care was necessary to protect the child's best interests.

FAILURE TO PROTECT

Termination of parental rights can occur in cases in which the parent does not inflict abuse himself or herself but fails to protect the child from abuse inflicted by another. Myers (1997) states, "A parent who knows his or her child is being abused by another adult, but who does nothing to protect the child, can be prosecuted under statutes expressly criminalizing such behavior, or under general principles of accomplice liability" (p. 363). He cites *In re Jonathan Michael D.*, a 1995 West Virginia case in which the court stated that "parental rights may be terminated on account of abuse even if the parent did not personally inflict the injuries" (Myers, 1997, p. 363). He also cites *In re Jeffrey R. L.* (1993), in which the court stated essentially the same conclusion. In *People v. Stanciel* (1992, cited in Myers, 1997) the court held that mothers have an affirmative duty to protect their children from the threat posed by abusive men. Myers (1997) discusses two cases of abused women who were prosecuted for failing to protect their children from murder at the hands of their abusive boyfriends. Both women offered expert testimony at trial on the effect of battered woman's syndrome on her ability to protect the child from abuse by the paramour, and this testimony was ruled admissible because its exclusion would deny the defendants their constitutionally guaranteed right to present a defense.

PERSONALITY DISORDER AND PARENTAL UNFITNESS

In addition to Axis I clinical syndromes listed in DSM-IV (American Psychiatric Association, 1994), there is another class of disorders coded in that manual's Axis II, labeled "personality disorders." Unlike Axis I disorders that tend to have well-defined symptoms that are troubling to the patient, Axis II disorders are longstanding maladaptive patterns of adjustment that may simply be experienced subjectively as part of the individual's "nature." In jargon terms, personality disorders tend to be more "ego syntonic" than "ego alien." In court there are often disagreements as to whether personality disorders qualify as "mental disorders" referred to in some statutes (McCann & Dyer, 1996). It is my experience that the majority of cases of neglect and abuse that proceed to the stage of a guardianship action involve birth parents who present personality disorders and not necessarily Axis I clinical syndromes.

There are a number of cases in which findings of termination on the basis of the birth parent's personality disorder have been upheld. The court in *In re C. S.* (1988) upheld a termination under a clear and convincing evidence standard in which a birth mother was diagnosed with narcissistic personality disorder. The examining psychologist cited factors, including antisocial behavior, drug abuse, and the birth mother's history of abuse and neglect as a child, that indicated a poor prognosis. The specific nexus between the diagnosed disorder and aspects of parental unfitness was that the defendant's narcissism prevented her from adequately responding to the needs of her children, as she put her own needs first.

The Nebraska Supreme Court in *Nebraska v. M. M.* (1988) found that a personality disorder constitutes a "mental deficiency" within the termination of parental rights law. Despite psychological testimony that the defendant, the birth father, did not have a mental deficiency (in the sense of mental retardation) and that he did not have a mental illness (in the sense of an Axis I type disturbance of reality contact), the court found that his personality disorder, which caused him to react violently when under stress, rendered him an unfit parent under the statute.

In *Louisiana ex rel. Townzen* (1988, cited in Ackerman & Kane, 1990) the Louisiana Court of Appeals found that the parental rights of a birth mother diagnosed with mixed personality disorder had been properly terminated under a clear and convincing evidence standard. The testimony of two psychologists was that the defendant had passive/aggressive, passive/dependent, and antisocial personality disorders. One of the experts indicated that the defendant's prognosis for improved parenting abilities through professional counseling was poor and that a continued relationship between the defendant and her son would exacerbate the child's psychological problems.

Over and above issues of parental unfitness, there is legal precedent addressing the issue of the needs and welfare of the children as they would be affected by a termination of parental rights. In *In re E. M.* (1993, cited in Ackerman & Kane, 1996) a state supreme court reversed a termination of a birth mother's parental rights on the grounds that the lower court did not adequately assess the impact of termination on the appellant's two children. In 1989 the trial court terminated the birth mother's rights on the basis of her mental retardation. The supreme court found that the trial court had erred in determining that there was no need to address issues of parent–child bonding in the case. A psychologist called by the state had testified that the children were bonded to their mother and that they had expressed a desire to live with both the foster mother and the birth mother. The court felt that the issue of whether a continuing relationship with the birth mother would meet the children's needs should have been addressed by the trial court.

AMERICANS WITH DISABILITIES ACT AND TERMINATION CASES

Many respondents in termination of parental rights actions are classifiable as disabled under the Americans with Disabilities Act (ADA). Because of the requirements of the act to accommodate individuals' disabilities in many settings, including social service interventions, it is incumbent upon child protective agencies that work with these families to be aware of clients' special needs. Recent decisions suggest that when social service agencies take steps to offer appropriate services to disabled birth parents, courts do not find persuasive the respondents' arguments in termination proceedings based on ADA issues.

Stone v. Daviess County Division of Children and Family Services (1995, cited in Ackerman & Kane, 1997) found that the state had provided numerous specialized social services to accommodate the special needs of two mentally retarded birth parents. The appeals court upheld the termination, noting that the birth parents did not avail themselves of the offered services because of their position that they were not deficient parents. Additionally, the court ruled that children's best interests outweigh ADA-related claims.

In re Welfare of A. J. R. (1995, cited in Ackerman & Kane, 1997) held that the state had offered necessary services to a moderately retarded birth mother and her borderline retarded husband. In this case the state presented testimony from 15 experts who stated that the services offered not only addressed the couple's special needs but also were modified to accommodate their specific disabilities. The court ruled that the state had not violated Title II of the ADA.

In a Maine supreme court decision, *In re Angel B.* (1995, cited in Ackerman & Kane, 1997) it was ruled that the birth mother had failed to demonstrate that the state had offered her services that were ineffective in affording her an equal opportunity to rehabilitate and regain custody of her children, given her disability. The court found that the respondent had indeed been offered numerous services and that her disability was properly taken into account in the service plan.

As sometimes occurs with federal legislation, laws that are passed for a specific purpose tend to be cited in litigation for purposes apart from the original intent of the legislators. In the case of the ADA, a law that provides valuable protections for the disabled in the areas of employment and public accommodation has been contorted into a defense for birth parents whose mental and emotional disabilities render them manifestly unfit to care for their children. This peculiar construction of the ADA has been soundly rejected by courts.

TERMINATION OF PARENTAL RIGHTS STATUTES

Neal (1989) notes that state termination statutes recognize criteria or factors for termination in three primary areas: parental conditions, parental conduct, and statutory duties of agency. Parental conditions include such long-term or chronic circumstances as parental incarceration with no possibility of parole in the foreseeable future, mental illness, mental retardation, and severe substance abuse. Parental conduct refers to the failure of birth parents to make the necessary adjustments to prepare for the child's return in spite of agency efforts to rehabilitate the family. This failure may also include parental disinterest in the child as evidenced by abandonment. Neal says that 28 states include language in their statutes, emphasizing the importance of the agency's input into compliance with the goals of the case plan. The failure of the state social services agency to provide support services to the family, to help birth parents with their rehabilitation, or to facilitate visitation with the children in placement is actually a common defense in termination actions.

In contrast to the historical perspective on children as chattel, 41 states have statutes that consider the best interests of the child when deciding on termination of parental rights. Some states also explicitly consider the child's preference; however, this is virtually never the case with younger children. California considers preference if the child is age 10 or older, and Massachusetts and Wisconsin when the child is 12 or older. In Hawaii, Louisiana, New Mexico, New York, Texas, Virginia, and West Virginia, only the preferences of children age 14 years or older are considered statutorily in termination actions.

A recent development in state statutes governing termination of parental rights is the inclusion of time frames as a consideration. Time frames are employed as part of the grounds for termination, as a reasonable parameter for family rehabilitation, and as a benchmark at which to initiate termination proceedings. Thirty-four states limit severing parental rights according to the child's length of time out of the home. Most of these states allow a year or more before either mandating or permitting a guardianship action. Some states such as Alabama and New Mexico have introduced shorter time frames where younger children are involved.

In 46 states there is a requirement that a guardian ad item be appointed to represent the child in termination of parental rights proceedings. In 5 states such an appointment is left to the discretion of the judge. In Hawaii the appointment of a guardian is permitted only in cases of abuse or neglect.

Various safeguards of the rights of birth parents appear in state statutes. For example, Illinois and Kentucky do not allow consideration of parental conduct that is not relevant to the parent–child relationship. This ruling is similar to the helpfulness requirement articulated in the Supreme Court's *Daubert* decision in which it was stressed that testimony must be relevant to the ultimate legal issue before the court and helpful to the court in rendering a decision on that issue. (The *Daubert* case is discussed at length in Chapter 10.) There are legal requirements for parental notification when a guardianship is filed. In some states it is mandatory for foster parents, other parties who have served as the child's caretaker, and other interested parties to be notified as well. Forty-six states provide appointed counsel for indigent birth parents. In 4 states such appointments are at the discretion of the judge. Forty-two states give birth parents the right to appeal a termination decision. Thirty-five states have adopted into their termination of parental rights statutes the clear and convincing evidentiary standard resulting from the 1982 United States Supreme Court decision in *Santosky v. Kramer.*

There is an emerging trend toward protection of the rights of putative fathers. A 1972 Supreme Court decision, *Stanley v. State of Illinois*, resulted in the requirement that states devise procedures for notifying putative fathers of any termination or adoption actions. A subsequent decision, *Caban v. Mohammed* (1979), was concerned with the right of a putative father to veto an adoption. As a result of this decision, putative fathers' registries were established, permitting putative fathers to receive all legal notices. This serves as a safeguard against later appeal of permanency planning decisions. Birth fathers' rights have been an increasingly contentious issue, as reflected in the Baby Jessica case, reviewed in Chapter 13.

Figure 2.1 (Neal, 1989) summarizes the major components of existing state termination statutes.

Hardin and Lancour (1996) note that state termination of parental rights statutes vary enormously in matters such as prescribed time periods and specification of circumstances that warrant termination of rights. They fault many states' laws as being excessively vague in regard to grounds for termination, citing the North Dakota statute that allows for termination on the basis of parental abandonment of the child without offering any explanation or definition of that term.

Hardin and Lancour (1996) state that there are two basic types of statutory schemes underlying the construction of termination statutes. The first allows for termination based on specific grounds; and if those grounds are established, then termination is decided according to the best interest of the child standard. They cite the Ohio statute as being a good example of this scheme. The Ohio law (Ohio Rev. Code Ann. 2151.414, 1996) includes such grounds as (1) the parents' failure to remediate problems that led to the initial placement outside the home despite reasonable efforts by the state to rehabilitate them, (2) severe and chronic mental illness, (3) parents' having committed additional neglect or abuse against the child since the date of the initial complaint alleging abuse or neglect, (4) parents' lack of commitment to the child, (5) parents' incarceration, and (6) parents' inability to protect the child against physical or sexual abuse.

The second type of statutory scheme provides a general framework, such as the impossibility of returning a child to the parental home within a reasonable time, rather than specific grounds for termination. Factors that assist in this determination are often spelled out in this second category of the statute; however, the difference is that when such factors are used all of them must be taken into account, and it is unclear whether a single factor might justify termination under this general standard. Hardin and Lancour (1996) note that reasonable efforts by state child protective agencies toward family reunification are occasionally included among the factors to be considered in the general framework of termination. They note that Maryland has a statute of this second type in which only abandonment appears as a specific ground for termination (Md. Fam. Code 5-313, 1996).

FIGURE 2.1. Summary of major components of state statutes concerning involuntary termination of parental rights. From Neal (1989, pp. A-1–A-2). Copyright 1989 by National Conference of State Legislatures. Reprinted by permission.

	AL	AK	AZ	AR	CA	CO	CT	DE		FL	GA	HI	ID	IL	IN	IA	KS	KY	LA	ME	MD	MA	MI	MN	MS	MO	MT	NE	NV	NH	NJ	NM	NY	NC	ND	OH	OK	OR	PA	PR	RI	SC	SD	TN	TX	UT	VT	VA	WA	WV	WI	WY
GROUNDS FOR TERMINATION[1]																					2																															
Parental incapacity to care for child	■		■		■	■		■			■	■	■	■	■		■	■		■	■			■	■		■	■	■	■		■	■	■	■		■		■	■	■	■	■	■	■	■				■	■	
Mental condition	■		■	■	■	■		■			■	■	■	■	■		■	■	■		■				■		■	■	■	■		■	■	■	■	■	■	■		■	■	■			■			■		■	■	
Alcohol/drug abuse	■		■	■	■	■					■	■		■	■		■		■		■						■	■	■			■		■	■	■		■		■	■	■		■				■		■	■	
Extreme disinterest/abandonment	■		■	■	■	■	■	■		■	■	■	■	■	■	■	■	■	■	■	■		■	■	■	■	■	■	■	■	■	■	■	■	■	■	■		■	■	■	■	■	■	■	■			■	■	■	
Failure to visit or communicate	■			■	■	■	■	■		■	■	■	■	■		■	■		■	■	■			■	■	■			■	■	■	■	■	■	■	■		■		■	■	■		■		■			■	■	■	
Failure to provide a home when able to do so				■	■	■					■	■	■				■	■	■				■	■	■	■		■			■	■	■	■	■				■	■	■			■					■	■	■	■
Infant abandoned—no ID for a specified time period	■			■	■	■		■				■	■	■	■		■			■			■		■	■		■		■		■	■	■		■		■	■	■	■				■				■			■
Extreme or repeated abuse or neglect	■		■	■	■	■	■	■		■	■	■	■	■		■	■	■	■	■	■		■	■	■	■	■	■	■		■	■	■	■	■	■	■	■	■	■	■	■	■	■	■				■	■	■	■
Long-term incarceration—early parole unlikely	■		■			■					■	■	■				■		■				■				■					■	■	■		■	■				■								■			■
Failure to improve in response to agency assistance	■		■	■	■	■	■	■		■	■	■		■	■	■	■	■	■	■	■		■	■	■		■	■	■	■		■	■	■		■	■	■	■	■	■	■		■				■	■	■	■	■
Case plan developed					■	■	■			■		■			■	■	■				■		■	■	■		■			■		■	■	■								■		■				■	■	■		
Services provided pursuant to plan			■	■	■	■	■			■		■			■	■	■	■	■		■		■	■	■		■	■	■	■		■	■	■		■						■		■				■		■	■	
Payment for portion of cost of care	■			■	■	■					■	■					■	■		■	■			■				■	■	■		■		■			■	■			■			■	■							
Specific length of time child is in placement considered			■		■	■	■	■		■	■	■	■	■	■	■			■		■		■	■	■	■	■		■	■	■		■	■			■		■		■			■		■			■	■	■	
Age of child a factor					■							■								■			■	■	■								■																			
More or less than one year in placement distinguished			■							■	■	■		■					■					■	■						■		■				■							■						■	■	
Expedited process under certain circumstances			■		■						■	■		■		■			■	■			■	■			■							■			■		■		■										■	

1. This chart indicates specific statutory language. Note that a number of states have specific requirements explicitly stated in their judicial decisions.

2. The information here applies to termination sought by a county agency. Other statutes allow any individual to petition for termination and adoption in the same proceeding, after having had custody of a child for six months.

	AL	AK	AZ	AR	CA	CO	CT	DE		FL	GA	HI	ID	IL	IN	IA	KS	KY	LA	ME	MD	MA	MI	MN	MS	MO	MT	NE	NV	NH	NJ	NM	NY	NC	ND	OH	OK	OR	PA	PR	RI	SC	SD	TN	TX	UT	VT	VA	WA	WV	WI	WY
ISSUES CONCERNING RETURN TO HOME[3]																																																				
Significant relationships	■				■		■	■		■	■						■			■	■	■	■	■	■	■	■		■	■		■				■	■			■			■	■		■	■	■		■	■	
Parent/parents	■				■	■		■		■	■			■							■		■	■	■		■		■	■		■				■				■			■	■		■	■			■	■	
Foster parents	■				■	■	■	■		■				■		■	■						■	■	■	■	■		■			■				■	■			■	■		■			■	■				■	
Child's preference			■		■	■		■		■		■		■		■				■		■	■				■		■			■				■	■				■					■				■	■	
Age of child a consideration			■		■	■						■				■				■		■	■		■				■				■				■													■	■	
Nature and depth of child's wishes are considered					■	■				■													■									■	■																		■	
Alternative placements	■		■		■	■				■		■				■				■		■	■	■			■	■		■		■				■	■			■			■	■		■	■				■	
Custody/guardianship--caretakers not adopting	■		■		■	■				■		■				■			■	■		■	■	■	■					■		■				■				■			■	■			■		■		■	
Other forms of long-term care (group home, etc.)	■		■							■										■		■	■	■	■		■	■								■				■			■	■		■	■		■		■	
Court ordered permanent foster placement	■				■	■				■						■			■	■		■	■	■			■								■	■							■	■			■				■	
Open adoption	■						■			■														■			■	■				■								■			■	■							■	
LEGAL PROCEDURES/ISSUES																																																				
Notice and hearing requirements	■	■	■	■		■	■	■		■	■	■	■			■	■	■	■	■	■	■	■	■	■	■	■	■	■	■	■	■	■	■	■	■	■	■	■	■	■		■	■		■		■	■	■	■	■
Right of appeal	■		■	■	■			■		■	■	■	■			■	■	■	■	■	■	■	■			■	■	■	■	■		■		■		■	■	■		■	■		■	■		■		■		■	■	
Right to counsel	■		■		■		■			■	■	■	■	■		■		■	■	■	■	■	■	■		■	■	■	■	■		■		■	■		■	■	■	■		■	■					■	■	■	■	■
For parents	■		■		■	■	■			■		■	■	■		■	■	■	■	■	■	■	■	■				■	■	■		■		■	■	■	■	■	■	■		■	■					■	■	■	■	■
For the child	■		■		■		■			■		■	■	■		■		■	■	■	■	■	■	■	■	■	■	■	■	■				■	■		■		■	■		■	■	■				■	■	■	■	■
Rights of putative fathers	■			■	■	■		■			■	■						■			■		■	■		■			■	■				■	■		■	■	■		■			■				■		■	■	
Proof by clear and convincing evidence	■	■	■	■	■	■	■			■	■	■	■	■		■	■	■	■	■	■	■	■	■	■	■		■	■	4		■	■	■	■	■		■		■	■		■	■				■	■	■	■	■
Time frames for completing termination litigation	■			■	■					■						■							■			■	■		■	■											■			■						■		
STATUTE RELATED TO INDIAN CHILD WELFARE ACT					■															■		■	■	■				■				■	■				■												■		■	

3. Note that a number of states specify that the best interests of the child must be considered. Although specific issues are not designated in the statutory language the factors listed on the chart are considered.

4. New Hampshire's burden of proof is beyond a reasonable doubt.

In cases not involving abandonment a complex set of factors must be applied. These factors include (1) timeliness of services to the family; (2) the extent to which the family and social services have fulfilled their respective obligations under the service agreement; (3) the child's feelings toward the parents and other family members who may affect the child's best interest; (4) the child's adjustment to home, school, and community; (5) the efforts toward rehabilitation displayed by the birth parents; and (6) the general picture of services offered to the birth parent.

NEW JERSEY STATUTES GOVERNING TERMINATION

The laws governing termination of parental rights in New Jersey reflect many of the considerations that appear in those of other states, as discussed above, as well as model statutes, which are reviewed below. In a review of New Jersey statutes that affect the work of mental health professionals, Wulach (1991) observes that involuntary termination of parental rights is an infrequent occurrence. Parents under New Jersey law must be afforded a range of procedural rights, which include receiving notice of proceedings and being provided with assigned counsel if they are unable to afford legal representation. Under New Jersey law, parents have the right to engage their own psychologist or psychiatrist to perform an assessment of them at the state's expense if their mental health is raised as an issue at trial.

Wulach (1991, p. 161) cites conditions under which the state can file a petition for termination of parental rights. These include the following:

1. Parents or guardian have been convicted of abuse, abandonment, neglect, or cruelty to a child.
2. Any child has been adjudicated as a delinquent.
3. The best interests of a child under the care or custody of the Division of Youth and Family Services require guardianship.
4. A parent or guardian has failed substantially and continuously or repeatedly for a period of 1 year to maintain contact with and plan for the future of a child whose care or custody has been transferred to the Division of Youth and Family Services or other authorized agency.

Wulach (1991) cites the case of *New Jersey Division of Youth and Family Services v. A. W.* (1986) in which four criteria governing termination were set forth. According to this decision, the trial court must determine whether (1) the child's health and development have been or will be seriously impaired by the parental relationship; (2) the parents are unable or unwilling to eliminate the harm, and whether the delay of permanent placement will add to the harm; (3) there are no alternatives to termination; (4) termination of parental rights will do more harm than good. All four of these requirements must be met in order for a trial court to grant termination. These standards include consideration of the harm to the child, the fitness of the parent, the child's relationship to the parent, the factor of passage of time, and issues of permanency planning.

A New Jersey bill approved in January 1996 adds language to the existing termination statute that reflects the *A. W.* decision. Notably, the language of the second criterion (i.e., parent is unwilling or unable to eliminate the harm to the child) is clarified by the addition of the following: "Such harm may include evidence that separating the child from his foster parents would cause serious and enduring emotional or psychological harm to the child" (N.J. Assembly, 1996a). This is important in regard to expert testimony in that an expert's prediction of severe and enduring harm, as opposed to a temporary grief reaction, may be used to demonstrate this portion of the state's burden as explicitly stated in the statute. Thus, judicial discretion as to whether to give any weight to attachment considerations is superseded by a legal requirement to do so.

The bill also lists a number of conditions that the birth parent must meet to avoid triggering the requirement that the state file a petition to terminate rights on the ground of abandonment. These include the following:

a. The maintenance of a relationship with the child such that the child perceives the person as his parent;
b. Communicating with the child or person having legal custody of the child and visiting the child unless visitation is impossible because of the parent's confinement in an institution or unless prevented for doing so by the custodial parent or other custodian of the child or a social service agency over the parent's objection; or
c. Providing financial support for the child unless prevented from

> doing so by the custodial parent or other custodian of the child or a social service agency. (N.J. Assembly, 1996b)

This language should eliminate situations such as the case *In the Matter of Guardianship of K. L. F., a Minor* (1991/1992), in which the New Jersey Supreme Court decided that a birth mother who had an infant daughter who had been in foster care since birth and who had made attempts to contact her caseworker, without actually succeeding, over the course of a year and a half had not abandoned the child and still had some sort of maternal relationship to her. (This case is discussed in detail in Chapter 3.) The language also tightens the requirements for visitation in that it stresses that the birth parent must maintain a relationship with the child that is of such a nature that the child perceives the individual as his or her parent. Thus, a birth parent's contact with the child that is so infrequent or of such poor quality that it does not lead to a perception on the part of the child that the individual visiting him or her is his or her parent cannot prevent the filing of a termination action.

NATIONAL STANDARDS FOR ADOPTION

Shapiro (1984, p. 108) cites the Uniform Adoption Act drafted by the National Conference of Commissioners on Uniform State Laws for delineation of the components of the adoption process. According to the draft, there must first be a termination of parental rights. This requirement has significance for experts in termination cases as it relates to the frequently introduced issue of "open adoption," which is usually defined as an adoption in which there is a judicial requirement that the adoptive parents permit some specified degree of contact between the child in question and the birth parents. Occasionally experts are heard to state on the stand that open adoption would be the preferred solution for the child. In actual practice, however, this rarely, if ever, occurs because of the requirement of state statutes that parental rights be terminated in order for the adoption to go forward. Termination, it should be recalled, is a complete severing of rights, with no legally enforceable residual power or influence over decisions regarding the child's welfare. (Open adoption is discussed more fully in Chapter 7.)

This issue of open adoption also raises important questions for both attorneys and mental health professionals who work with birth parents in such matters. Despite detailed explanation of the terms of a surrender of parental rights, practical experience has shown that birth parents often come away from the conference with the impression that if the adoptive parents state that the birth parents will be permitted to see the child after adoption, the birth parents have some sort of legally enforceable right to that visitation. A proper orientation for birth parents as to all of the ramifications of signing a surrender of rights is essential from the point of view of protecting the parents' rights. State child welfare agencies must avoid soliciting birth parents' agreement to something that they do not fully understand. This thorough orientation of birth parents is also essential to protect the validity of an adoption based on a surrender document that permits severance of parental rights. If it can be demonstrated at some future time that the birth parent was under the impression that visitation rights were legally guaranteed, the adoption decree might be nullified on appeal.

Other stages in the adoption process cited by Shapiro (1984) include a decree granting the adoptive parents custody. The final component is a decree of adoption based on the criterion of best interests. The Uniform Adoption Act requires that birth parents consent to the proposed adoption, except in cases where they are either incapable of consent or have had their parental rights terminated by a court. Shapiro notes that there are provisions in the act for the adoption of children of severely mentally disabled parents without their consent under the theory that individuals who are judged or presumed to be incompetent cannot give legally valid consent. Shapiro (1984) also cites provisions in the act that allow for adoption without parental consent if the parent has a history of mental illness extending more than 3 years into the past if two evaluators testify that the individual is unlikely to recover within the foreseeable future. However, Shapiro notes that even the severe mental disability of a birth parent does not in and of itself constitute sufficient grounds for termination if the parent has arranged alternative care for the child.

Shapiro (1984, p. 112) states that judicial criteria for parental fitness can be summarized as follows:

1. Parents' capacity to provide the child with nurturance.
2. Parents' capacity to maintain the home.
3. Parents' capacity to care for the child's physical needs.
4. Parents' capacity to provide sufficient intellectual stimulation for the child.

He cites a California Appeals Court case upholding a state statute granting termination of a mentally disabled parent's rights when the parent cannot, by virtue of the disability, support or control the child. This decision imposed the requirement that, by a standard of clear and convincing evidence, it is established that the parent suffers from a mental disability that will continue indefinitely, regardless of treatment, and that immediate severance of the parental relationship is the least detrimental alternative for the child. This latter requirement is an especially important consideration for older children or for children who have been placed after they have developed a clear sense of being the birth parent's child and have memories of having lived with the birth parent. As Bush and Goldman (1982) point out, many children in that position prefer to spend the rest of their childhood years in foster care rather than undergo an adoption that would change their name and sever for good any relationship that they may have had with the birth parent.

However, in other decisions cited by Shapiro (1984), the passage of time and judicial findings go against leaving children in indefinite foster care. He cites a 1979 Washington Court of Appeals matter in which a termination of parental rights was affirmed because the birth mother's progress in rehabilitation was so slow that her children would remain in foster care indefinitely if the state continued to work toward a return of custody (Shapiro, 1984, p. 114). Similarly, the case of *H. A. C. v. D. C. C.* heard in Colorado in 1979 resulted in a termination because the birth mother was not following her treatment plan and the court felt that the passage of time was injuring the children in question (Shapiro, 1984, p. 114).

GOLDSTEIN, FREUD, AND SOLNIT'S MODEL LEGISLATION

Permanency planning is a central theme of the seminal work by Goldstein et al. (1979) in which the authors introduce model legislation that addresses child placement and parental rights. Their selected provisions for a child placement statute include definitions of *wanted child*, *psychological parent*, *child's sense of time*, and *least detrimental alternative* (pp. 98–99). A *wanted child* by this definition is a child who receives affection and nourishment on a continuing basis from at least one adult and who feels that he or she is and continues to be valued by those who take care of him or her. A *psycho-*

logical parent is one who fulfills the child's psychological and physical needs on a day-to-day basis. The *child's sense of time* refers to the fact that the urgency of a child's instinctual or emotional needs makes the sense of time different from that of adults who have the capacity to anticipate the future and manage delay. Thus, intervals of separation that would not seem significant to an adult constitute important breaks in continuity for young children. Finally, Goldstein et al. define *least detrimental alternative* as that child placement that maximizes in accord with the child's sense of time, the child's opportunity for being wanted and for maintaining on a continual, unconditional, and permanent basis, a relationship with at least one adult who is or will become that child's psychological parent. They further urge adoption of a standard that reads: "It is the policy of this state to minimize disruptions of continuing relationships between a psychological parent . . . and the child" (p. 99). Other recommendations by Goldstein et al. are that the child be made a party to the custody dispute represented by independent counsel and that trials and appeals be conducted as rapidly as is consistent with responsible decision making (pp. 100–101).

The child's sense of time is represented in the Goldstein et al. proposed legislation in the definition of *longtime caretaker*, who is defined as an adult who has cared for a child (1) for 1 year or more, in the case of children under the age of 3 at the time of placement, or (2) for at least 2 years, in the case of children 3 or older at the time of placement. There is a presumption that longtime caretakers are the psychological parents of the child in their custody because, according to the time perspective of the young child, it is as if that child had been with those caretakers since birth.

NATIONAL COUNCIL OF JUVENILE COURT JUDGES' MODEL STATUTE ON TERMINATION

Language from the above standards appears in the Model Statute for Termination of Parental Rights developed by the Neglected Children Committee of the National Council of Juvenile Court Judges (Lincoln, 1976). The introductory section of the statute notes that "children have their own built-in time sense based on the urgency of their instinctual and emotional needs" (quoted in Lincoln, 1976, p. 5). Echoing Goldstein et al. (1979), the statute notes that what seems like a short wait to an adult can be an intolerable separation to a young child. Protection of children's attachments to foster caretakers is mentioned in the introduction, which asserts that repeated uprooting of children in placement who have become attached to surrogate parents is "seriously detrimental to their physical, mental, and emotional well being" (quoted in Lincoln, 1976, p. 5). The statute also mandates that there shall be prompt and final adjudication in order to ensure stable and ongoing care of the child and that appeals from an order terminating parental rights shall have first priority in the higher court.

The language of the statute sets stringent standards for the success of such appeals that require proof of legal error in the lower court's decision to the substantial prejudice of the appellant, gross abuse of judicial discretion, or judgment clearly and manifestly against the weight of the evidence. The statute specifies a preponderance of the evidence standard for the actual termination proceedings within the family court. In general, the majority of state statutes currently provide for a "clear and convincing evidence" standard for termination of parental rights. This standard emerged after the United States Supreme Court decision in *Santosky v. Kramer* (1982) overturned the more lenient "preponderance of the evidence" standard that had been employed for termination actions in many state courts.

The National Council of Juvenile Court Judges' Model Statute also mandates appointment of an attorney to represent the child as counsel and as guardian ad litem, consistent with the recommendation by Goldstein et al. (1979) that the child be made a party to the termination action and be represented by independent counsel. It is also consistent with due process protection built into the termination statutes of 46 states, in which the law provides for the appointment of a guardian ad litem to represent the child in termination actions (Neal, 1989).

Among the criteria proposed by the Model Termination of Parental Rights Statute for severing birth parents' rights are emotional illness or mental deficiency of such duration or nature as to render a parent incapable of caring for the child. This is consistent with case law that recognizes such conditions as legitimate grounds for termination but that rejects termination solely on those grounds, absent a demonstrated nexus between the condition and a parent's capacity to care for the child. Other factors that demonstrate parental unfitness under the standards of the statute include physical, emotional, or sexual abuse of a child; excessive use of drugs or alcohol; neglect; conviction of a felony and imprisonment; and unexplained injury or death of a sibling.

The statute also recognizes the duty of birth parents to cooperate in the efforts of social service agencies to rehabilitate them. It cites the failure of reasonable efforts along these lines as constituting another factor in establishing unfitness. Also mentioned is the parents' failure to maintain regular visitation with children in placement and failure to maintain reasonable consistent contact or communication with a child. Parents' lack of effort to adjust their circumstances, conduct, or conditions to meet the needs of the child is noted.

Integration of the child into the foster family constitutes another dimension of the child's situation that courts are to consider in deciding on termination of parental rights, as per the Model Statute. It mandates that courts take into account "whether said child has become integrated into the foster family to the extent that his familial identity is with that family" (quoted in Lincoln, 1976, p. 7). This is consistent with the purely psychological consideration of protecting the child's mental health and personality development by supporting the placement alternative that causes the least harm to the child's developing a positively valued sense of personal identity. The statute also strives to protect the other chief pillar of personality development, the child's object relations. As part of this determination, the statue instructs courts to note "the love, affection, and other emotional ties existing between the child and the parents, and his ties with the integrating family," as well as "the capacity and disposition of the parents from whom he was removed as compared with that of the integrating family to give the child love, affection, and guidance and continuing the education of the child" (quoted in Lincoln, 1976, p. 7).

Other factors that the Model Statute specifies include the length of time that the child has been in the placement and the "moral fitness, physical, and mental health of the parents from whom the child was removed and that of the integrating family or person" (quoted in Lincoln, 1976, p. 7). The statute mandates that courts consider the child's preference, if the child is deemed capable of expressing such a preference. Finally, as an overriding consideration, the proposed statute makes clear that it is "the physical, mental, or emotional condition and needs of the child" (quoted in Lincoln, 1976, p. 8) that are to receive priority.

CHAPTER 3

National Legislation and Case Analysis

RECENT NATIONAL LEGISLATIVE EFFORTS

As noted in the Introduction, on November 19, 1997, President Clinton signed into law an important piece of legislation entitled the Adoption and Safe Families Act of 1997. This act includes a number of measures geared toward increasing the number of children moved from foster care to adoption and rewarding states monetarily for demonstrated progress in this area. While federal law does not determine state statutes and case law in an absolute fashion, it typically exerts a strong influence on events at the state level. This effect is accomplished by providing a model for state legislation and occasionally, as in the present case, by including financial incentives for states to conform their laws to the federal model. It should be noted that there is often considerable variation among states in matters of law and that it is necessary for practitioners to familiarize themselves with the requirements of the law in their particular state when consulting in termination of parental rights cases. Figure 2.1 in Chapter 2 gives an overview of the termination of parental rights statutes across states.

The Adoption and Safe Families Act removes the requirement that the state make reasonable efforts toward reunification of foster children with their birth parents under certain conditions. (This "fast-track" adoption issue is discussed more fully in Chapter 7. The act states that

> if a court of competent jurisdiction has determined that the child has been subjected to aggravated circumstances (as defined by State law, which definition may include abandonment, torture, chronic abuse, and sexual abuse) . . . or that the parental rights of a parent with respect to a sibling of the child have been terminated involuntarily . . . reasonable efforts of the type described [above] shall not be required to be made with respect to any parent of the child who has been involved in subjecting the child to such circumstances or such conduct, or whose parental rights with respect to a sibling of the child have been terminated involuntarily.

The section goes on to state that "in determining the reasonable efforts to be made with respect to a child and in making such reasonable efforts, the child's health and safety shall be of paramount concern." Whether this includes the child's mental health as well as physical health is not made explicit; however, it is certainly arguable that mental health considerations such as the possibility of severe and enduring psychological harm associated with severing the child's relationship with caretakers to whom the child has become attached falls under this section of the statute.

One of the most important sections of the act is one that mandates that the state file a petition to terminate parental rights in the case of any child under the age of 10 years who has been in foster care for 15 out of the most recent 22 months. The only exceptions to this specified in the bill are if (1) the child is already in the care of a relative, (2) a state child protective agency has documented a "compelling reason" that a petition for termination would not be in the child's best interests, or (3) the state has not met its burden of providing rehabilitative services under the reasonable efforts requirement. The act rewards states with adoption incentive payments of $4,000 for each foster child moved into adoption during the fiscal year in excess of the base number of adoptions and an additional $2,000 for each adoption of a special needs child in excess of the base number for the fiscal year. The act requires states that seek these funds to provide baseline figures for foster care adoptions and special needs adoptions in a report to the federal government. The importance of this section of the act is that it furnishes a powerful legislative remedy to the practice of allowing children to languish in the indeterminate status of foster child for years on end.

The act replaces the current requirement of dispositional hearings for foster children 18 months after placement under the Social Security Act with a 12-month requirement. The terminology also changes from "dispositional" to "permanency" hearings that are no longer to address the "future status of" the child but are instead to create

> a permanency plan for the child (including whether and, if applicable when, the child will be returned to the parent, the child will be placed for adoption and the State will file a petition to terminate the parental rights of the parent, a legal guardian will be appointed for the child, or the child will be placed in some other planned, permanent living arrangement, including the custody of another fit and willing relative).

The next section of the act mandates that foster parents or relatives caring for a child be provided with notice of reviews or hearings concerning the child's status. The act does not, however, permit foster parents to become parties to termination litigation or to participate in the status review process beyond merely being heard as witnesses.

One provision of the Senate version of the bill that was dropped in the final version of the act mandated that the Department of Health and Human Services prepare and submit a report to the House Ways and Means Committee that describes the extent and scope of the problem of substance abuse in the child welfare population, types of services provided to this population, and outcomes of service delivery. Also mandated in the earlier form of that bill was that recommendations be developed for coordinating drug abuse interventions and child welfare interventions.

The Adoption and Safe Families Act of 1997 also eliminated provisions in the previous Senate bill that would have mandated priority substance abuse treatment for child welfare cases and that would have provided payments to support children residing with a parent in domestic violence shelters or drug rehabilitation programs. The act added a provision specifying that nothing in the act is intended to intrude inappropriately into family life, prohibit the use of reasonable methods of parental discipline, or prescribe a particular method of parenting.

ANALYSIS OF TWO ILLUSTRATIVE CASES

In the Matter of Guardianship of J. T.

Two recent New Jersey cases illustrate the present state of litigation in this area, providing insight into the reasons for many of the provisions of the above legislation. In particular, these cases cast light on some of the themes common to all of the above bills, including the timeliness of a permanent resolution of a child's situation, the reduction of the movement of children through a succession of foster placements, and the responsibility of the birth parent to maintain a relationship with the child instead of abandoning that child. Further, in both of the following cases there was extensive involvement of mental health professionals, resulting in both positive and negative consequences, according to the level of expertise and professional judgment of the individual practitioner. One of the cases, J. T., also illustrates the efforts of foster parents to become involved as litigants in a termination action.

In the Matter of Guardianship of J. T. (1993) the state appeals court commented on the history of a case that dragged on through the legal system from October 1991 to November 1993 and beyond. Between November 1987 and July 1989 the Division of Youth and Family Services was involved with this family because of homelessness and alleged neglect of their then two children, E. T. and M. T. On July 19, 1989, these two children were voluntarily placed with their maternal grandmother in Puerto Rico by the birth mother, S. S. The infant in question, J. T., was born in November 1989, at which time she presented with congenital syphilis and was unable to breathe on her own, requiring respiratory stimulation. The child weighed 3 pounds 5 ounces at birth and was born at 30 to 31 weeks gestation. According to hospital records, the birth mother was a cocaine user and in fact used the drug 2 hours before being admitted to the hospital to deliver J. T. The Division of Youth and Family Services inquired with the maternal grandmother in Puerto Rico about placement of J. T.; however, the grandmother stated that as she was already caring for S. S.'s 1½- and 2½-year-old children she would not be able to take on the responsibility of caring for J. T.

On December 18, 1989, the Division of Youth and Family Services filed a Complaint for Protective Services. The complaint alleged that the birth father of J. T. was "crazy" and that the couple had no place to live. On February 1, 1990, the Division of Youth and Family Services was granted an Order for Protective Services.

On January 4, 1990, J. T. was discharged from the hospital and placed in a foster home. On February 1, 1990, the birth parents were court ordered to visit the child twice per month. Neither parent complied with any aspect of the order, nor did either parent attend a hearing of the Child Placement Review Board. The Division of Youth and Family Services subsequently made other attempts to place J. T. with relatives, none of whom were interested in caring for her.

From December 27, 1989, until December 7, 1990, the birth parents failed to express an interest in J. T. or to arrange a permanent plan for her. An action for termination of parental rights was filed in Superior Court on March 12, 1991. A state child protective services worker spoke with the birth mother on February 26, 1991, at which time the birth mother stated that she wanted her daughter back. This was the first time that the birth mother had shown any interest in the child. The birth mother was informed that a Guardianship Complaint was about to be filed and that she would have to await the outcome of the litigation. In response to the Guardianship Complaint and Order to Show Cause, the birth mother appeared in court after she was assigned an attorney. A default judgment was entered against the birth father on May 21, 1991.

I performed a bonding assessment (see Chapter 6 for a discussion of bonding assessments) of J. T. with her foster mother on July 31, 1991, at which time J. T. was 20 months old. The foster mother was observed to be a competent, attuned caretaker who appeared to be emotionally invested in the child. J. T., despite her adverse birth history, appeared developmentally normal, happy, and content. The parent–child interaction indicated that this child was selectively attached to her foster mother. My recommendation was that the state continue to pursue a case goal of foster home adoption for this child, as removal from that home and placement with the birth mother would inflict a traumatic loss that would result in impairments of the child's basic trust, self-esteem, capacity to form intimate emotional ties to others in the future, and capacity for normal self-confidence and optimism.

A termination hearing was held in Superior Court in October 1991. At the conclusion of the evidence, the trial judge stated that he was not satisfied that the state had established by clear and convincing evidence that the Division of Youth and Family Services had considered other reasonable alternatives to terminating the mother's rights as required by case law, particularly *New Jersey Division of Youth and Family Services v. A. W.* (1986).

On December 18, 1991, the trial judge considered written summations and evidence addressing the above issue and concluded that the New Jersey Division of Youth and Family Services had not conducted a satisfactory investigation of other alternatives to termination. On January 2, 1992, the judge ordered the Division of Youth and Family Services to investigate other alternatives to termination and to arrange biweekly visitation between the birth mother and J. T., who was now 25 months old. On March 11, 1992, the judge ordered the Division of Youth and Family Services to "conduct an in-depth study regarding the [natural mother's] proposed alternatives to termination of her parental rights," which specifically referred to the birth mother's proposed alternative of placing J. T., with her and her new boyfriend, with whom she was residing and whom she subsequently married.

On August 20, 1992, the foster mother was permitted limited intervention in the case, and on September 25, 1992, the trial judge appointed another psychologist to conduct an immediate evaluation of all parties to examine "the bonding and relationship between [J. T.] and her biological mother as well as the bonding and relationship with her foster mother." The judge cited another New Jersey decision, *In the Matter of K. L. F.* (1992), in support of the order. At this point J. T. was nearly 3 years old and had resided with her foster mother since her discharge from the hospital 6 weeks after birth. The court-appointed psychologist testified on October 30, 1992, a full year after the initial termination of parental rights hearing. This psychologist told the court that in his opinion the best interests of J. T. would be served by placing her with her birth mother, provided that the latter could furnish an appropriate upbringing for her.

On December 4, 1992, the trial judge signed an order dismissing without prejudice the complaint for termination, that is, without precluding an action based on new or additional evidence. Provisions of the order included the state's undertaking a plan for gradual unification of J. T. with the birth mother, arranging for therapy for the birth mother and her new husband, and arranging for visitation between J. T., the birth mother, her two other children, and her husband. The judge denied the foster mother's application for a stay. On December 4, 1992, the foster mother filed an appeal of the order. The appellate court monitored the case during 1993, during which period the trial court issued several new orders modifying the visitation schedule and establishing new dates for the transfer of J. T. to the birth mother. The lack of progress toward reunification prompted the appeals court to issue a remand decision, directing a review of the entire matter by the trial court.

On remand, the expert appointed by the trial court testified that he had observed four visits between J. T. and the birth mother as of September 23, 1993. On one of these visits the child refused to enter her birth mother's home. This occurred again on a subsequent visit. On another occasion the foster mother transported J. T. for the visits, but the birth mother called and canceled. When asked to describe the relationship between J. T. and her foster mother, the psychologist stated that the child was bonded to the foster mother and that the parent–child bond between them was becoming stronger with the passage of time. The expert also noted that, although J. T. did not seem to be fearful of her birth mother, there were times when she would stay near the foster mother and not approach the birth mother. On September 23, 1993, the psychologist expressed the following opinion: "I think that at the point of transfer it would be very, very traumatic. . . . The support systems are really going to have to work very hard to help at this point now. Harder than they would have maybe a year or two ago, whatever. But they're going to have to work very hard to help this child though this transfer."

After meeting with J. T. on September 27, September 28, and September 29, 1993, the court-appointed expert gave the following opinion on unification: "I feel that at . . . almost age four, . . . I think there is a question now as to what a separation will do to this girl. . . . At this point in a child's life the maternal parent is a very important person for that child. . . . And if the direction and guidance from that person isn't in the same direction as the court has been working for, it's going to be—I feel would end up possibly being harmful to her down the road, yes." However, when asked whether the harm involved in a transfer would be serious and enduring (the statutory test for a level of harm to a child that would persuade the court not to remove that child from the foster placement), he stated, "It is very difficult to say exactly that there will not be harm later on." The expert also expressed the opinion that there were "too many factors" to consider to ascertain the degree of harm that would result from transferring J. T. to her birth mother. The appeals court opinion notes that during five visits between September 27, 1993, and October 4, 1993, J. T. had to be reassured all the time that the foster mother was not far away, and the door to the waiting room where the foster mother remained could not be closed. The child constantly asked, "Where's mother?"

A third psychologist, appearing on behalf of the foster mother, testified that he had treated J. T. 20 times between December 30, 1992, and April 16, 1993. He expressed the opinion that, at age $3\frac{1}{2}$ years, J. T., who had never lived with the birth mother, would certainly be traumatized by a transfer to another caretaker, no matter how good that caretaker might be. He further opined that J. T. would continue to require psychotherapy regardless of whether a transfer occurred. He stated that if J. T. were removed from the foster mother, he was certain that "there would be harm to the child." Echoing the predictions contained in my report on this child at age 20 months, the foster mother's expert predicted that J. T. would suffer an impairment of her ability to trust and that this would carry over to future relationships. He stated, "I don't think that she would be able to, as she grows up, be able to have relationships with other people without, intimate relations with other people without being absolutely terrified that they will leave as well."

A fourth psychologist provided seven sessions of psychotherapy to J. T. at the request of the foster mother and submitted a report dated September 10, 1993. The trial judge excluded this report from evidence, but the appeals court considered it to be legitimate evidence and ruled that the trial judge's failure to consider it amounted to a mistaken exercise of discretion. The appeals court directed that it be made a part of the appendix. The appeals court also ruled that the trial court's failure to consider it as evidence was a mistaken exercise of discretion. Concurring with me and with the foster mother's expert, this fourth psychologist, who had provided seven sessions of therapy to J. T. at the request of the foster mother, stated, "Removing J. T. from the only psychological parent and home she has ever known would likely cause irreparable harm to her emotionally and developmentally. . . . The probability of irreparable damage to this child in the event the transfer takes place is overwhelming. . . . Separating from [the foster mother] and her children will in all probability cause [J. T.] severe and permanent emotional damage which no amount of therapy will rectify."

Given the above expert opinions on the consequences of removing J. T. from the foster mother who had raised her since the age of 6 weeks, it is of interest to review the reasoning of the trial judge in issuing the order for transfer of this child to her birth mother. The trial judge stated, "There is no doubt it will be difficult. There is no doubt that there would be some trauma and therefore some harm. And there is no doubt that bonding has taken place because of—and has probably solidified because of delays by the court system, by DYFS [state child protective services], by the legal machinations and maneuverings, but Dr. [foster mother's expert] has a recommendation, yet what is it based on? On a possible attention disorder, on certain self-esteem problems, or flirtatiousness. I just don't think that's enough. There's trauma in every case such as this. . . . Certainly there will be harm. But does the harm reach the level talked about in these cases, and has it been shown to this court clearly and convincingly?"

In its legal analysis of the case, the appeals court noted that cases in which a child has bonded with excellent foster parents and in which the birth parents are rehabilitated are always difficult to decide. The appeals court felt that at the conclusion of the original termination hearing on October 31, 1991, the trial court should have dismissed the guardianship complaint on the grounds that the state had not established through clear and convincing evidence that the birth mother's request for unification had been fully explored. This was based on the requirements of New Jersey's *A. W.* case that unless all reasonable alternatives to termination had been considered, the complaint for guardianship should be dismissed. The appeals court added that not only should the complaint have been dismissed but the state child protective services should have been left with the responsibility of managing the case, including drafting a plan for the child's permanent placement. The court stated: "*A. W.* recognizes that DYFS [state child protective services] is especially better equipped to provide these services than judges. . . . In the process of effectuating the legislative policy, a judge must be careful not to usurp the function delegated to DYFS."

It is noted that such close judicial oversight of a case is typical of divorce/custody matters that come before the family court; custody and visitation are issues that are considered together with division of the marital assets, alimony, and many other divorce-related issues on which the court makes a variety of rulings. However, this model is inappropriate to handle parental fitness matters that are not concerned with who gets weekends, vacations, and school holidays with the children but that center on manifest parental unfitness at the time of removal of the child, the child's subsequent attachment pattern, rehabilitation of the birth parent, and special needs of both the parent and the child. One might speculate that the trial judge in J. T. handled the case as though it were a divorce matter without being fully aware of the special psychological and social casework aspects of termination cases.

In regard to the issue of psychological bonding of the child with the foster parent, the opinion of the appeals court was quite direct. The court cited another New Jersey Supreme Court case, *Matter of Guardianship of J. C.* (1992), in which it was stated that "bonding that takes place before a termination petition has been decided serves to decrease the potential for eventual reunification." The court went on to note that in J. T. a substantial portion of the child's bonding with the foster mother as her psychological parent was caused by the birth mother's lack of interest in J. T. for the first 15 months of the child's life. The birth mother made no attempts to visit the child or to take custody of her between the time that the mother was discharged from the hospital on November 25, 1989, and February 26, 1991, when she informed the caseworker of her desire to pursue custody. Indeed, the appeals court felt that the trial judge had gone so wide of the mark as to warrant an intervention by the appellate court that went beyond its usual limited scope in a nonjury case. The appellate court also expanded the traditional scope of its review of this case because of "alleged error in the trial judge's evaluation of the underlying facts and the implications to be drawn therefrom."

The court noted in its opinion of November 22, 1993, that it had made clear in its original remand decision that J. T. should not be given to her birth mother if "separating the child from her foster mother would cause serious and enduring emotional or psychological harm." While acknowledging that the child's relationship with the birth parents must be considered in deciding such cases, the appellate court stated: "We agree with the foster mother and DYFS [state child protective services] that the trial judge's evaluation of the evidence submitted by the experts and the implications to be drawn therefrom went so wide of the mark, that the interests of justice demand intervention and correction. All four experts agree that J. T.'s relationship with the foster mother is excellent, and that a very intense emotional bond exists between J. T., the foster mother, and her children." The court also cited my opinion, along with that of the foster mother's expert and of the psychologist who had treated J. T. for seven sessions at the foster mother's request, namely, that a transfer would cause serious and enduring emotional or psychological harm. Also cited was the opinion of the trial judge's expert who, "though less specific, stated that the transfer 'would be very, very traumatic.'"

The appellate court stated that the trial judge was apparently of the view that absolute certainty of serious and enduring harm was required to satisfy the state's burden of proof. The appellate court noted that "such long-term predictions cannot be made with absolute certainty" and that under New Jersey law the proofs in family court matters are not required to rise to that level. Noting this, the appellate court characterized the psychological evidence in J. T. as "overwhelming" and determined that it met the clear and convincing standard. On that basis, the court reversed the trial court's order for transfer of J. T. to the birth mother.

In the Matter of Guardianship of K. L. F., a Minor

Although the New Jersey appellate court's opinion in J. T.'s case reflected several aspects of the federal legislation now being considered regarding facilitation of adoptions, including speedy resolution of the situation of each child in foster care, taking into account the child's attachment to foster caretakers and the abandonment of children by biological parents, a New Jersey Supreme Court case, *In the Matter of Guardianship of K. L. F., a Minor* (1991/1992), represents the judicial antithesis of these congressional efforts. The case points up the complexities of judicial interpretation of behavioral science evidence in these matters, especially when the state has proceeded in a manner contrary to statute and the higher court must as a matter of law correct the injustice, even though this may adversely affect the child psychologically. B. F., the biological mother of K. L. F., became pregnant with the child as a result of being gang raped in New York City. She came to New Jersey to have the child, believing that New York City was too dangerous a place to rear children. She gave birth to a healthy daughter, K. L. F., in November 1988.

At the time she gave birth, the biological mother was homeless and therefore entered into an arrangement with the state child protective services to place the child into temporary foster care. The agency arranged for B. F. to live at a shelter that did not allow infants or children. B. F. visited the baby twice during December 1988 at the state offices. When she came for a third visit she was unable to see the child because the caseworker was ill. Shortly after this, B. F. returned to New York City in search of permanent housing, leaving the baby under the care of New Jersey's child protective services.

The New Jersey Supreme Court noted that during the following year and a half the biological mother was unemployed and homeless. She testified at trial that she had made numerous attempts to contact the New Jersey caseworker responsible for her child but was unable to reach an agency worker who was able to help her. Workers for the state child protective services sent letters to various state agencies and made many telephone calls in an attempt to locate the birth mother, all to no avail. In May 1990, which was 18 months after K. L. F. had entered foster care, the state concluded that the child needed a permanent home and transferred her to a new set of preadoptive parents, removing her from the foster parents with whom she had been residing since birth. K. L. F. remained in the custody of the preadoptive parents until shortly after June 30, 1992, the date of the state Supreme Court's decision. K. L. F. was then 3½ years old.

The New Jersey Supreme Court noted that under the voluntary placement agreement that the birth mother signed, she had the right to take back custody of her child at any time. The court stated that if the state wished to retain custody of K. L. F., despite the birth mother's request, then it was necessary to seek a court order authorizing it to do so. The court stated: "DYFS [state child protective services] was not empowered to displace B. F. as a parent without judicial approval."

Less than one month after the state filed a guardianship action in this case, the birth mother reached K. L. F.'s new caseworker and requested to see her child so that she could eventually regain custody. The caseworker informed B. F. that the agency was bringing a legal action to terminate her parental rights and that she would have to release medical information, undergo a psychiatric evaluation, and wait for a court to decide if she could visit the child. B. F. attempted to bring suit without an attorney to recover her child, but became frustrated and did not pursue that course.

B. F. found a stable living situation and signed a 3-year lease on an apartment in Staten Island, New York, where she was living with another daughter. The New Jersey Supreme Court noted that, despite the birth mother's stability, the state nevertheless petitioned the court for guardianship of K. L. F. and for termination of parental rights based on abandonment of the child and the best interests of the child. The state concluded that K. L. F. had bonded with the preadoptive parents, with whom she had been living for 10 months and that moving her again would cause her psychological and emotional harm.

The trial court refused to grant guardianship on the grounds that the state had not met its burden of demonstrating by clear and convincing evidence that K. L. F. would suffer serious and enduring harm if removed from the preadoptive parents and given over to her birth mother. Further, the trial court found that B. F. had not abandoned the child and that she had rehabilitated her lifestyle to the point where she was a fit parent for her daughter K. L. F.

In its opinion on this case, the New Jersey Supreme Court set forth its bases for supporting the above findings, which were also affirmed by the appellate court. In regard to the issue of abandonment, the New Jersey Supreme Court found that B. F. had no income and no home and was therefore unable to receive telephone calls from caseworkers who were attempting to locate her. The court also found that B. F. had made "numerous" and "persistent" attempts to communicate with the state child protective services. This finding was based on the birth mother's testimony that she had telephoned the agency from pay telephones during the child's term in foster care and that she had attempted to file pro se legal actions in two separate New Jersey counties to regain custody of her daughter. The New Jersey Supreme Court mentioned in its opinion that "no phone calls were separated by more than a year." This criterion for concluding that abandonment had not occurred contrasts dramatically with the language of the New Jersey bill cited in Chapter 2 concerning abandonment. The New Jersey bill states that in order to avoid triggering the requirement that the state file a guardianship petition, a birth parent must demonstrate the following:

a. The maintenance of a relationship with the child such that the child perceives the person as his parent;
b. Communicating with the child or person having legal custody of the child and visiting the child unless visitation is impossible because of the parent's confinement in an institution or unless prevented from doing so by the custodial parent or other custodian of the child or a social service agency over the parent's objection; or

c. Providing financial support for the child unless prevented from doing so by the custodial parent or other custodian of the child or a social service agency.

Thus, under the subsequent New Jersey legislation, the fact that B. F. attempted to contact the state child protective services on many occasions, with none of the calls separated by more than a year, would not be sufficient to preclude the filing of a termination action.

Myers (1992) defines abandonment as "parental conduct indicating a conscious disregard of the obligations of parenthood" (p. 187). He cites a Nebraska case (*In re J. S.*, 1987), particularly relevant to K. L. F., in which the court held that "voluntary departure from the state may be viewed as abandonment of one's children and cannot be used as an excuse for the impossibility of compliance with a court-ordered plan of rehabilitation" (p. 187). Myers states that, while some birth parents may at a later time attempt to reestablish a relationship with children whom they have, in effect, abandoned, "abandonment is not washed away by minimal efforts to reestablish a relationship" (p. 188). He cites *Matter of Loretta Lynn W.* (1989) in New York and *In re Adoption of T. M.* (1989) in Pennsylvania as examples of courts' refusals to accept token efforts on the part of birth parents to reestablish contact with their children as sufficient grounds to negate a finding of abandonment. On the other hand, *Black v. Gray* (1988), a private custody case in Delaware in which the child's mother filed a petition to terminate the biological father's parental rights because of abandonment, resulted in a state supreme court decision to reverse the lower court's termination decision on the grounds that, under Delaware law, "an abandonment is not an irrevocable act." It is noted that this case did not involve foster placement of the child in question and that the legal action was between two birth parents, not between the birth parent and the state.

In regard to the finding that the state had not met its burden of showing that K. L. F. would suffer serious or enduring harm if removed from the preadoptive parents, the New Jersey bill contains language that echoes the language of the decision. The bill states: "Such harm may include evidence that separating the child from his foster parents would cause serious and enduring emotional or psychological harm to the child" (N.J. Assembly, 1996a). It is of considerable interest, then, to examine the court's basis for concluding that such harm would not befall K. L. F. if she were removed at age 3½ years from foster parents with whom she had been living for 2 years and placed with a birth mother with whom she had never lived.

The state's expert, a psychologist with considerable experience in child protective services cases, testified that the cumulative effect of another change of custody "could be permanent" and that the child's history of two separations from caretakers with whom she had formed an attachment would have effects amounting to "long-term time bombs." However, according to the New Jersey Supreme Court opinion, the state's expert acknowledged that K. L. F. had apparently adapted successfully to the change in caretakers at age 18 months. As a basis for her conclusions, the state's expert expressed her general views on the impact of disruptions and changes on child development. The expert testified that children who experience multiple changes in custody tend to fall below other children in development because the former spend their energies on acclimating to the continual changes. The state's expert predicted that children who do not bond psychologically will suffer from an inability to form lasting relationships and will become disruptive and distrustful. The written opinion does not make reference to the citation by either expert in the case of any empirical or clinical literature. Thus, it appears that the K. L. F. case involved a classical "battle of the experts" in which both experts testified from the position of individual authority and experience without introducing any relevant professional or scientific literature to support any of their conclusions.

The defendant's expert, a psychiatrist, testified that the detrimental effect of removing K. L. F. from the preadoptive parents and giving her over to the birth mother would be "minimal." This expert's explanation for such a conclusion was that "the vulnerability of a child in moving is very concentrated between 9 months and 18 months because this is the time in which the child generally learns who is stranger and who is home base." According to the defense psychiatrist, if the child has successfully bonded with a primary caretaker during the critical early years of life, in this case the foster placement from birth to 18 months and the preadoptive placement from 18 months to 28 months, the child acquires a set of adaptive skills that allow her to absorb significant changes successfully. In fact, the New Jersey Supreme Court opinion noted "The trial court accepted the testimony of [the defense expert] that K. L. F. could readily overcome any problems associated with leaving her preadoptive parents." The trial court also stated that the records of the state child protective services covering the transfer of custody from the foster home to the preadoptive home at age 18 months indicated that "her reaction and her adjustment was marvelous, was appropriate, was normal, was suitable." Therefore, the trial court was persuaded by the testimony of the defense expert that this child's "successful" experience of being transferred from the foster parents to the preadoptive parents indicated that she would similarly adjust to being given to her birth mother.

The New Jersey Supreme Court opinion noted that the appellate court determined that even if the testimony of the state's expert were credited and accepted, it was insufficient for a showing of the required degree of harm by clear and convincing evidence. The appellate court stated: "In short, [the state's expert] found K. L. F. had handled with substantial success two major moves in her young life, but she was concerned about the child's ability to respond well to yet another move. That is a legitimate concern: surely it would be preferable for a child not to be so disrupted. But the fact that another such move inevitably carries some risk is not clear and convincing evidence that the return of the child to her mother would be "so injurious" as to justify terminating the mother's rights." Noting that they were "acutely mindful of the controversy that surrounds the competing psychological theories of the effects of bonding," the judges on the New Jersey Supreme Court stated that, while the state's expert felt that a transfer of custody would cause K. L. F. harm, "based on her assumption that change itself was harmful," they found that "the record supports the contrary conclusion of the trial court." This conclusion was based on the defense expert's "beliefs that after a certain age children can absorb change, particularly if it takes place under the right circumstances."

Taken from the perspective of the existing literature on infant attachment, separation, loss, and personality development, the New Jersey Supreme Court's citation of "competing psychological theories of the effects of bonding" amounts to elevating the remarks of one expert witness to the status of a "theory," although there is nothing in the record to suggest that the defense expert's views represented anything other than his own clinical observations. Indeed, the review of the research and theoretical literature presented in Chapters 8 and 9 indicates that there is virtual unanimity on the point that the loss of a child's central parental love objects during the period prior to age 5 years, especially if this event is repeated with new sets of caretakers to whom the child has formed an attachment, constitutes a severe blow to that child's personality development and subsequent mental health.

The defense expert's testimony to the effect that K. L. F.'s "successful experience" of adjusting to new parent figures after losing her first set of caretakers at age 18 months would enable her to "readily overcome any problems associated with leaving her preadoptive parents" at age 28 months (in the middle of a developmental subphase in which children are thought to be especially vulnerable to psychic harm if traumatized) is, in my opinion, contrary to every theoretical formulation reviewed in Chapter 8 and to every empirical research and clinical study reviewed in Chapter 9. It is therefore puzzling that the New Jersey Supreme Court would cite this type of testimony (which, in my opinion, does not even comport with common sense) as a primary basis for their finding of no severe and enduring harm associated with a new transfer of custody of this child.

Other jurisdictions tend to view such matters differently. The Texas Supreme Court, for example, in *E.I. du Pont de Nemours and Co. v. Robinson* (1995) stated, "Even an expert with a degree should not be able to testify that the world is flat, that the moon is made of green cheese. . . . If for some reason such testimony were admitted in a trial without objection, would a reviewing court be obliged to accept it as evidence? The answer is no." The elevation of the individual views of the defense expert in K. L. F. to the status of a "competing psychological theory" could have been precluded by the trial court's insistence on both experts' citation of some research or theoretical literature in support of their testimony.

Another factor that the trial court stressed in the original decision in this case was that the state's expert discounted the significance of the difference between the child's racial background and that of the preadoptive parents. The decision does not specify what the racial background of either was, or exactly how that should have been factored into the expert's opinions. A commentary on this issue in K. L. F. would have been very helpful, as the issue of transracial adoptions is quite controversial among certain professional groups. Two policy statements of the Association of Black Social Workers on the social and individual impact of adoption of African American children by white families are presented in Chapter 7, which also reviews the empirical literature in this area.

My interpretation of the dynamics of this case is that the New Jersey Supreme Court seized on the defense expert's testimony to justify their remedying the wrong to the birth mother of the state's having moved to place her child for adoption without according her due process through first filing for an Order to Show Cause. Unfortunately the remedying of this injustice had the side effect of inflicting another traumatic loss of a child of 3½ years who had already suffered the loss of her central parental love objects at age 18 months. This is much easier to do if one minimizes the perception of harm to the child by unquestioning acceptance of expert opinion to the effect that the first experience of separation (actually loss) strengthened her so that she could readily tolerate a second blow of this type. The recent signing into law of the Adoption and Safe Families Act of 1997, discussed above, will cause judges at all levels to place greater weight on avoiding this type of psychological harm to the child and less weight on the rights of birth parents who allow their children to languish in the foster care system for lengthy periods of time without making genuine efforts to become involved in their lives.

CHAPTER 4

Ethical Considerations in Parental Fitness and Related Evaluations

The American Psychological Association (APA; 1998) released its *Guidelines for Psychological Evaluations in Child Protection Matters* relating to children in the foster care system. The guidelines recognize that parents have a fundamental civil and constitutional right to care for their children and that the child has a fundamental interest in being protected from abuse and neglect. Citing the doctrine of *parens patriae*—or the role of the state as protector of interests such as health, comfort, and welfare of citizens—the guidelines note that states have the right to intervene in private family matters when a child is at risk.

The APA guidelines indicate that such interventions typically occur in three stages. At the first stage, when there is a report of child abuse or neglect to a state agency, the matter is investigated. At the second stage, if the findings of the investigation indicate that the child is at sufficient risk, then that child may be placed outside of the home, and the state may make recommendations for the parents' rehabilitation. At the third stage, if rehabilitative efforts have failed to create a sufficiently safe environment for the child or if the child has been returned unsuccessfully, then the state may request a hearing for final disposition. This action may result in termination of parental rights.

The guidelines mandate that psychologists engaged in child protection evaluations make themselves aware of relevant standards for removal and termination of parental rights proceedings. The guidelines note that termination of parental rights is an extreme disposition and that the United States Supreme Court has instituted a clear and convincing evidentiary standard for such proceedings (*Santosky v. Kramer*, 1982).

According to the guidelines, the primary purpose of a child protection evaluation is "to provide relevant, professionally supportable results or opinions in matters where a child's health and welfare may have been and/or may in the future be impaired by the parental relationship." An additional dimension of the assessment in cases in which the state is seeking to terminate parental rights is whether rehabilitation efforts for and by the parents have succeeded in providing a safe environment for the child's return. Curiously, while the guidelines state that the child's interest and well-being are paramount, the only additional focus in termination evaluations that the guidelines cite is whether the parents have been or can be successfully rehabilitated. The guidelines are silent on the subject of the potential of devastating psychological harm to the child in cases in which, after a lengthy stay in foster care in which the developing child forms a profound attachment to the caretaker, a return to the birth parents inflicts upon that child the loss of the central parental love object.

Other salient topics treated in these guidelines include an emphasis on the maintenance of an objective and impartial stance; necessity of acquiring specialized competence in child development; family dynamics; impact of separation on children; and child abuse issues. The guidelines also stress sensitivity to "human differences" (gender, race, ethnicity, religion, national origin, sexual orientation, disability, language, or socioeconomic status) in performing child protection assessments. For example, psychologists are to be aware of variations in child-rearing practices among cultures and to weigh these practices against the requirements of existing state law in rendering opinions concerning the parent–child relationship.

The child protection evaluation guidelines stress avoidance of multiple relationships and confusion concerning role boundaries. This would include such practices as refusing to accept any of the parties being evaluated as a psychotherapy patient during the assessment period and only accepting such an involvement with caution following a child protection evaluation. However, the guidelines do permit testimony as a fact or expert witness regarding information that the psychologist has become aware of in a professional relationship with a client. Permitted also is testimony on child development and similar topics about which the psychologist provides expertise to the court without relating this information specifically to the parties involved in a particular case.

As is the case generally with clinical and forensic assessments, the guidelines mandate that evaluators obtain informed consent from all adult participants and explain the situation to the child, as appropriate. Psychologists are to inform clients of the nature of the evaluation, its purpose, to whom the results will be provided, and the role of the psychologist as the referring party. Children are to be informed that their safety is of primary importance and that because of this the information generated by the examination will be shared with others. Psychologists are to inform participants of the limits of confidentiality.

Other procedural requirements set forth in the guidelines include multiple methods of data gathering, clarification of financial arrangements, maintenance of adequate written records, and the exercise of appropriate caution in interpreting assessment data. In regard to the first of these, multiple methods of data gathering, it goes without saying that psychologists who deal with individuals who are involved with state child protective services should avail themselves of as much information as possible in documenting harm to the child; parents' attitudes toward social service personnel; rehabilitation efforts; medical treatment; arrests; handicapping conditions; and similar concerns that are documented in the case record of the referring agency.

Finally, the guidelines mandate formulating conclusions according to well-established professional and scientific standards with clearly articulated reasoning and disclosure of all relevant data pertaining to all sides of the issues that are being evaluated. Noting that the profession has not reached consensus about the advisability of making dispositional recommendations, the guidelines advise psychologists who choose to offer such recommendations to do so on the basis of sound psychological data and of the child's health and welfare.

The *Ethical Principles of Psychologists and Code of Conduct* of the American Psychological Association (APA; 1992) includes a section listing ethical standards specifically applicable to forensic psychology. Not only is psychological consultation in termination cases governed by these principles, but there is also a subset of ethical standards for family court work that affects termination cases as well.

Standards 5.01, 5.02, and 5.05 of the APA's (1992) *Ethical Principles* deal with confidentiality issues. Psychologists have an obligation to discuss with clients the limitations on confidentiality and have a primary obligation to respect the confidentiality rights of those with whom they work. Psychologists may disclose confidential information with the consent of the client or under certain limited circumstances without the client's consent for such purposes as providing needed professional services to the client, obtaining appropriate professional consultations for the client, or protecting the client or others from harm. As far as child protection evaluations are concerned, the psychologist must inform the client that there is no confidentiality in the evaluation session and that whatever the client says could find its way into the examiner's report. This is an important consideration, since it is not uncommon for clients to ask, well into the process, if some fact that they are about to disclose will be treated in confidence. It is also important to inform clients that the report and any other information generated by the assessment, such as notes and test data, will only be disclosed to the referring agency and will not be used for any other purpose.

The principles are silent regarding such specific situations as the psychologist's being served with a subpoena by private attorneys in a civil action for records of clients examined for a state agency in connection with child protection issues. Generally, the psychologist has a duty to resist such subpoenas, since the client has not waived confidentiality. While subpoenas issued by an attorney's office carry official warnings in the name of the court, specifying civil penalties and a contempt citation for failing to provide the subpoenaed materials, in reality, disclosure of privileged records can only be compelled by court order. When confronted with a court order, psychologists do indeed face judicial sanctions if they do not comply. However, even at that level of coerced disclosure there is still a further step available to practitioners that may provide additional client protection. Rather than simply turn over the subpoenaed materials to counsel, the preferred procedure is to contact the judge who issued the order and request that a provision be made for the records to be delivered directly to the judge for review in chambers as to relevance to the ultimate legal issue. It may result that the judge will exclude some or all of the material on the basis that it has no relevance to the issue to be decided by the court, thus sparing the client needless disclosure of confidential information in open court.

Standard 7.05 (a) of the APA's (1992) *Ethical Principles* states that prior professional relationships do not preclude psychologists from testifying in legal proceedings as "fact witnesses" to the extent "permitted by applicable law" (American Psychological Association, 1992, p. 1610). Perrin and Sales (1994) note that this standard leaves psychologists to discover what testimony is permissible. The authors state that the problem with the vagueness of that standard is that most psychologists who are called to testify in such circumstances are not forensic experts and are thus unaware of the differences between fact and expert witnesses and of the laws applicable to fact witnesses.

There is some case law regarding the disclosure for court purposes of privileged information by mental health professionals who have treated clients in psychotherapy. A Connecticut decision, *In re Romance M.* (1993, cited in Ackerman & Kane, 1996) ruled that privileged information could be admitted. In that case, a state appeals court found that it was proper to disclose privileged communications between a birth mother and her treating psychiatrist because the birth parents' mental health was at issue in the termination action. In New Jersey, there is case law ruling that the best interests of the child prevail over both the psychologist's privilege (*Fitzgibbon v. Fitzgibbon*, 1984; *Arena v. Saphier*, 1985) and the marriage counselor privilege (*M. v. K.*, 1982).

However, a Mississippi case (*Lauderdale County Dept. of Human Services v. T. H. G.* (1992, cited in Ackerman & Kane, 1996) ruled that information concerning mental health treatment received by parents of a 5-year-old child could not be admitted as evidence in the termination action without the consent of the patients. Treatment records and testimony by a psychiatric nurse and a psychologist who had treated the birth parents were excluded on the basis of doctor–patient privilege. The court weighed the value of such evidence in child protection against the importance of facilitating access to mental health treatment without concerns over violation of confidentiality relating to litigation. The parents had objected that such evidence was inadmissible unless a party had filed pleadings that placed his or her mental state at issue or had waived privilege.

The essential factor is therefore whether the court determines that the birth parent's mental health is of such relevance or significance in the termination action that the issue of potential harm to the child associated with some feature of the parent's contended psychological condition outweighs the parent's privilege. And the clear implication for practitioners is to protect the confidentiality of therapy patients unless a court decides that disclosure is of overriding importance and issues an order compelling such disclosure.

Standard 7.01 of the APA's (1992) *Ethical Principles* calls for psychologists to base their forensic work on appropriate knowledge and competence. Perrin and Sales (1994) point out that the guidelines do not follow up this precept with an indication of what constitutes appropriate knowledge and competence for this specialty area. They offer a general set of topics with which psychologists engaged in forensic work should be familiar. Perrin and Sales state:

> Whether the service is clinical, consultative, research, or teaching, competent forensic service provision requires some degree of competence in the forensic forum and in the interface between the forensic forum and psychological practice . . . competence in forensic psychology should include formal training in the following core areas: substantive and procedural laws affecting practice, the operation of legal systems, psycholegal research, expert witnessing, and consulting with legal and law-related practitioners (e.g., law enforcement officials) and policy makers. To this list, training in areas specific to the forensic psychologists' practice should be added (e.g., forensic clinical assessment and therapeutic procedures). (p. 376)

The New Jersey Board of Psychological Examiners' (1993) *Specialty Guidelines for Psychologists in Custody/Visitation Evaluations* provides a lengthy list of recommended competencies for psychologists who perform divorce/custody evaluations. Those areas that are relevant for termination of parental rights assessments include knowledge of child growth and development; knowledge of parent–child bonding and the effects of disrupted attachments and separations; knowledge of the scope of parenting, including parental involvement, parental capacity to provide for the child's physical and psychological needs, such as love, security, affection, valuing of the child, attunement/responsiveness, moral development, intellectual stimulation, development of autonomy, and peer/family socialization.

Furthermore, in the New Jersey guidelines, other recommended competencies for psychologists who perform divorce/custody evaluations are knowledge of adult development and psychopathology, specialized knowledge relating to abuse and impairment, including awareness of trauma responses, victimization, and general sequelae of child abuse and domestic violence; and knowledge of substance abuse and alcohol-related issues. The guidelines also mandate that evaluators possess competence in psychological testing that enables them to formulate independent clinical conclusions from personality tests and similar instruments rather than rely solely upon the results of computerized narrative reports without being able to interpret scores yielded by the measure. The guidelines expressly state: "Psychologists recognize that the ultimate responsibility for interpreting the meaning of test results and their relevance to parental capacity rests with the psychologist and not with the formulators of the computerized narrative report . . . regardless of how authoritative the output of such instruments may appear" (p. 5).

Both the *Specialty Guidelines for Psychologists in Custody/Visitation Evaluations* (New Jersey Board of Psychological Examiners, 1993) and the *Guidelines for Child Custody Evaluations in Divorce Proceedings* (American Psychological Association, 1994) stress the avoidance of what are termed "dual relationships" in the New Jersey guidelines and "multiple relationships" in the APA guidelines. The APA guidelines state that psychologists should generally avoid conducting a child custody evaluation in cases in which the psychologist has served in a therapeutic role for the child or the immediate family, nor should the psychologist accept any of the parties as a therapy client during the course of such an evaluation. The New Jersey guidelines state that under no circumstances should a treating psychologist agree to assume the role of evaluator, although under special circumstances, usually under court order, a psychologist whose initial involvement with the case was as an evaluator may agree to function subsequently as a therapist with periodic reporting to the court, with confidentiality limitations clearly explained to all parties. In regard to the provision of court testimony by treating therapists, the APA guidelines state: "A psychologist asked to testify regarding a therapy client who is involved in a child custody case is aware of the limitations and possible biases inherent in such a role and the possible impact on the ongoing therapeutic relationship" (p. 678). The APA guidelines advise treating psychologists to decline the role of an expert witness who gives a professional opinion regarding custody and visitation issues.

An issue that is treated in detail in the New Jersey guidelines is that of reasonable psychological certainty versus clinical speculation. The guidelines state: "Psychologists recognize the obligation to formulate conclusions based on a reasonable degree of psychological or scientific certainty or probability" (p. 16). The commentary section for this guideline explains the distinction as follows: "Reasonable psychological certainty is defined for purposes of these guidelines as certainty that is based on either substantive clinical observations, empirical research results, well-accepted theoretical propositions, or an integration of all three, and that is clearly not speculative" (p. 17). Distinguishing conclusions based on reasonable psychological certainty from clinical hypotheses in the ongoing treatment of a psychotherapy patient, the New Jersey guidelines state:

> Psychologists recognize that qualification as an expert witness constitutes an explicit recognition by the court that the psychologist's capacity to deliver an opinion in the matter under consideration exceeds that of the lay public. Psychologists therefore recognize that offering clinical hypotheses as though they were scientifically valid conclusions is inappropriate. Psychologists recognize the obligation to weigh carefully all conclusions and recommendations against the standard of reasonable psychological or scientific certainty or probability. (p. 17)

The case of *Snyder v. Scheerer* (1993, cited in Ackerman & Kane, 1996) illustrates this principle. In this matter, a birth mother with a 15-year history of bipolar disorder was hospitalized shortly after the birth of her baby. A month after her release, she attempted suicide and was readmitted to the hospital, where she remained for several months. She signed an agreement granting temporary custody to her sister and brother-in-law. Six months after her release from the hospital following the suicide attempt, the birth parent attempted to regain custody of the child; however, her sister and brother-in-law refused to relinquish custody. The trial court found that the sister and brother-in-law had become the baby's psychological parents. The case was appealed to the state supreme court, which found that speculation by the trial court regarding the future mental health of a mother was not an appropriate ground for denying her petition for return of custody. The court noted that other jurisdictions had found that speculation regarding a parent's future mental condition was not an appropriate basis for denying custody.

One major difference between a child protection evaluation in a termination of parental rights action and a divorce/custody evaluation is that in the latter the psychologist is asked to determine which of the parties is the better parent in a situation where custody and visitation terms can always be renegotiated or relitigated, while in the former the ultimate legal issue is permanent severing of the individual's rights to the child. It is therefore inappropriate for psychologists who perform assessments in termination actions to frame conclusions as though the matter amounted to a parenting contest between rival litigants. Comments regarding the superiority of the environment that the foster parent can provide for the child as opposed to the more modest circumstances of the birth parent are prejudicial rather than probative with respect to the ultimate issue. The court is to decide not merely whether the foster parent could do a better job of rearing the child, but whether the birth parent has failed the child so egregiously that ending the individual's legal status as that child's parent would be in the child's best interests. Psychologists who routinely testify in divorce/custody matters and begin working with child protection cases that proceed to the termination phase must adopt a new perspective. Given the severity and finality of a judgment against the birth parent, the superiority of the foster home relative to the birth parent's home cannot in and of itself be a factor in formulating conclusions and recommendations in such cases. Justice Ginsburg in writing the majority opinion in *M. L. B. v. S. L. J.* (1997) stated that the loss of a parent's relationship with her children is of such "magnitude and permanence" that it is "barely distinguishable from criminal condemnation" ("Needy Who Lose Parental Rights," 1996, p. A22).

The American Pychology–Law Society (APLS; 1991), constituted as Division 41 of the APA, published a set of aspirational specialty standards for forensic psychologists: *Specialty Guidelines for Forensic Psychologists* (1991). These standards echo those of the APA's *Ethical Principles* (1992) and *Guidelines for Psychological Evaluations in Child Protection Matters* (1998) to a great extent. The APLS guidelines stress limiting practice to areas in which the psychologist possesses competence, possessing a fundamental and reasonable level of knowledge concerning those aspects of the legal system in which the psychologist becomes involved, and understanding and protecting the civil rights of parties in legal proceedings in which the psychologist participates. In contrast to other guidelines and standards that expressly prohibit the provision of both evaluation and treatment services to the same client, the APLS guidelines state: "When it is necessary to provide both evaluation and treatment services to a party in a legal proceeding (as may be the case in small forensic hospital settings or small communities), the forensic psychologist takes reasonable steps to minimize the potential negative effects of these circumstances on the rights of the party, confidentiality, and the process of treatment and evaluation" (p. 659).

The APLS guidelines stress the obligation of the forensic psychologist to ensure that clients are informed of (1) their legal rights with respect to the service, (2) the purpose of any evaluation, (3) the nature of the procedures to be employed, (4) the intended uses of the product of the psychologist's services, and (5) the party who has employed the forensic psychologist. The guidelines further mandate that, unless an evaluation is court ordered, forensic psychologists obtain client's informed consent before proceeding with the assessment.

The APLS guidelines state that forensic psychologists have an obligation to be aware of legal standards affecting confidentiality and to conduct their professional activities accordingly. The standards state: "Forensic psychologists establish and maintain a system of record keeping and professional communication that safeguards a client's privilege" (p. 660). Further: "Forensic psychologists maintain active control over records and information. They only release information pursuant to statutory requirements, court order, or the consent of the client" (p. 660). The standards also require that forensic psychologists inform clients as to the limitations of the confidentiality of their services.

There are additional important considerations in this area in the case of evaluations of birth parents who are facing criminal charges of child abuse, child endangerment, or related offenses. The guidelines state:

> Because forensic psychologists are often not in a position to know what evidence, documentation, or element of a written product may be or may lend to a "fruit of the statement," they exercise extreme caution in preparing reports or offering testimony prior to the defendant's assertion of a mental health claim or the defendant's introduction of testimony regarding a mental condition. Consistent with the reporting

> requirements of state or federal law, forensic psychologists avoid including statements from the defendant relating to the time period of the alleged offense. (p. 663)

This requirement relates to a Federal Rule of Procedure (12.2[c]) that states that no statements made by a defendant in the course of an examination and no testimony by the expert based upon such statements nor any other fruits of the statements can be admitted into evidence against the defendant in any criminal proceeding, except in those instances in which the defendant has raised mental state as an issue.

In other words, when examining a birth parent for purposes of child placement issues, an expert may jeopardize that birth parent's defense in a related criminal action by including in the report statements made by the birth parent relating to the charged offense. On the other hand, such information may be of vital importance to the family court action in which the safety of the child is at issue. It is therefore of singular importance that birth parents who are facing criminal charges be informed about the limitations of confidentiality to the point where they are virtually "Mirandized"—in other words, informed that anything they disclose during the evaluation could be used against them in any subsequent litigation to terminate their parental rights.

According to the APLS guidelines, the standard for documentation of services is higher for forensic psychologists than the normative standard for general clinical practitioners, since the work products of forensic psychologists are routinely subjected to judicial scrutiny. The guidelines state that the standard to be applied to such documentation anticipates such scrutiny and that forensic psychologists, with the foreknowledge that their professional services will be used in an adjudicative forum, incur a special responsibility to provide the best documentation possible under the circumstances.

Melton et al. (1987) argue that mental health professionals should refrain from offering testimony couched in language that reflects the ultimate legal issue. They state that witnesses should simply assert the limitations of mental health expertise and state that it is beyond the witnesses' competence to offer opinions on matters of law. Regarding the question of testimony relating to the ultimate legal issue, in the APA's (1998) *Guidelines for Psychological Evaluations in Child Protection Matters* it is noted:

> The profession has not reached a consensus about whether making dispositional recommendations in child protection evaluations is within the purview of psychological practice. However, if the psychologist chooses to make dispositional recommendations, the recommendations should be derived from sound psychological data and must be based on considerations of the child's health and welfare in the particular case. (p. 16)

In the APLS (1991) *Specialty Guidelines for Forensic Psychologists* it is stated:

> Forensic psychologists are aware that their essential role as expert to the court is to assist the trier of fact to understand the evidence or to determine a fact in issue. In offering expert evidence, they are aware that their own professional observations, inferences, and conclusions must be distinguished from legal facts, opinions, and conclusions. Forensic psychologists are prepared to explain the relationship between their expert testimony and the legal issues and facts of an instant case. (p. 665)

Perrin and Sales (1994) note that the latest APA ethical guidelines are completely silent with respect to ultimate-issue testimony and ultimate-issue conclusions in written reports. Furthermore, these authors state: "Although psychologists performing forensic examinations are commonly asked for, and frequently give, opinions on the ultimate legal issue (e.g., was the defendant insane at the time of the crime), some laws prohibit such testimony" (p. 380). Whereas the APA guidelines do not address the issue at all and other guidelines are equivocal, the *Specialty Guidelines for Psychologists in Custody/Visitation Evaluations* (New Jersey Board of Psychological Examiners, 1993) expressly state that ultimate-issue conclusions properly rest with the legal system and not with psychological experts. According to the New Jersey *Specialty Guidelines*:

> Psychologists distinguish between recommendations as to the ultimate legal issue, which are the province of the legal system, and expert opinions, which are based on direct inferences from scientific data. Expert opinions are based exclusively on direct inferences from the scientific data collected in and of relevance to the custody evaluation. However, psychologists recognize that the provision of scientific, psychological data represents only one component in deciding the ultimate legal issue. (p. 18)

Psychologists who testify on termination hearings face an interesting dilemma with regard to the ultimate legal issue. In order to adhere to professional ethics as to making recommendations that will maximally benefit the child in question, psychologists frequently conclude that the child's best interests would be served by a severing of parental rights in order to permit adoption. However, the question of whether to sever parental rights is the ultimate legal issue before the trier of fact in a termination hearing. Thus, it would be an intrusion into the province of the court for the psychologist to state in the recommendations section of the report that parental rights should be terminated to permit adoption. However, it would also be something of an ethical lapse for the psychologist to refrain from making any recommendations regarding the permanent plan for the child in cases in which, from a mental health perspective, it is clearly in that child's interests either to remain permanently with a caretaker other than the birth parents or to return to the birth parents.

One way of couching such recommendations without making an unwarranted intrusion into the court's prerogative is for the psychologist to recommend a case goal to the referring party: for example, "In light of the above findings, it is recommended that Child Protective Services pursue a case goal of adoption for Johnny." This is not a recommendation as to the ultimate legal issue, but simply a recommendation to the agency charged with looking after the welfare of the child as to what course of action it should pursue. For psychologists engaged by attorneys who represent the birth parents in such actions, such recommendations may also be phrased with respect to the preferred course of action for agencies charged with the welfare of the child. The underlying principle is that termination of parental rights is a complex decision, with mental health considerations forming only one component of the decision process. Certainly, it should be understood that in order for the court to give this component its appropriate weight in making a decision, it is necessary for mental health experts to convey clearly and accurately their assessments of the parent–child dynamics, risk of harm to the child, need for services, prognosis for birth parents' rehabilitation, and other related factors.

CHAPTER 5

Assessments of Birth Parents, Foster Parents, and Other Potential Caretakers

INITIAL REFERRAL QUESTIONS

Experience has shown that one of the most common shortcomings of psychological evaluations in child protection matters is that the practitioner uncritically accepts a case from a referring party who couches the reason for referral in general terms—for example, "We want a psychological on this birth parent." In fact, this is a common complaint from casework supervisors, whose supervisees have made this type of amorphous assessment request. When the evaluator accepts the case without clarifying what the agency needs from the testing, casework supervisors, who must decide on appropriate intervention strategies, find such "generic" or "vanilla" psychological reports to be of little value in providing guidance. Before accepting the referral at all, it is important for psychologists to ascertain what specific issues the examination is to address. If the referring party is unable to formulate a set of referral questions, then this must be done jointly by the psychologist and the referring party.

The reason for this practice is that evaluations of birth parents in child protection matters are essentially forensic psychological evaluations, as opposed to clinical ones. Forensic psychological reports must be carefully worded to insure precision of expression, appropriate conservatism in framing conclusions, and attention to all salient issues of the case that can be addressed by psychological means. Conclusions must be governed by the standard of reasonable psychological certainty, and documentation of the assessment must anticipate judicial scrutiny. While it is certainly necessary to attend to purely clinical issues in order to assist the child protective service agency in working with the birth parent or to assist the birth parents' counsel in recommending what rehabilitative activities the client should undertake, in many cases the clinical issues are subordinate to the forensic ones.

The following is offered as an example of the consequences of neglecting to formulate specific referral questions. Psychologist *X* assesses birth parent *Y* at the request of child protective services, which states that it wants to have an opinion from a psychologist as to whether the client is capable of caring for her two children. Birth parent *Y* has two children who have been in the foster care system for nearly one year, and she is seeking to have them returned. The children were originally removed because of neglect. The psychologist finds *Y* to be a mildly depressed young woman of low borderline intellectual ability, but otherwise unremarkable. Psychologist *X* feels that the removal was due to the client's being unable to cope by virtue of her intellectual limitation and mild depression, and he recommends that *Y* be considered for a return of the children once recommended services are in place. Psychologist *X* advises psychotherapy and a psychiatric consultation for medication-needs assessment. These conclusions and recommendations are included in a report submitted to the agency. The psychological report has done a good job of focusing on *Y*'s depression and formulating strategies to address the problem.

In actual fact, the removal of *Y*'s children was only partially based on neglect. The younger child, age 18 months, is severely asthmatic and has other chronic medical problems as well. This child, who is classified "medically fragile" and is in a specialized foster home, requires administration of a precise dosage of two different asthma medications through a device that mixes and mists the medication, delivering it to the child through a mask. The child has had three emergency room visits because of asthmatic crises.

In a subsequent hearing to decide whether the client's children should be returned to her care, Psychologist *X* is asked by the state to testify on the basis of the report. While the state's attorney attempts to elicit further opinions regarding *Y*'s capacity to care for the asthmatic child, her court-appointed counsel effectively negates this in cross-examination. *Y*'s attorney asks Dr. *X*, "Doctor, you identified a problem that my client was having with depression and, according to your recommendations, she sought help for the condition and is no longer regarded by anyone as being depressed. Now, at the last moment, the state's attorney is attempting to place yet another roadblock in *Y*'s path to regaining her children. If the state's attorney is making my client's intellectual level out to be an issue of earth-shaking proportions, why did you not offer any conclusions or recommendations whatsoever in your report relating this to her capacity to care for the children?" The attorney also asks, "If the state is so concerned about my client's level of literacy with respect to administering medications, why did you fail to mention this at all in your report? Can you even give an opinion as to the client's level of literacy if you did not administer any specific tests for it?"

Had Psychologist *X* formulated a set of specific referral questions at the outset by consulting with the caseworker, the questions might have included the following:

1. What is the assessment of the client's current intellectual and personality functioning?
2. Does the client's depression interfere with her ability to parent her children, and, if so, what is her prognosis and what services are necessary to address the condition?
3. Would the client's intellectual limitation, if any exists, prevent her from properly following the directions in administering medication to her asthmatic child?
4. Does the client possess a sufficient level of literacy to understand dosage and administration directions for any medication that her child may require?
5. Does the client have the intellectual ability, alertness, and judgment to recognize the signs of an impending asthmatic crisis and to respond appropriately either by giving the child additional medication as indicated or by seeking emergency medical attention?

Framing the psychological report around the above specific referral questions would have saved Psychologist *X* considerable difficulty in responding to able cross-examination by Y's attorney.

The APA's (1998) *Guidelines for Psychological Evaluations in Child Protection Matters* list a number of typical referral questions, listed below, for psychologists in such cases. It has also been my experience that the following questions are quite common.

First, the guidelines ask how seriously the child's psychological well-being has been affected by parental actions. This is a complex question that relates to both objective medical findings and subtle intrapsychic factors that may be overlooked by caseworkers. The latter may involve self-esteem; level of anxiety; vigilance; rumination; traumatic sexualization; deficits in intellectual, social, or emotional development resulting from inadequate stimulation; and similar factors. From the perspective of the parent's examination, the psychologist should attempt to formulate an estimate of the parent's capacity to provide adequate stimulation, to empathize with the child, to respond to the child's physical and emotional needs, to set limits appropriately, and to relate to the child in a nonpunitive manner.

Second, the guidelines ask what therapeutic interventions would be recommended to assist the child. From the point of view of assessing the parents, it is important to determine whether they are capable of profiting from therapy and whether they are capable of contributing positively to the child's therapy either through collateral sessions or in family therapy.

Third the guidelines ask whether the birth parents can be rehabilitated; if so, how; and if not, why? Such questions frequently entail a specialized knowledge of drug and alcohol issues in addition to basic psychopathology. Questions of DSM-IV diagnoses are important here as well, since the issue of whether an individual can be rehabilitated is inextricably tied to a specification of the pathology that the individual presents. A related question that is not listed in the APA guidelines, but appears in the case law in this area, is whether the birth parent can be rehabilitated within a reasonable period of time, considering the developmental needs of the child. Many judges who see children languishing in the foster care system for many years are particularly sensitive to the passage of time in these cases. Thus, it is important to distinguish acute conditions with a reasonable probability of near-term remission from chronic conditions, including both clinical syndromes and personality disorders, that can be expected to remain refractory to rehabilitative interventions until the child in question reaches the age of majority.

Fourth, the guidelines ask about the psychological effect on the child if returned to parents. From the point of view of the birth parent's psychological examination, it is important to arrive at a sense of how the birth parent would react to a child who has suffered the loss of foster parents to whom that child may have become attached and who presents behavioral problems such as aggression, regression, or withdrawal. Such behaviors may be the result of a traumatic loss of former caretakers or simply a reaction to the stress of being moved at all, or it may be a means of testing the behavioral limits as part of the process of readjustment to birth parents who have already failed the child once. It is important to assess the birth parent's capacity to respond in an attuned and empathic manner to children who are exhibiting behavior problems and to refrain from punishing the child for affectionate references to the foster parent or for making unfavorable comparisons between the birth parent and foster parent upon being returned to the former's home. It is also important to assess the birth parent's capacity to refrain from interpreting the child's negative behaviors as a personal attack or as deliberate provocation.

The components of an adequate parental fitness examination include a review of the history, a clinical interview with the client, questioning the client as to the specifics of the case, psychological testing that is appropriate to the referral questions posed, assessment of deceptiveness, and review of collateral data. The weight given to any of these components will vary according to the specific facts and issues of the case.

Before the client is seen in person, it is necessary for the examiner to review the available background information on the case. The history should include the reasons for the child's placement into foster care; medical information on the child's injuries if there is physical abuse involved; previous psychological and psychiatric reports on the children and birth parents, including records of any psychiatric hospitalizations; and other pertinent facts of the case. Where the matter has reached the stage of a filing for termination of parental rights, the state's complaint is often the most useful source of information. It is extremely difficult to conduct a satisfactory interview with birth parents who employ denial and minimization, and who omit crucial details as well, in the absence of a comprehensive history of the case to guide the focus of the inquiry.

The clinical interview serves the purposes of establishing rapport with the client, educating the client about the testing process and issues of confidentiality, making observations about the client's behavior and attitude, and eliciting the client's perceptions of his or her personal history and involvement with child protective services. Standard rapport-building techniques should be employed at the outset to put the client at ease. The purpose of the examination should be clearly explained to the client in terms that he or she can comprehend. The client should be made aware of who it was who requested the evaluation, should be told about the nature of the procedures (interview alone or interview plus testing and/or observation with the child), and should be informed that the examiner will be issuing a report based on the results. The client should be apprised of the limits of confidentiality; and if there are criminal charges pending, it is important for the examiner to stress that any statements that the client makes could find their way into the report. The client should also be informed that the resulting report will be furnished to the referring agency, but that it cannot be released for any other purpose without the client's consent. This should be memorialized through the client's signing of a consent form authorizing release of the information to the named party.

It is especially important to respond to clients' requests to divulge something to the examiner "off the record" by underscoring that anything the client says could become part of the report. Occasionally, clients will respond to an empathic examiner by treating the session as though it were psychotherapy and seeking relief by disclosing material that would work against them in a termination or other child protective court action or that is frankly self-incriminating. If the client volunteers this information after an appropriate orientation regarding the limits of confidentiality, then it is permissible for the examiner to record the information and incorporate it into the report. However, if the client precedes the disclosure in any way with a request for the material to be treated in confidence, then the client should be "Mirandized."

The interview normally progresses from emotionally neutral topics, such as education and work experience, to more sensitive areas, such as family background. It is important to ask whether the client was reared by both birth parents or by a single mother or father, or whether the client spent childhood in the care of relatives or in the foster care system. The atmosphere of the home should be discussed, and the client should be asked if there were any particular family problems as he or she was growing up. In cases in which the child was removed because of physical abuse, it is important to elicit details about the client's own experience of parental discipline. The response "We got hit" should be followed up with "What did your mother (father, stepfather, etc.) hit you with?" It is also important to inquire about the types of behavior that were punished at home and about whether the physical punishment had more to do with the parent's state of mind (e.g., a client might say of his or her father: "He used to hit us when he came home drunk. We didn't really have to do anything to get hit."). The examiner should also attempt to elicit any history of sexual abuse. If the client was sexually abused, it should be determined whether the abuse was disclosed, and to whom, and what the reaction of the parents was if they learned of the abuse.

The client should be asked, "Have you ever had any psychological or psychiatric treatment?" and whether he or she has ever had to be hospitalized because of a psychiatric crisis. The examiner should also inquire about any history of arrests. It is especially important to follow up with detailed questions if the client reports an arrest. The most important follow-up question is, "Have you ever been arrested for anything else?" The examiner should get an estimate of the number of arrests and should question the client about each charge. Clients should also be asked routinely about incarceration if they report a history of arrests. Any discrepancy between the seriousness of the charge and the length of incarceration or place of incarceration should be explored. For example, if a client relates that he was incarcerated in a maximum security prison for 5 years because he was convicted of "assault," the examiner might express surprise that he received such a long sentence for such a minor offense and that the time was served at a maximum-security institution. It is also important to inquire what the actual sentence was for each charge and to inquire about the amount of time served. If a client reports that he served 5 years of a 5-year sentence for a minor offense, the logical question to ask is why he remained incarcerated for the entire time rather than being paroled at some point. This could lead to disclosure of another conviction for which the client was serving time during that incarceration. The examiner should also inquire about the client's disciplinary record within the institution.

The client should be questioned about his or her use of alcohol. This inquiry should include questions about the age at which the client began to drink alcohol, whether the drinking remained constant or progressed to greater amounts, what types of alcoholic beverages the client consumed, and whether the client feels that he or she has ever had a problem with alcohol. It is especially important to ask about current use and when the client last drank any alcohol. If the client admits to a problem with drinking, it should be ascertained whether the client has undergone any type of rehabilitation, such as detoxification, 28-day inpatient program, outpatient treatment, and/or Alcoholics Anonymous. Clients' attitudes toward drinking alcohol in front of their children should be elicited, and clients should be asked if alcohol played any part in the problems that resulted in the children's placement.

As with questions about alcohol, the examiner's inquiry into a client's drug use should include the age at which the client began to use drugs and whether the client progressed to larger quantities of drugs. The types of drugs used by the client should be ascertained, as well as whether there was a progression from "soft" drugs like marijuana to more powerful agents like cocaine and heroin. The means of drug ingestion should be determined as well, especially whether the client has engaged in intravenous drug use. The evaluator should also ask about the quantity of drugs consumed during the period of heaviest use. In inquiring about quantity of drugs consumed, the examiner should ask the client for dollar amounts rather than allow the client to respond with number of "bags" or "bottles" consumed.

If the client reports using a substantial quantity of drugs, such as a $50-per-day heroin habit, then the follow-up question should ask how the client was able to afford the habit. Specifically, the examiner should ask if the client ever had to resort to drug selling, robbery, or prostitution in order to finance the drug habit. If a client replies that he or she "did whatever I had to do" to obtain drugs, this should be regarded as a distinctly pathological sign. A client who describes his or her criminal activity with a tone of impersonal necessity ("If he had given me the money like I asked him, I wouldn't have had to hit him so hard.") tend to be among the most resistant to rehabilitative efforts. This cognitive strategy of deemphasizing personal responsibility in favor of the idea that the person simply "has to" engage in criminal behaviors to obtain drugs or money reflects severe superego defects and a narcissistic self-involvement in which other people are regarded as merely objects who serve the purpose of providing gratification of the person's need of the moment. Another cognitive strategy for maintaining the drug addiction is to compare oneself favorably to other addicts who are one step beyond oneself in their degree of criminal activity. One severely addicted young woman, who financed her $100-per-day drug habit by selling cocaine, related to me that she did not feel that she had a drug problem because she saw other women engaging in robbery to support their habits and she did not have to resort to that.

Birth mothers of drug-exposed children should be asked for their feelings about using drugs while pregnant. It is important to employ follow-up questioning when discussing this subject with clients. For example, a drug-addicted mother whose daughter was born with heroin in her system denied having taken drugs during her pregnancy with that child. When confronted with the contradiction between this assertion and the fact that she delivered a drug-exposed child, the mother replied, "Well, I wasn't getting high like I was before I got pregnant." When asked for more detail about the amounts of drugs that she had ingested before, as compared to during, her pregnancy, the mother was vague and described her drug activity as "dipping and dabbing." When confronted again with the fact that her daughter had registered positive for heroin at birth, the mother admitted to having taken "a whole bag" of heroin on the day she delivered, adding, "I didn't think it would get into her system like that. I was wrong." Some mothers have a nonchalant attitude toward their use of drugs while pregnant. They may minimize the seriousness of the behavior ("He was born with just a trace of cocaine in his system.") or engage in crude denial of consequences. My colleague and I (McCann & Dyer, 1996) report a case in which a birth mother proudly stated to the examiner that although her youngest child had been found to have drugs in his system at birth, he was not born *addicted* to drugs as her older children had been, implying that this was an indication of progress on her part.

Clients who admit to having problems with drugs should routinely be asked when their last use of drugs occurred. It has been my experience that a surprising number of clients, who are undergoing evaluation for the express purpose of attempting to regain custody of their children, will admit to having used drugs shortly before the examination, sometimes on the very day of the session ("I needed something this morning to deal with the stress."). It is also important to be alert for behavioral signs of drug intoxication during the session, including elevated mood, loquaciousness, lethargy, and any change in behavior following trips to the bathroom.

In general, parents referred for evaluation because of abuse or neglect of their children tend to be much more defensive than are parents seen for more routine clinical evaluations. This observation is consistent with the experiences of evaluators in a variety of forensic contexts in addition to child welfare matters (McCann, 1997). Wright (1980) states that many abusing parents, although disturbed, possess the capacity to appear normal and unlikely to abuse their children. He labels this the "sick but slick syndrome." Wright found a pattern of sophisticated defensiveness and greater tendency toward psychopathy in the test records of child abusers as compared to nonabusing parents in a study that included the Rorschach, MMPI, and other measures. Wright notes that the child abusers seemed to be highly attuned to social desirability factors in responding to the test instruments and, in fact, registered significantly less bizarre content in their Rorschach responses than did the comparison sample.

PSYCHOLOGICAL TESTING

Psychological testing is an important component of parental fitness evaluations, provided that the instruments used are appropriate to the referral questions posed and provided that the examiner does not overstep the bounds of conservative interpretation of results according to generally accepted criteria for forensic test use (Heilbrun, 1992). A number of commonly employed psychometric instruments are discussed below with regard to their use in parental-fitness examinations.

The Bender Gestalt Test (Bender, 1938) is a highly structured, nonthreatening procedure that is commonly used by psychologists as a warm-up test that assists the subject in acclimating to the examination setting. The subject is given a pencil and a stack of unlined white 8½″ × 11″ paper and is asked to copy a series of nine geometric designs presented individually on cards by the examiner. Many examiners follow this copy phase of the test with a recall phase in which the test paper and stimulus cards are removed and the subject is instructed to try to reproduce from memory as many of the designs as can be recalled. The Bender is useful beyond its warm-up function in that it is an excellent test of visual perceptual abilities (Boll, 1978). Clinically, the test serves as a screening device that can raise a red flag for psychological conditions such as organic brain damage, mental retardation, and gross perceptual problems.

There is a good deal of controversy in the profession regarding the test's validity in diagnosing organic brain damage. While most neuropsychologists regard the Bender Gestalt Test as inferior to more recent procedures in assessing organic impairment, Lacks (1984) cites studies in which the Bender Gestalt Test compares favorably with several other diagnostic procedures in assessing organicity. For purposes of the typical parental fitness evaluation, the Bender should be employed as a screening measure of organicity; however, in situations in which the subject produces an unusually poor test record that contains classical indicators of organicity, this result should receive due attention in the report.

Less well documented, but often clinically striking, are features of the Bender Gestalt Test record that are associated with emotional and behavioral pathology such as narcissism and explosiveness. Hutt (1969) presents a detailed system for such projective interpretations of features of the Bender record. These types of interpretations of the Bender record should be approached cautiously and are perhaps best treated as generating hypotheses that are better tested with other instruments that were designed for that purpose. As a general rule in parental fitness and in all forensic evaluations, it is wise to keep in mind Heilbrun's (1992) admonition that the results of a particular test should not be used for that which it was not intended.

Intellectual Ability Measures

The Wechsler Adult Intelligence Scale—Revised (WAIS-R) (Wechsler, 1981) is the most popular measure of adult intelligence in the United States. It consists of 11 component scales known as subtests, each of which measures a different aspect of intellectual functioning. The subtests are grouped into two scales: the Verbal Scale, which includes six subtests that are heavily dependent upon language skills, and the Performance Scale, which includes five subtests that are relatively language free and that emphasize perceptual and motor skills as well as nonverbal reasoning. The WAIS-R requires between 60 and 90 minutes to administer. Given this lengthy administration time, the test should not be routinely employed with subjects for whom assessment of intellectual impairment is not a referral question. However, for those subjects whose fitness to parent their children cannot be adequately assessed without determining their intellectual capacities, the WAIS-R is the test of choice. Apart from its psychometric superiority as a measure of general intellectual functioning, the test's open-ended response format also lends it clinical utility. While interpretations of the content of examinees' responses to individual test items on the Wechsler must be approached with caution in a forensic setting, such analysis often illustrates mental limitation or deviant thought processes in a way that psychometrically derived scores cannot.

For example, an examinee who is asked to explain the meaning of "Strike while the iron is hot" and who responds, "You got to hit them before they hit you back," is disclosing more about himself or herself than a simple lack of facility with verbal abstraction. Similarly, when asked to point out the essential similarity between a boat and an automobile, the subject who responds, "They both can be used to transport dead bodies," is demonstrating that, although he or she can allocate both components of the item to a common category, there is also an invasion of morbid content and primary process thinking into the normal stream-of-conscious thought.

For situations in which a full-scale intellectual assessment is not warranted but the examiner wishes to address the issue with a less elaborate and less time-consuming procedure, there are some useful alternative measures available. The Slosson Intelligence Test—Revised (SIT-R) (Johns & Van Leirsburg, 1994) provides a reliable measure of verbal cognitive ability that usually takes between 10 and 15 minutes to administer. Correlations between the SIT-R and the WAIS-R Verbal Scale scores range from .83 to .91, indicating a very substantial relationship that permits the SIT-R to be substituted for the WAIS-R when intellectual ability is not a central focus of the assessment. Correlations with Wechsler performance IQs are quite modest. Johns and Van Leirsburg (1994) in their review of the SIT-R consider the test to be a valid measure of crystallized intelligence that is most useful as a screening measure.

The Broad Cognitive Ability Brief Scale of the Woodcock–Johnson Psycho-Educational Battery (W–J) (Woodcock & Johnson, 1977) is a brief test of overall cognitive ability based on 2 subtests, Quantitative Concepts and Antonyms–Synonyms, taken from the 12-subtest Tests of Cognitive Ability section of the battery. The Brief Scale correlated .85 with the WAIS-R Verbal Scale for a sample of 78 students from the 12th grade and performed as well as the WAIS-R Verbal IQ in predicting Wide Range Achievement Test reading achievement scores for a sample of 75 students from the 12th grade. The scale was found to have internal consistency reliabilities in the mid- to high .90s for three adult samples. The Broad Cognitive Ability Brief Scale takes approximately 10 minutes to administer. Experience has shown that with samples of adults of limited educational background the W–J Broad Cognitive Ability Brief Scale substitutes quite acceptably for the WAIS-R Verbal Scale. Unfortunately, the revision of the W–J Battery (Woodcock & Johnson, 1990) does not contain a counterpart to the original tests's Broad Cognitive Ability Brief Scale, and examiners who wish to rely on the Brief Scale as a screening measure will have to be content with a very useful measure that has been superseded by a revised parent scale.

Parenting Skills and Abuse-Specific Instruments

In this day of more specialized psychological assessment and greater emphasis upon empirical validity relating to specific referral questions, there has developed in the area of child welfare an increasing interest among psychologists in abuse-specific instruments. Grisso (1986) cites the need for specific assessments of this type in cases in which (1) simple lack of sophistication is responsible for the circumstances that lead to the child's removal and (2) the situation can be remedied through education and counseling. It is arguable, however, that in all evaluations relating to child welfare matters the clinician's battery should be composed exclusively of instruments that measure abuse potential and parenting skills, since assessment of the individual's overall personality profile is inappropriate for testimony relating to termination of parental rights. I strongly disagree with this line of reasoning on the grounds that in a termination action the case has reached the point where the state decides to end the birth parent's tie to the child because of the parent's chronic failings that are reflective of deep-seated personality problems. Those core personality dysfunctions should be the focus of the assessment, not specific parental competencies. Of course, as noted in Chapter 2, there must be a nexus demonstrated between the individual's psychopathology and specific deficiencies in parenting capacity. In certain situations, however, the following instruments with a more narrow focus on specific parenting skills will be useful.

Grisso (1986) cites a number of possible causes of parents' inadequacies in rearing their children; for example, temporary life stress, simple lack of information about topics such as children's health and appropriate means of discipline, and serious mental disorder or disability. Grisso notes that the question of remediability of the parents' deficits is salient in assessments that bear on the question of termination of parental rights. He states:

> One must look beyond the measurement or observation of current parenting abilities, of course, to obtain data with which to address these explanatory possibilities. Some of these optional interpretations may be considered with data obtained from a broad, clinical assessment of the parents' intellectual and personality characteristics, mental status examination, and interview exploration of the parent's motives and desires. (p. 204)

Thus, while Grisso views specific measures of abuse and of parenting skills as complementing the standard clinical assessment in child protection evaluations, he argues against regarding those measures as the exclusive sources of data in such cases.

The Child Abuse Potential Inventory (CAP) (Milner, 1986) is a 160-item self-report instrument designed for use with male and female parents or primary caregivers who are suspected of physical child abuse. The current form of the CAP has a readability level of third grade. An examinee with a high school degree can complete the inventory within 15 to 20 minutes. The inventory has 3 validity scale indices: the Lie Scale, the Random Response Scale, and the Inconsistency Scale, each of which has a recommended cutoff score listed in the test manual. In addition to yielding an "abuse" score that predicts the subject's potential for child abuse, the inventory has a number of factor score scales measuring "distress," "rigidity," "unhappiness," "problems with child and self," "problems with family," and "problems from others." The thoroughly crafted test manual contains (1) extensive documentation of reliability and stability for the scales, all of which are acceptably high for an instrument of this type; (2) factor analysis results; and (3) a number of concurrent and predictive validity studies. A separate interpretive manual (Milner, 1990) discusses issues involved in practical application of the inventory. This is the best-researched instrument for detection of child abuse instrument that is currently available, with the greatest degree of empirically demonstrated validity for its stated purpose.

The Parent Awareness Skills Survey (PASS; Bricklin, 1990) was originally developed as a tool to assess relative parental strengths in child custody and visitation cases in the context of a divorce action. More recently, this impressionistic instrument, which includes an optional quantitative scoring system based on rather subjective criteria, has come to be used in parental fitness assessments as well. In administering PASS, the examiner conducts a structured interview with the subject that is based on a series of 18 vignettes illustrating typical parent–child problems. Themes presented in these vignettes include children's stealing, defiance, violent behavior, special educational needs, and related problems. The parent is read the vignette and is then asked to respond by stating how the parents should handle the situation, what additional information might be needed to intervene more effectively, what possible needs of the child are being expressed in the situation, and other dimensions of effective parenting. The parent's initial responses are amplified through two additional levels of probes to elicit material that can be evaluated according to PASS criteria. The free responses and responses to probes are assessed within six dimensions or aspects of parenting, including critical issues, adequate solutions, ability to communicate to children in understandable terms, ability to acknowledge feelings, ability to appreciate relevant history, and ability to employ feedback data.

The Parenting Stress Index (PSI) (Abidin, 1986) is an attitudinal measure that has some demonstrated statistical relationship to risk of abuse. It is a 101-item self-report instrument that addresses various sources of parental stress in child rearing and asks subjects about the extent to which the stressors apply to them. This may be supplemented by an optional 19-item checklist to assess the presence of environmental stressors during the preceding 12 months. Rodriguez and Murphy (1997) found that, according to the PSI, 33 low-income mothers of developmentally delayed children reported a great deal of parenting stress. The study also disclosed a significant correlation between (1) PSI total, PSI child characteristic scores, and PSI parent characteristic scores and (2) potential for abusiveness as measured by CAP. The PSI manual cites studies by Johnson, Floyd, and Isleib (1983) and Mash, Johnston, and Kovitz (1983) in which PSI discriminated between samples of abusive and nonabusive parents. In the Mash study, significant differences between abusive and nonabusive mothers were found on all PSI scales. The Mash study also found significant correlations between PSI stress scores and negative aspects of the subjects' interactive behaviors toward their children. Milner (1995) notes that, while the PSI has distinguished between groups of physical child abusers and nonabusing comparison parents, no data are available on classification rates of the PSI in groups of "abusers" and "nonabusers."

Application of the PSI to the assessment of birth parents who have children in placement is a sensitive and complex matter because the inventory discusses current stressors and the parent might not have interacted with the child in any situation beyond supervised 1-hour visitation for months or years. It may be of value, however, if the birth parent has other children in his or her custody whom she or he is raising at the time of the assessment. One issue that often appears in termination hearings with a birth parent who has apparently successfully reared other children during the period of another child's placement in foster care is that the additional stress imposed by returning that child to the birth parent would be more than the parent could manage, even given the fact that he or she has reared the other children in the interim without incident.

Milner (1995) cites the Michigan Screening Profile of Parenting (MSPP) as an abuse-specific instrument that has validation and cross-validation data on concurrent classification rates. He cautions, however, that although individual classification rates for physical abusers of children are adequate and are equal to other measures, the test tends to yield high false positive rates, even in nurturing-parent groups. Grisso (1986) points out that the parenting-specific scales of the MSPP do not discriminate between abusive and nonabusive parents, although the more general clinical scales of the instrument that are indexes of cognitive or emotional strength do consistently differentiate between groups. Grisso states: "If these are the main contributions of the MSPP, one wonders why examiners in clinical or forensic cases would prefer the MSPP to some other, more refined psychological measures of stress, coping, and personal dissatisfaction" (p. 255). Likewise, Holden and Walker (1985, pp. 400–407) state that the scoring difficulties of the MSPP, limited information on reliability and validity, and the small number of items used in screening dysfunctional parenting are major obstacles. They recommend using the CAP and PSI until the psychometric deficiencies of the MSPP have been satisfactorily resolved.

Standard Clinical Instruments

The Minnesota Multiphasic Personality Inventory–2 (MMPI-2) (Butcher et al., 1989) is the first revision of the original MMPI since its development in the 1940s. The original test was the most widely used clinical personality inventory in the world, with literally thousands of research studies on it in the professional and scientific literature. A review of the MMPI-2 by Duckworth and Levitt (1994) states that the reliabilities of the numerous validity, clinical, supplementary, and content scales of the inventory are generally in the acceptable range. They note that the test manual presents some validity studies relating scale scores to criteria such as number of recent life changes, a social readjustment rating scale, and partner ratings on an adjustment scale. They state that preliminary studies show that the MMPI-2 does about as good a job of diagnosis in clinical settings as did the original MMPI. Duckworth and Levitt also note that many clinicians are staying with the original MMPI until a satisfactory body of research evidence about the revision is accumulated. The MMPI-2 requires a reading level of eighth grade and takes from 60 to 90 minutes for most individuals to complete. Testing time is lengthy because the test contains 567 items.

McCann and Dyer (1996) point out that the presentation of reliability evidence in the MMPI-2 test manual is deceptive because the text gives a range of values for both stability and internal consistency coefficients that in fact only applies to the stability of the test. The internal consistency statistics for the MMPI-2, which can only be found in an appendix in the back of the test manual, indicate that many of the test's scales fall well below accepted standards of internal consistency, including some that have more error variance than true score variance. A more positive treatment of the usefulness of the MMPI-2 for forensic purposes may be found in Pope, Butcher, and Seelen (1993).

The Millon Clinical Multiaxial Inventory–II (MCMI-II) (Millon, 1987) and the Millon Clinical Multiaxial Inventory–III (MCMI-III) Millon, 1994) are becoming increasingly popular in all types of forensic assessment contexts, including parental fitness evaluations. Both instruments, consisting of 175 items based on content related to the diagnostic criteria of the American Psychiatric Association's *Diagnostic and Statistical Manual of Mental Disorders* (DSM), measure constructs related to DSM Axis I clinical syndromes and Axis II personality disorders. The content of the MCMI-II is associated with the revision of the manual's third edition (DSM-III-R), and the content of the MCMI-III is rather directly and literally tied to the diagnostic criteria of the fourth edition (DSM-IV), lending the latter instrument considerable content validity for diagnosing mental disorders. Both instruments require an eighth-grade reading level and can be administered in less than an hour.

The stability and internal consistency of all scales of the MCMI-II are above the level of .80 recommended for forensic work (Heilbrun, 1992). The MCMI-II manual presents an elaborately designed criterion-related validity study of the test for a sample of more than 700 therapy patients and evaluation subjects, with clinicians' ratings as the criterion. Results are presented as classification efficiency statistics, and are impressive. The MCMI-III manual lacks such validity evidence; however, a recent study by Davis, Wenger, and Guzman (1997), employing a psychometrically sophisticated clinician-rating criterion, demonstrates validity for all scales that equals or surpasses that of the MCMI-II.

The MCMI-II and MCMI-III have utility in parental fitness evaluations in that they provide diagnoses of DSM-IV disorders and are particularly effective in assessing Axis II personality disorders. McCann and Dyer (1996) describe procedures for relating MCMI-II results to specific referral questions concerning behavior, cognition, interpersonal relations, and other characteristics via the extensive work that Millon has done in the area of personality disorders as part of his general formulation of a clinical science of psychopathology (Millon, 1969; Millon & Davis, 1996).

The Rorschach Technique

A special difficulty arises in the case of assessment of individuals who do not possess the requisite level of intellectual ability or educational achievement to complete the standard objective clinical inventories. While projective techniques such as the Rorschach inkblot method are valuable adjuncts in the evaluation of more able subjects, when dealing with those subjects who are not functionally literate such techniques are the only alternative to actually reading each personality inventory item to the subject and recording the response, a method of questionable validity and practicality. The Rorschach has enjoyed great popularity since its introduction into American clinical psychology in the 1920s. While initially regarded uncritically by psychologists as being virtually an X-ray into the human psyche, the Rorschach method is now viewed with more scientific conservatism as an instrument with a good deal of psychometric utility for certain purposes, but less than the mental X-ray/neuropsychological/cognitive measure that it was previously touted to be. However, McCann (1998) notes that there are skeptics such as Dawes (1994) who categorically deny the validity of the Rorschach for any assessment purpose.

The Rorschach is used in two primary ways by psychologists in assessing personality traits. The more popular method among practitioners trained in the 1960s and 1970s is a content-based approach in which the subject's individual responses to each of the 10 inkblots are the focus of interest. While this approach has the advantage of yielding rich clinical data, it suffers from a reliance on subjective methods of interpretation. The second method, which has always enjoyed some popularity among clinicians, but has recently been refined by Exner (1993) and others to the point of being accepted as the dominant method, relies upon statistical analysis of stylistic features of the test record, such as whether form, color, shading, and other aspects of the blot determine the subject's responses. This approach suffers from the defect of attempting to analyze the unstructured Rorschach method as though it possessed the properties of a pencil-and-paper test; however, the research has documented the statistical adequacy of this method of interpretation to the satisfaction of a substantial number of clinicians.

Weiner (1996), in a review of some of the more promising studies of quantitative Rorschach variables, reports that the Rorschach has adequate validity as a measure of emotional maturity, egocentricity, personality change in psychotherapy, and other clinical phenomena. Clearly attributes such as emotional maturity and egocentricity are of considerable interest in assessing parental fitness. There is a good deal of contemporary debate as to whether the psychometric approach to the Rorschach championed by Weiner and Exner rests upon an adequate research basis. Wood, Nezworski, and Stejskal (1996), for example, assert that the interrater reliability of most of the scales of Exner's Comprehensive System has never been adequately demonstrated, that the major scales or indices of this system are of questionable validity, and that the research base of the Exner system consists chiefly of unpublished studies that have not been made available for peer review. Meyer (1997a) has responded to these and other criticisms of the Comprehensive System and has presented a meta-analysis of published Rorschach reliability studies in the *Journal of Personality Assessment* from 1992 through 1995 using the Comprehensive System. Meyer's meta-analysis has yielded kappa reliabilities ranging from .72 to .96 for various Rorschach indices. Meyer's (1997a) article was followed by a response piece by Wood, Nezworski, and Stejskal (1997) who argued that there were numerous deficiencies in Meyer's analysis, particularly the meta-analysis of reliabilities. Meyer's (1997b) rejoinder piece, which presented counterarguments, followed this response.

McCann (1998) reviewed the literature on the Rorschach from the perspective of its admissibility as a basis for psychological expert testimony. McCann notes that 85% of APA-accredited training programs taught the use of the Rorschach in 1993 and that this instrument remains one of the most popular assessment procedures among psychologists in the United States, employed by more than 80% of practitioners who engage in evaluation. Regarding forensic use, McCann indicates that the Rorschach is usually not challenged in court and that in fact it has been given legal weight by appellate courts throughout the United States. McCann reviews the Rorschach in light of test standards developed within the forensic psychological community (Heilbrun, 1992) and legal standards for scientific evidence based on the Federal Rules of Evidence, in particular the *Daubert* decision (*Daubert v. Merrell-Dow Pharmaceuticals*, 1993). McCann presents arguments in support of the sufficiency of the Rorschach's reliability, validity, standardization, and relevance for admissibility in court under existing standards. Although McCann notes that the relevancy of the Rorschach may be less clear in situations in which parent–child relationships are being assessed, he states that the instrument can nevertheless be of value in providing information on the personality characteristics of parents that may affect their parenting capacity. And although McCann concludes that the Rorschach generally meets accepted standards for admissibility in court, he states that there are still significant questions about the instrument's capacity to detect deviant response styles, including both "faking good" and malingering. McCann further cautions that in those instances cited in the literature in which testimony based on the Rorschach was limited or excluded, the problem was due to invalid inferences made by the psychologist who was relating the findings to specific psycholegal issues rather than any intrinsic scientific flaws in the instrument. It should be noted that McCann's analysis addresses the Exner system of Rorschach scoring and interpretation, and does not apply to earlier scoring systems or to more impressionistic interpretive methods such as content analysis.

My view of the ramifications of the debate over the Rorschach's scientific adequacy is that, in a curious parallel to psychologists' initial uncritical acceptance of and subsequent cooling toward the Rorschach as the ultimate psychic X-ray device, the profession has now abandoned its initial unbridled enthusiasm for the Comprehensive System as the panacea for the Rorschach's psychometric deficiencies. However, the Comprehensive System does seem to provide some decided advantages with respect to documenting the precision of measurement and validity of major Rorschach indices that have been clinically recognized for several decades as trustworthy measures of certain types of psychopathology. Regarding the argument that the Comprehensive System has actually elevated the Rorschach to the level of psychometric sophistication that characterizes most well-constructed psychological tests, I am of the opinion that this argument is so obviously fallacious as to require the type of suspension of disbelief that well-written fiction induces in its readers.

As with virtually all psychological measures, extreme deviations from the norm are the most consistent and trustworthy indicators of pathology. This principle limits the effectiveness of the Rorschach in typical divorce/custody assessments, in which examinees are frequently character disordered but free of major Axis I psychopathology and where the level of sophisticated defensiveness produces rather bland Rorschach records. In parental fitness evaluations, however, in which the parties to be evaluated often present considerable pathology, it is common to obtain Rorschach records with relatively rare clinical signs, such as morbid content, contaminations, odd confabulations, pure color responses, and the like, that are encountered almost exclusively in disturbed or severely maladjusted patients. In such cases, the forensic expert can place more confidence in the results of the unstructured and impressionistic Rorschach procedure than in instances in which the task is to make relative judgments among less disturbed subjects, as would be the case in many divorce/custody evaluations.

Thus, in my opinion, for this type of forensic application the Rorschach is best viewed as essentially a type of structured-interview procedure in which the subject responds, not to questions, but to visual stimuli that tend to elicit particular types of responses in persons with serious emotional or characterological problems. Thus, just as a psychological or psychiatric interviewer would infer the presence of a thought disorder from an interviewee's loose associations and use of neologisms during an interview, the Rorschach examiner would draw a similar inference from the presence of Rorschach indicators that are both rare and specific to thought disorder. The Rorschach is best employed as a search for such unusual and blatant phenomena that are clearly associated with psychopathology. This means that not all Rorschach records are determinative. Those records that do not contain extreme response patterns should not be subjected to a minute analysis that employs the ratios and percentages of the Comprehensive System as though these indices were psychometrically adequate for forensic application. While this approach will probably not sit well with purists of either the X-ray or psychometric Rorschach camps, I feel that the approach affords the best method of capitalizing on the amply demonstrated clinical utility of a proven assessment instrument without misrepresenting its scientific precision in a manner that could prove prejudicial in court.

ADDRESSING SPECIFIC PSYCHOLEGAL QUESTIONS

In contrast to a custody/visitation evaluation in which the examiner is asked to draw conclusions as to the relative fitness of the litigants to care for the children in question, a parental fitness evaluation deals with a more fundamental and momentous issue. In a parental fitness evaluation, the bottom-line referral question is usually whether the individual is fit, in an absolute rather than a relative sense, to serve as the caretaker of his or her children. This determination presents something of a problem in forensic evaluation since there is no psychometric instrument that has been validated for the express purpose of determining whether an individual is fit to parent a child. CAP comes close because an individual who is deemed to be at significant risk for inflicting abuse on a child would be universally considered as unfit to serve as that child's primary caretaker, at least for the period during which such a risk exists; however, even CAP has not undergone any validation research with that specific psycholegal question as the criterion variable. Grisso (1986) states the problem as follows:

> Courts have sometimes used a parent's diagnosis as the primary or sole factor for inferring inadequacy in parenting ability. This practice ignores current legal precedent requiring consideration of functional consequences of mental disabilities, rather than presuming incapacity on the basis of mental disability alone. Thus, forensic assessments describing only diagnoses, personality characteristics, or general intel-

> lectual abilities of parents do not assess directly the law's concerns about caretaker's child-rearing abilities. Diagnoses may be relevant, but the competency concept requires a description of what the caretaker understands, believes, knows, does, and is capable of doing by way of child caretaker functions. (p. 201)

Thus, the forensic evaluator is left with an obvious need to develop a satisfactory nexus between clinical data that may indicate psychopathology, on the one hand, and the conclusion that the individual is fit or unfit as a parent, on the other. As is noted in Chapter 2, the nexus between (1) the diagnosed psychopathology and (2) specific parental behaviors has been found to be of critical importance in many cases, and the lack of such a showing has been the basis for reversal of lower courts' termination decisions. In one of its decisions (*In re C. P. B. and K. A. B.*, 1982) a Missouri court of appeals stated that "unlike neglect, abandonment, abuse, or nonsupport, the mental illness of a parent is not per se harmful to a child" (cited in Ackerman & Kane, 1990, p. 364). What should be avoided, to the extent that this is possible in the legal system, is a battle of the experts in which one expert testifies on the basis of a conclusory report that considers the birth parent as fit to rear the children and another expert testifies on the basis of an equally conclusory report that considers the birth parent as unfit, with neither expert providing any useful information to the court as to the external bases for such opinions (Dyer, 1996).

Ackerman and Kane (1990) conceptualize the above dilemma in the context of the birth parent's capacity to meet the child's needs. Ackerman and Kane distinguish between (1) parents who have only a short-lived mental disorder or a single stress-induced psychotic episode and (2) parents who have a series of psychotic episodes or are chronically psychotic. Ackerman and Kane state that the former type of parent can be expected to adequately address his or her child's needs, whereas the latter, by virtue of chronic impairment of reality testing, emotional control, and behavioral stability, presents a threat to his or her child's welfare. Ackerman and Kane cite a list of specific needs of children who were examined in a 6-year study of children of patients with bipolar disorder (McKnew, 1987, cited in Ackerman & Kane, 1990). I regard Ackerman and Kane's list as constituting a useful set of criteria for assessment of parental fitness, according to whether a birth parent or foster parent, or other potential caretaker, is capable of meeting the needs enumerated by Ackerman and Kane.

These needs include the following (Ackerman & Kane, 1990, pp. 362–363):

1. Parental affection, protection, and guidance
2. Feeling valued and cared for
3. Limit setting and role modeling of coping techniques
4. A value system that accommodates self-interest to social realities
5. Parental awareness and acceptance of the child as a unique person
6. Physical care that is responsive to the child's individual needs
7. Sufficient parental involvement so that the child's emotional needs are fulfilled
8. Parents who are suitable models for identification
9. Parents who will exercise the proper amount of control over the children, neither too much nor too little
10. Parents who enforce rules and demands consistently and with appropriate vigilance
11. Parents who can differentiate the child's needs and feelings from their own and who acknowledge and support the child as a separate person
12. Parents who can teach the child to tolerate anxiety and frustration by acting as models for handling stress and anxiety

Grisso (1986, p. 202) cites the following list of parenting tasks by Clausen (1968), derived from a consideration of children's developmental needs:

1. Provision of nurturance and physical care;
2. Training and channeling of physiological needs in toilet training, weaning, provision of solid foods, etc.;
3. Teaching and skill training in language, perceptual skills, physical skills, self-care skills in order to facilitate care and insure safety;
4. Orienting the child to his [*sic*] immediate world of kin, neighborhood, community, and society, and to his [*sic*] own feelings;
5. Transmitting cultural and subcultural goals and values and motivating the child to accept them for his [*sic*] own;
6. Promoting interpersonal skills, motives, and modes of feeling and behaving in relation to others; and

7. Guiding, correcting, and helping the child to formulate his [*sic*] own goals and plan his [*sic*] own activities.

Using these standards, as well as other specific needs that may play a role in the individual child's situation, it is possible for the forensic evaluator to draw rational conclusions about the birth parent's fitness. This is best accomplished through an examination of the specific DSM-IV diagnostic criteria for disorders with which the evaluation subject is diagnosed.

McCann and Dyer (1996) note that DSM-IV has the status of being the ultimate learned treatise for forensic psychologists. Each disorder listed in the DSM-IV has a number of diagnostic criteria as well as a description of typical presentations of individuals who have the disorder. There are extensive behavioral and interpersonal descriptions associated with DSM-IV personality disorders, many of which relate directly to issues of parental fitness and the ability of the individual to meet children's needs as cited in the above list. If the examinee meets the criteria for a specific personality disorder or presents traits and features of more than one disorder, the DSM-IV can be a useful bridge from the clinical data underlying the diagnosis to citation of specific defects in the individual's parenting capacity that would signal unfitness. As noted above, the evaluator is on safest ground when using diagnostic instruments such as the MCMI-II or MCMI-III that are closely tied to DSM criteria.

CHAPTER 6

Assessment of Children's Psychological and Attachment Profiles

In addition to whether the birth parent is capable of caring for the child appropriately, the other major referral question in termination cases, or cases in which the child protective agency is deciding whether to pursue a guardianship action or work toward a return of custody, concerns the attachment profile of the child. It is routine for psychological consultants to perform what are termed "bonding evaluations" in these cases. A bonding evaluation is a specialized type of assessment whose goal is to determine the nature and quality of the child's attachments to birth parents and foster parents, especially to address the question of who occupies the position of greatest centrality in the child's emotional life. This is roughly equivalent to Goldstein et al.'s (1979) concept of the psychological parent, although current thinking is more flexible on the subject than Goldstein et al.'s original formulation of this concept. The specifics of theoretical issues relating to psychological bonding are discussed in Chapter 8. Conditions that create a disturbance in a child's capacity to form attachments, or to bond with caretakers, are discussed in Chapter 9.

There are some evaluators who employ highly structured procedures for conducting bonding assessments, such as the Strange Situation devised by Ainsworth (Sasserath, Witt, & Weitz, 1988). In this procedure, the evaluator places the parent or other caretaker and child in a room where they can be observed through a one-way mirror. The parent is told that she is being observed and is given specific instructions concerning the observational protocol. The parent is told to play with the child, then to leave the child alone in the room, and then to return to the child. The child's degree of discomfort, clinging, attempts at following the parent, self-soothing in response to the loss, and so forth, are assessed in order to classify the child as either securely or insecurely attached, with some investigators adding various subclasses of insecure attachment. This can be an extremely stressful experience for some children since it is impossible to predict the child's degree of upset in advance, even going by parental reports. It should be noted that the Strange Situation is only valid in the assessment of children below age 18 months. For older children, less structured observational methods are indicated. My preference is to allow the parties to acclimate to the observation situation and then to use a passive technique to elicit spontaneous interaction.

Often a great deal can be learned about the child's reactions to separation by simply conducting a brief individual interview with the child after the conjoint observation with the parent. In this procedure, the separation is not something artificially staged for the purpose of the assessment but rather occurs naturally as a necessary concomitant of the individual interview. This procedure also has the advantage of taking place once the child has had the maximum opportunity to acclimate to the new situation of the examiner's office. At the point when it is announced that the conjoint observation has concluded and the child is to be seen individually, the examiner should note how the parent responds to this new phase of the examination. Does the parent reassure the child that the former will be right outside? Does the parent give a parting hug or kiss? If the child reacts by attempting to follow the parent out to the waiting room, does the parent display any evidence of attunement to the child's anxiety, or does the parent mechanically command the child to remain in the room with the examiner? Does the parent bring the child back to the interview area by brute force, showing indifference to the child's protests, or does the parent employ competent strategies to reengage the child, offering rewards, reassurances, or explanations to facilitate the child's adjustment? Such considerations are particularly important in the case of a child who has experienced numerous separations and losses, especially ones for which the child was not adequately prepared, having been taken somewhere and left there, unceremoniously and precipitously abandoned by the caretaker. Such a child obviously has object constancy and security concerns that require a special approach, which the parent who is being assessed may or may not be capable of providing. It should also be noted whether the child who is being interviewed individually displays any apprehension over the presence or absence of the caretaker and how the child greets the caretaker upon returning to the waiting room. Does the child, for example, head for the social worker or transportation aide rather than the birth parent? Is there any display of physical affection upon the reunion?

Whitten (1994) cites the Marschach Interaction Method (MIM) as one structured means of assessing attachment in children from neonate to adolescent. The MIM consists of a list of activities and a structured observation guide. The activities promote various forms of parent–child interaction that reveal patterns of parental behavior and attachment-related behavior in the child. The evaluator selects 7 to 10 activities that are developmentally appropriate from the MIM list and directs the parent to carry out the activities with the child. The evaluator then unobtrusively records the concrete actions that constitute the observed interactive process. Whitten states that this exercise elicits information about the child's attachment-enhancing behaviors, deviant or paradoxical interactions, and overall ability to respond to any specific adult, as well as the adult's assumptions about the child. Whitten concludes that this technique is an effective means of assessing the child's working model of interaction and the parent's assumptions about his or her own role and expectations about the child. Whitten also advocates the use of such structured checklist methods as the Conners Behavior Rating Scales and the Child Behavior Checklist as an adjunct to the direct observation of interaction processes in assessing the child's attachment profile.

It should be noted that Goldstein et al. (1979) do not recommend relying upon the child's expressed preferences in formulating opinions about that child's attachment profile. Goldstein et al. state that "The words of children, their overt actions, and even their allegiances are often too fickle for experts to evaluate correctly" (p. 43). I sharply disagree with this view. In the case of a young child who has been with foster parents since infancy and who has had minimal contact with a birth parent, or who has had upsetting contact with a birth parent, one usually sees a distinct and firmly fixed preference for remaining in the foster home with "Mommy and Daddy." On the other hand, in the case of older children who have maintained a tie of some sort with birth parents, one frequently sees that the child is reluctant to have all ties with that parent severed by adoption and expresses a well-founded preference for remaining in foster care status in order to permit the continuation of this relationship with the birth parent, as inconsistent and conflicted as it may be. This view is in accord with the opinions of Bush and Goldman (1982), who state that children's descriptions of their situations and prospects often mesh with adult views of their situations and that differences between children's and adults' views could be accounted for on the basis of differences in interests and perspective.

One fact that does limit the value of individual interviews with some children is that the children have developed an awareness of the threat to the stability of their placement posed by contacts with birth parents and probing by interviewers, and the children therefore become distressed and uncommunicative. Another phenomenon that is occasionally observed in such interviews is that when the interviewer sees the child immediately after the child has had a pleasant visit with a birth parent the child will express a preference for living with the birth parent; and when the interviewer sees the child after the child has had a pleasant session with foster parents the same child will express a preference for living with the foster parents. This contradiction may be accounted for in four ways, depending upon individual factors.

In the first scenario, the child is genuinely ambivalent about remaining in the custody of the foster parents as opposed to reunification with the birth parents. In the second scenario, which applies either to young children who have not developed sufficient cognitive skills or to mentally retarded older children, the child simply does not grasp that the examiner is attempting to elicit a preference regarding permanent placement and responds in the context of continued visitation or weekend or overnight visits, even if the examiner stresses that the question refers to a permanent home. In the third scenario, the child has been so threatened and upset by the process that he or she does not wish to express a preference regarding permanency. One usually encounters this phenomenon in "parentified" children who have served virtually as the caretaker of a dysfunctional birth parent and who are severely affected by guilt that prevents them from saying anything that, in their opinion, could injure either set of parents. In the last scenario, the child has actually been coached by the foster parent to give a particular answer under threat of dire consequences for deviating from the prepared script. This is quite rare, although defense attorneys routinely inquire as to this possibility if the child expresses a preference for remaining with the foster parent. In such cases, further questioning about the child's understanding of the purpose of the interview and about what the child has been told about how to respond to questions may expose the fact that the child has been coached.

Sasserath et al. (1988) recommend that evaluators pay attention to certain phenomena during bonding assessments of young children. These phenomena include the frequency and nature of touching between child and parent as an index of comfort level, comfort seeking and guidance seeking behavior by the child, and the capacity of the parent to engage the child effectively and to respond to the child's expressed needs in an appropriate manner. Other behaviors cited by these authors that permit inferences about the child's attachment profile include whether the parent and child make eye contact and smile at each other; whether the child displays signs of upset if a separation occurs during the session; how the parent responds to the child's signals of hunger, thirst, or need to use the bathroom; and whether the child is willing to explore the environment while the parent is in the same room.

Other indicators that should be considered when performing bonding assessments reflect the specificity of the child's attachment to the adult in question and the adult's competence in parenting. If, for example, a preschool child engages in game playing with the foster parent or birth parent, it is often useful for the examiner to attempt to engage the child in the same sort of interaction. If the child responds immediately to the examiner in a manner identical to that in which the child responded to the parent, it raises the question of whether the child is only capable of a diffuse, superficial connection to virtually any friendly adult while lacking the capacity for profound attachment to specific figures. A history of multiple placements and descriptions such as "He'll go to anybody" would confirm the hypothesis, taking into account, of course, specific behavioral expectations about the child's developmental subphase.

Another consideration that is particularly revealing is the child's willingness to accept physical affection from the parent. Does the child eagerly approach when asked to give the birth mother a kiss? Is there joyless, passive compliance? Does the child actively resist the physical affection or show discomfort with it? A related question is the competence of the parent in seeking to give physical affection to the child. For example, one birth father who was observed with his 4-year-old son alternated verbal requests for a kiss with criticism such as, "You aren't going to talk to me today, are you? You're just going to be like that!" or with threats such as, "Okay, I'm leaving. I'm going to McDonald's to get a hamburger and french fries, and I'm going to eat them all myself, and you aren't going to get any!"

It is particularly important to observe the child's affective tone while being observed with the foster parent and with the birth parent. Children who are securely attached to a caretaker usually appear relaxed, happy, and enthusiastic while interacting with that figure. Stereotyped reactions such as a forced laugh and severely limited range of responses during the session are much more likely to be present in conflicted relationships. At the pathological extreme of the spectrum, it is not uncommon to see openly hostile behavior on the part of children who are interacting with birth parents whom they perceive as a threat to the security of their placement with the foster parents.

Sasserath et al. (1988) note that a common misconception in this type of bonding assessment is that the parties will be on their best behavior and will thus be able to fool the examiner. Sasserath et al. state that attachment cannot be faked and that the bonding assessment will distinguish between behavior and emotion in the child that has been reinforced over time as opposed to the child's short-term reactions to the immediate behavior of the parent.

A thorough bonding assessment should include (1) an interview with the adult to provide background information and to assess the adult's attitude toward the child; (2) an observation of the child with the adult; and (3) in the case of children who are capable of meaningful verbal communication, an individual interview with the child. The interview with the child should elicit the child's concept of the role of the adult with whom the child has been observed, for example, "Mommy," "Ellen," "Mrs. Jones," "Grandma." The child should be questioned about any "other mommy" whom the child has, and the child should tell the examiner all the child can about this other figure. The child should be asked whether he or she enjoyed the observation session and whether he or she enjoys visits with the birth parent in general. The question of preference for a permanent living arrangement, depending on the child's capacity to grasp the implications of this, should be raised. The child should also be questioned about missing the present caretaker if placed with the birth parent and about missing the birth parent if allowed to remain permanently with the current caretaker. Care should be taken to sift out the child's genuine preferences from mere socially desirable responses. Symmetrical questioning about the foster and birth parents sometimes elicits contradictory socially desirable responses that are not very informative with regard to the child's real preference. In the case of younger children, it is also not that unusual to elicit contradictory expressed preferences depending on which adult has just been observed interacting with the child. Certainly, the child's wishes give valuable clues about the attachment profile; however, the element of saying things merely to please the examiner must be taken into account.

One often neglected element of the bonding assessment is the review of the history. In many respects, this is the most important part of the procedure. Evaluators should try to gain access to as much information about the case as possible from a number of different sources, including a review of the case record of the child protective services; school records of the child; previous psychological, psychiatric, learning disabilities, and other evaluations of the child; and information supplied by the adults who are observed with the child.

A measure of adaptive behavior such as the Vineland Adaptive Behavior Scales (Sparrow, Balla, & Cicchetti, 1984) should also be routinely included in the assessment procedure. For cases in which the birth parent is marginal and there is a question as to how self-sufficient a school-age child may be or whether that child is relatively helpless and totally dependent, an instrument to measure adaptive behavior is a useful component of the assessment. Adaptive behavior refers to the nonintellective aspects of meeting the challenges of daily life. For young children this would include feeding, dressing, and toileting skills; elementary social interaction skills; and basic communication skills.

The Vineland Adaptive Behavior Scales can yield a decent estimate of the child's adaptive behavior skills, can disclose the informant's attitudes toward the child, and can elicit collateral information that standard interviewing techniques may fail to pick up. For example, there is a difference between a foster parent who responds mechanically to the Vineland's items as they are presented by the examiner and the foster parent who elaborates and displays a sense of delight in the child's developmental accomplishments during the administration of this procedure. Anastasi and Urbina (1997) note that internal consistency, interrater, and test–retest reliabilities for the domain and composite scores on the Vineland are satisfactory. Validity information is presented in the form of factor analyses; correlations with other adaptive behavior inventories; and correlations with formal, general mental ability measures. The Vineland also possesses good content validity since the test items address common areas of self-help, social, motor, and communications skills appropriate to various age levels.

Where possible, the child should be observed with the foster or preadoptive caretakers and also with the birth parents. The latter observation may not be advisable in cases in which there has been visitation that the child has resisted and it is felt by the examiner that the observation would simply inflict an unpleasant experience on the child without providing any additional useful information.

The evaluator must gain access to all of the available information concerning the child's history. Especially vital are details concerning the child's early experiences with the birth parent and the child's placement history. There is an enormous difference between a child who was left with inappropriate caretakers during infancy while the inadequate parent "ran the streets" looking for drugs and a child who remained with the birth parent in a stable home environment during the first 2 years of life until a precipitous disruption of the family situation (parent's arrest; eviction from apartment, causing homelessness) resulted in a placement. If possible, the evaluator should review information pertaining to the child's reaction to placement(s). These data provide important clues about the specificity of the child's attachment to the birth parent as well as the child's capacity for specific attachment in general. The capacity to form specific attachments is a precondition for separation trauma following removal from a placement. The issue of attachment disorders is discussed in detail in Chapter 9.

The more extreme the circumstances of the case, the greater the importance of the history in assisting the evaluator in formulating conclusions about bonding. In many cases, the history is the single most important element in formulating conclusions. It is always to be borne in mind that the best predictor of future behavior has consistently been shown to be the individual's prior behavior. Thus, when we are presented with an apparently rehabilitated birth parent who is functioning normally in meeting the challenges of independent living in the community without children to care for, we should not be unduly swayed by this fact if there has been an extreme failure of parental duty toward the child in the past and no other evidence of a spectacular shift in the individual's mental life except for the apparent good adjustment without the responsibility of child care.

In many cases, a child who is placed in foster care directly from the hospital after birth and who remains in a continuous placement with the same caretaker for several years, with only sporadic contact with the birth parent, is extremely unlikely to have any sort of positive emotional connection to the birth parent and is extremely likely to be profoundly bonded to the foster caretaker. Furthermore, a child who has undergone four or five different foster placements within the first few years of life is highly likely to have a damaged capacity for selective attachment, and the central factor of the case becomes the resolution of the child's emotional problems.

Other factors of the history that should not be overlooked are the child's medical condition and learning handicaps. Medical problems should be assessed in the context of the required level of care. Severe asthma, for example, may require several administrations per day of a precise mixture of medications through a nebulizer, with life-threatening consequences if the child does not receive the medication consistently. This is a frequently encountered factor because foster children are much more likely to have serious medical problems than is the population at large because these children often have been exposed to intrauterine drug toxicity, no prenatal care, physical and emotional deprivation during infancy, physical abuse, and other assaults on the physical organism and immune system. (See, e.g., the case of S. C. in Chapter 12.)

Diabetic children may require daily injections of insulin, and children with severe allergies need to be protected from exposure to the allergen. Unusual stress, particularly the stress of a parental separation, may aggravate such children's physical conditions and this factor should certainly be raised as an issue affecting the ultimate placement of the child.

Learning handicaps frequently require competent and consistent reinforcement of learning at home by the caretaker. Learning-disabled children frequently display subtle or gross neurologically based behavior disorders that call for an appropriate modification of the caretaker's behavioral expectations. Such children are frequently managed through a delicate balance of behavior modification and other interventions in the home, complementing the structure provided by the school program. These interventions often require a high level of competence and commitment on the part of the caretaker, and the result of an interruption of this care is to derail the child's academic progress and capacity for appropriate behavior in the community. As with medical problems, learning and behavior disorders should also figure heavily as factors that affect the child's ultimate placement and also as factors that bear on the quality of the child's attachment to the foster caretaker.

Another important element of a child's history is the involvement of the birth parent with the child. Even in the case of a child who has been placed at birth, a fairly deep attachment is possible if the parent visits consistently and displays a responsive and loving attitude toward the child. Children know intuitively when someone is genuinely emotionally invested in them; and in such cases, the consistent contact with the birth parent through regular visitation enables the young child to internalize an image of the birth parent as a caring and helpful figure. It is far more easy for such a parent to assume a position of centrality in the child's life in the event of a return of custody than it is for a birth parent who has previously occupied an extremely peripheral position in the child's inner mental life. It is far easier for a child to reconnect to a birth parent who is a well-defined, positively invested figure in the child's inner mental world than to a birth parent who has been a nebulous image and toward whom the child has been ambivalent or overtly hostile because of prior frustrations and traumatic experiences.

PSYCHOMETRIC TESTS IN THE ASSESSMENT OF CHILDREN IN PLACEMENT

There are situations in which the examiner's interview and bonding assessments should be supplemented with an individual psychological examination of the child. These situations most frequently involve special-needs children whose condition requires special vigilance, parental involvement, or other intervention that the birth parent or other proposed caretaker may or may not be able to supply.

The Bender Gestalt Test, discussed in Chapter 5 in connection with adult assessments, is also very useful as a developmental measure of perceptual–motor skills in children. Koppitz's (1964) scoring system and children's norms for the Bender provide an objective means of assessing visual–motor integration in children. As with adult subjects, the Bender is a nonthreatening way of introducing the child to the assessment situation.

The Wechsler Intelligence Scale for Children—Third Edition (WISC-III) has come to supplant its predecessor, the Wechsler Intelligence Scale for Children—Revised (WISC-R), as the standard instrument for assessment of children's intellectual abilities. The Wechsler scales are based on Wechsler's definition of intelligence as "the overall capacity of an individual to understand and cope with the world around him [*sic*]" (Wechsler, 1974, p. 5). The WISC-III measures a number of intellectual abilities, ranging from the more abstract ones, such as verbal reasoning and expressive language ability, to qualities that are more related to common sense, such as "social intelligence" and discrimination of perceptual details in common objects and situations.

Several clinical evaluations of score profiles on this instrument have been developed, with various authorities claiming to be able to assess personality and behavioral propensities based on subtest score patterns. Some of these pattern-interpretation systems, such as the relationship of Performance IQ over Verbal IQ to juvenile delinquency and other behavioral problems, have a degree of empirical support (Witt & Dyer, 1997).

It has been my experience that detailed clinical analyses of intelligence test data gleaned from children in termination cases are generally more accepted in court than are conclusions about defendant birth parents based on similar data. Family-court judges seem to be willing to grant experts substantial latitude to express clinical opinions that may be somewhat speculative if the experts' opinions can provide insights into the psychological functioning of children as the children cope with the multiple stresses of separations, traumatic experiences, and other disruptions during the course of their stay in the foster care system or in kinship care.

Kamphaus (1993) states that WISC-III is "yet another milestone in the development of the Wechsler series that promises to receive widespread acceptance" (p. 155). Kamphaus also notes that the popularity of the Wechsler tests testifies to the accuracy of Wechsler's understanding of the practical needs of clinicians who perform intellectual assessments. However, Kamphaus is critical of the lack of attention to modern cognitive theory that has developed since the original publication of the children's version of the Wechsler test in the 1940s.

Zachary (1990) states that the strength of the entire Wechsler series of tests lies in its ability to differentiate between subjects who are high and subjects who are low in general mental ability. This observation is consistent with Wechsler's formulation of intelligence as a "global capacity." Zachary also notes that there is considerable empirical support for another facet of Wechsler's theory of intelligence, namely, the verbal–performance dichotomy. This dichotomy is quite useful in the clinical interpretation of Wechsler records, especially in predicting subjects' tendencies toward behavioral acting out. This is not merely a piece of clinical lore. My colleague and I (Witt & Dyer, 1997) note that there is a good deal of empirical support for a verbal less than performance pattern in juvenile delinquents.

Zachary (1990) and McDermott, Fantuzzo, and Glutting (1990), state that the common practice of profiling subjects' abilities through subtest analysis, especially through "ipsatization" methods involving computation of mean subtest value and deviations of individual subtests from this mean, do not have any empirical basis. In fact, such ipsatization removes most of the variance associated with general mental ability, causing a reduction of two-thirds to three-quarters of the predictive validity for academic success criteria.

While these psychometric considerations may be a handicap with respect to assessments that are more focused on school issues than on clinical ones and assessments focused on learning disability, the advantages associated with the clinical richness of this instrument far outweigh its having fallen behind in theory-related modifications of scale content. The fact that WISC-III requires verbatim recording of subjects' responses permits qualitative analysis of performance that provides specific insights that may relate to issues involving cognitive style and other clinical elements. In my opinion, WISC-III is clearly the instrument of choice in termination cases in which intellectual assessment of the child is a primary referral question and in which the examiner wishes to develop insights into the child's logical thought processes.

For those cases in which a more refined diagnosis of cognitive abilities relating to specific learning disabilities is warranted, then the instrument called the Differential Ability Scales (DAS) is more suited to the assessment task. DAS, while omitting the measurement of social comprehension as found in the WISC-III Comprehension and Picture Arrangement subtests, contains several measures on both the basic scales and supplementary scales that address learning problems in a rather direct way. Because of the greater amount of unique variance in individual scales of this instrument and greater *g* loading of the common variance, DAS not only is a better assessment of general intelligence, but also is a more sharply focused assessment of individual abilities than is WISC-III. The greater amount of specific variance in individual subtests of DAS facilitates the identification of reliable intertest differences in a profile.

Elliott (1990) rejects the term "intelligence" altogether, preferring instead the more neutral term "abilities." Elliott states that DAS has value as a measure of (1) a general intellectual factor, relating to Spearman's *g* factor; (2) clusters of abilities that tend to change somewhat depending upon children's ages; and (3) individual specific abilities, as measured by individual subtests.

Kamphaus (1993) states that the DAS manual is of very high technical quality and that the psychometric properties of the test are strong. Kamphaus also notes that the DAS's low floor makes it an appropriate instrument for the assessment of subjects suspected of having mental retardation, especially at the lower levels of the retarded range.

Anastasi and Urbina (1997) describe the standardization of DAS as exemplary, adding that the sample size of 3,475 individuals was considerably larger than usual for an individually administered test. They also note that a substantial item bias analysis was conducted by using samples of African American and Latino children. Anastasi and Urbina characterize DAS as a state of the art instrument that is as yet unsurpassed in the advantages that it affords to users.

The Goodenough–Harris Drawing Test (Harris, 1963) is a language-free measure of intellectual maturity through developmental analysis of human figure drawings. Anastasi and Urbina (1997) note that this procedure has found major applications in the armamentarium of clinical and counseling psychologists. The authors cite a study of the Goodenough–Harris Test in Iran in which the scores of 6- to 13-year-old children were found to be comparable in many respects to the score patterns found among United States children. Because of the fact that drawing a human figure is virtually a universal experience of childhood, the Goodenough–Harris Drawing Test is useful as a culture-fair test, which makes the test a useful tool in the assessment of children who have undergone environmental, economic, and educational deprivation, like many children in the foster care system.

Naglieri (1988) has developed an updated version of the Goodenough–Harris Drawing Test that eliminates some of the outdated scoring and uses more recent norms. The Naglieri scoring system is also designed to be less ambiguous than the Goodenough–Harris Test. Anastasi and Urbina (1997) note, however, that the Naglieri Test has been criticized for its lack of evidence concerning the advantages of this revised scoring system. I employ developmentally scored drawing procedures as a means of determining whether a child possesses a true intellectual potential that may not be reflected in the results of standard intellectual measures. Clinical experience has shown that the Naglieri scoring system has several advantages over the older Goodenough–Harris procedure; however, there is much more of a ceiling effect in the Naglieri norms than in the Goodenough–Harris norms that reduces the usefulness of the Naglieri Test with children above the age of 11 years.

Although highly subjective methods of personality assessment such as the Thematic Apperception Test would be poor candidates as psychometric procedures under present federal standards (see Chapter 10 on *Daubert/Frye*), my view is that such methods are appropriate for the assessment of children in termination cases. The Children's Apperception Test for younger children, up to the age of 8 years or so, and the Thematic Apperception Test for older children and adolescents, yield valuable clinical information that can provide a legitimate basis for experts' conclusions about children's current adjustment and emotional needs. As noted above, family court judges tend to grant greater latitude for experts in testifying about their assessment of the children who are the subjects of this litigation than in the assessments of birth parents.

A variant of the standard House–Tree–Person projective drawing technique is the Kinetic Family Drawing (KFD). This procedure requires the child to draw a picture of his or her family, including the child him- or herself, and to depict everyone in the drawing as engaged in some type of action. Although some records of this type are rather bland, others can be quiet revealing: for example, when a child draws himself between two foster parents who are engaged in a nurturing activity, such as cooking dinner or playing ball with the child, but relegates the birth parent to the periphery of the drawing where the birth parent is engaged in a self-absorbed activity, such as smoking a cigarette, and is facing away from the child. Whitten (1994) also recommends KFD as an important tool in assessing the attachment profiles of children who are old enough to draw and associate to the drawings.

PSYCHOMETRIC PROCEDURES IN THE ASSESSMENT OF SEXUAL ABUSE

Many foster children who are being considered for adoption have experienced sexual abuse. Clinical assessment of such children serves two purposes: (1) determining whether sexual abuse has occurred and (2) assessing the impact of sexual abuse trauma on the child's psychological functioning. Assessment of whether sexual abuse has occurred typically takes place in the initial stages of the case, well before circumstances have progressed to the point where termination of parental rights is being considered. Assessment of the impact of sexual abuse trauma on the child is valuable in addressing clinical questions about the child's capacity to attach, about attitudes toward the birth parent if the parent or a partner of the parent was the perpetrator, and about intrapsychic matters such as mood regulation, capacity for signal anxiety versus incapacitating anxiety, behavior problems, and self-esteem/self-concept.

Faller (1996) states that psychological tests are neither necessary nor sufficient to determine whether a child has been abused, but that testing can provide valuable information in making such determinations and in assessing the child's overall situation. Faller notes that there have been several studies employing measures of self-esteem to investigate the hypothesis that sexual abuse lowers children's self-esteem. The results of this research have been mixed, and there is no justification in inferring that sexual abuse has occurred simply because a child presents with impaired self-esteem. Although many sexually abused children have poor self-esteem, such low self-esteem is not specific to sexual abuse, and the probability that an abused child has impaired self-esteem should not be confused with the probability that a child has been sexually abused because he or she has impaired self-esteem.

Friedrich (1990) addressed the problem of symptoms specific to sexual abuse through the development of the Child Sexual Behavior

Inventory. This instrument has been shown to discriminate reliably between sexually abused and nonabused children. Faller (1996) notes, however, that some sexual abuse victims are nonsymptomatic and that even the most common symptom of abuse, pathologically sexualized behavior, occurs in only 40% of sexually abused children. Another promising instrument for assessing sexual abuse is the Trauma Symptom Checklist for Children (Briere & Lanktree, 1992). It has been demonstrated that this instrument has adequate reliability and has validity against a criterion of clinical judgments about whether a child has or has not been sexually abused.

Faller (1996), in summarizing the research on the use of projective drawings in sexual abuse assessments, states that predictive validity is modest at best. Faller does not regard the use of drawings as being of value in addressing the question of whether sexual abuse has occurred. Drawings do have value, however, in the overall clinical assessment of sexually abused children and as a collateral source of information in determining whether abuse has occurred. Faller cites a number of techniques that employ free drawings and kinetic family drawings and that have been found helpful in such assessments.

The assessment of sexually abused children, especially with respect to confirming that abuse has occurred, is a specialized field. Practitioners who undertake such assessments should be familiar with the literature in this area, especially as it pertains to interviewing practices. Difficult questions involving traumatic memory, children's suggestibility, cognitive capacities of young children, and related issues pose daunting problems for evaluators in this area, especially if the results of the assessment are to be presented in court. On the other hand, in assessing children with substantiated sexual abuse in connection with termination of parental rights litigation, it is crucial to address the impact of the sexual abuse trauma on the child's psychic functioning.

FACTORS TO BE CONSIDERED IN FORMULATING OPINIONS

In deciding the best placement of a child, a number of child-specific and adult-specific factors should be integrated. Those factors specific to the child include the child's attachment profile; the age at which the child was placed in foster or kinship care; the number of placements to which the child has been subjected; and any behavioral, emotional, intellectual, or physical handicaps of the child that would impose an increased burden of care. Parent-specific factors, some of which have been discussed in the preceding chapter, include the parent's ability to respond to the child's normal and special needs, the consistency with which the parent has maintained a tie with the child through visitation and other forms of contact, and the parent's motivation to resume (or, in some cases, to assume) a parental role vis-à-vis a particular child.

In considering what weight to give to the child's attachment profile, it is useful to take into account the child's age and developmental level. It has been my experience that qualitatively different sets of consequences are involved in deciding upon a permanent placement for an older (age 8 and above) as opposed to a younger child.

In the case of a younger child whose personality is still very much in the process of formation through the development of basic identifications and emotional connections, separations and losses can have a traumatic effect that produces profound structural defects in the personality that lead to severe personality disorder and depression as an adolescent or adult. The extreme example of this, as typified by the case of Dee-Dee presented in Chapter 12, is the child who is placed out of the home at an early age and is repeatedly moved from one foster home to another, perhaps with an attachment to a foster parent who might have been interested in adopting, interrupted by an unsuccessful return to the birth parent and placement with yet another foster parent upon returning to foster care. Such children develop a pseudo-self-sufficiency that protects them from exposure to the crushing emotional pain associated with further losses of love objects in whom they have allowed themselves to become invested emotionally.

A less serious, but nonetheless potentially destructive, situation is that of the young child, below 5 years of age, who has been placed early and has developed an attachment to foster caretakers with little or no contact with the birth parents. To disrupt the child's attachment to the foster caretakers and give the child over to birth parents who are virtual strangers to the child will have an adverse effect upon delicate processes of personality formation.

In the child's immature and egocentric view of the world, the loss of the central parental love objects will be processed as an event precipitated by that child's own actions. This type of immature reasoning is poignantly reflected in the parting words of Baby Richard as he was being taken from his adoptive parents by his biological father, with whom he had had minimal contact: "Please don't make me go. I'll be good." The key factor is that one is observing the operation of a developing, as opposed to an intact, personality structure whereby the child does not feel entirely psychically separate from the psychological parents, tends to have an egocentric view of cause and effect, and has not acquired the capacity for logical reasoning, independent mood regulation, anxiety management, or stable behavioral controls.

In the case of older children, especially those who have spent their preschool years in relatively stable circumstances that permitted a substantial degree of healthy personality development, there is often a substantial identification with the birth parents and an emotional tie to them. In such cases, adoption of the child, with its concomitant severing of all contact with the birth parents, risks depriving the child of a significant object tie and of an aspect of personal identity that are important for subsequent mental health. Another situation that is frequently encountered in older foster children is that of the pseudo-self-sufficient child who has been through a number of foster homes and possibly a failed adoption. In these children, there is an extremely limited capacity to form new attachments because of pervasive mistrust, negativism, and hostility, as well as a deep fear of intimacy resulting from prior devastating experiences of rejection. In these cases, therapeutic considerations are paramount, and it is futile to look to adoption per se as a solution to the child's problems.

CHAPTER 7

Special Situations

TRANSRACIAL ADOPTIONS

Of the estimated 50,000 children who are legally free for adoption, fully half are minority group children, primarily African American. In order for the African American community to absorb all of these children, adoptions within that community would have to proceed at a rate of 44 per 10,000, whereas the actual rate is less than half of this (Vroegh, 1997). This imbalance between the availability of African American adoptive families and the needs of African American children in placement has led to the practice of placing such children with white adoptive families.

The practice of placing African American children outside their own community has been criticized by the Child Welfare League of America (1993) and has been vehemently condemned by the National Association of Black Social Workers (1972, 1994). In general, white professionals are not aware of the extent to which some black professionals view the practice of transracial adoption of black and mixed race children as an assault on the black community. The argument advanced by opponents of transracial adoption of African American children is that these children are entitled to an African American racial identity as a birthright and that placing them outside the black community precludes their adequately developing such an identity. Opponents of these adoptions stress that the African American child adopted into a white family will always be viewed as different from his or her siblings and other family members because of the noticeable difference in skin pigmentation and is therefore condemned to the status of an oddity. Furthermore, these opponents envision a scenario in which the white adoptive family becomes estranged from the extended family because of having adopted an African American child, who is consequently blamed as being the cause of this estrangement. Opponents regard the efforts of white adoptive families to become knowledgeable about black culture, to learn how to take care of black children's hair, and to form relationships with African Americans (whom they would otherwise have avoided) as unnatural accommodations to an essentially unworkable situation. This, according to detractors, casts a pall of artificiality and superficiality on the relationships within such an adoptive family and on that family's external relationships.

Opponents of transracial adoptions contest the assertion that African Americans will not adopt sufficient numbers of black children. They state that the adoption gap is the result of the inhospitability of the social service/adoption system to minority candidates and to economically disadvantaged candidates who cannot negotiate the bureaucracy that favors white and middle-class adoptive families. That the practice of transracial adoption is seen as destructive to black children and as an infringement on the rights of African Americans generally is apparent in the following excerpts from the original statement of the National Association of Black Social Workers (1974):

> Overt ethnic identification, especially for Blacks, was long suppressed by the social and political pressures speaking to total assimilation of all peoples in that great melting pot. We were made, by devious devices, to view ethnic identification as a self-defeating stance, prohibiting our acceptance into the mainstream. Black people are now developing an honest perception of this society; the myths of assimilation and of our inferiority stand bare under glaring light. We now proclaim our truth, substance, beauty and value as ourselves without apology or compromise. The affirmation of our ethnicity promotes our opposition to the trans-racial placements of Black children. (p. 1)

> We fully recognize the phenomenon of trans-racial adoption as an expedient for white folk, not as an altruistic humane concern for Black children. The supply of white children for adoption has all but vanished and adoption agencies, having always catered to middle class whites, developed an answer to their desire for parenthood by motivating them

> to consider Black children. This has brought about a re-definition of some Black children. Those born of Black–White alliances are no longer Black as decreed by immutable law and social custom for centuries. They are now Black–White, inter-racial, bi-racial, emphasizing the Whiteness as the adoptable quality; a further subtle, but vicious design to further diminish black and accentuate white. We resent this high-handed arrogance and are insulted by this further assignment of chattel status to Black people. (p. 2)
>
> The visceral feeling underlying the "would you want your daughter to marry one syndrome" still pervades the socialization concerns of white parents. Despite pronouncements of the universality of children a Black boy's entry to adolescence prompts his white mother's panic state call for help as she ponders whom he will date. On the other hand, it is testimony to the absence of a preponderance of Blacks in his social circle; a serious void in his psycho-social development creating a point of trauma in this crucial stage of his psycho-sexual development. (p. 3)

A more recent statement by the National Association of Black Social Workers (1994) is entitled "Preserving African-American Families." As in the 1972 statement, the association asserts that black children are most appropriately raised in same-race homes and that there can be damage to black children's self-concept and general welfare if they are inappropriately placed with white adoptive families. The position statement criticizes the practice of placing children in foster care because of correctable and temporary problems, such as homelessness or neglect resulting from poverty. The statement notes that in states such as Michigan foster parents receive a much more generous stipend for maintaining a foster child than do parents attempting to raise their biological children on a welfare grant.

The paper also criticizes the widely held view that African Americans do not adopt in sufficiently large numbers. Citing bureaucratic barriers to African American adoptions, the position paper states "there is something seriously defective with the current adoption system as relates to African-American children, particularly given that African-Americans adopt at a rate of four times faster than any other racial group given equal income" (p. 4).

While the 1994 position statement acknowledges that transracial adoption may be a suitable strategy for a small minority of children, it states that this should only be considered "after documented evidence of unsuccessful same race placements has been reviewed and supported by appropriate representatives of the African-American community" (p. 4). The paper also criticizes the lack of attention paid to family reunification efforts relative to adoptive placement efforts and also the insufficient use of kinship care as an alternative to adoption by unrelated individuals, especially across racial groups.

Howze (1996) presents the perspective of an African American child-advocate attorney on the impact of transracial adoption. Howze cites the case of an African American mother who became enraged upon learning that her child had been placed with a white foster mother and subsequently consented to that child's adoption by a single African American woman. Howze continues:

> In the meantime, the mother had another child. A new case was opened and she relapsed and began using drugs again. This child was placed with a white family. Social workers and attorneys should have taken a hard look at the case history before placing the infant. The race of the family caring for the child matters to this mother. She does not trust white people. The issue in this case is not whether that mistrust of whites is founded or unfounded. The issue is what will help resolve permanency issues for this child. If placement with an African American family will make consent to adoption easier for the mother who truly loves her children but is not capable of rearing them, why can't her attorney advocate for such a placement? Is there some benefit in allowing the mother to have some choice in this wrenching end of the abuse and neglect process? (pp. 66–67)

Singer, Brodzinsky, Ramsay, Steir, and Waters (1985) found that when placed within the first few months after birth, interracially adopted infants did not differ in their attachment capacity from nonadopted infants. These investigators did find, however, that the interracially adopted infants in their study tended to be somewhat more insecure than nonadopted infants.

Brodzinsky, Smith, and Brodzinsky (1998) reviewed the literature on transracial adoption. They note that recent studies, designed with greater experimental rigor than were the classical studies in this area, have yielded results similar to the earlier studies, namely, that transracially adopted minority children felt strongly attached to their adoptive families and that they did not differ from their nonadopted siblings in self-esteem.

Regarding the question of racial identity among such children, the picture is a complex one. Although Brodzinsky et al. (1998) cite research indicating that transracially adopted 3- to 8-year-old African American children (and their nonadopted white siblings as well) did not demonstrate a preference for white over black dolls, other research has shown that white parents of transracially adopted children tended to avoid identifying their children as "black" whereas the African American parents of in-racially adopted children did not. This pattern was also evident in the children themselves.

Brodzinsky et al. (1998) also note, however, that the overall pattern of results in the research cited in their review indicates that parents of transracial adoptees who do not isolate their children from the African American community and who accept their children's racial identification raise children who have a positive self-image as African American. However, the authors also discuss studies that indicate that transracial adoptees' psychological difficulties increased over the duration of a large longitudinal study and that the decreased adjustment appeared to be related to decreases in Afrocentric cultural beliefs, which in turn were related to the ways in which adoptive families handled these issues as the children matured.

The effect of transracial adoption on the self-concept of African American children is the subject of a longitudinal study of 52 adolescents of black descent adopted in infancy and reported by Vroegh (1997). This article reports the fifth phase of the study at a point 17 years after the original research was undertaken. Vroegh found that overall adjustment was not related to either transracial versus same-race adoption or to the subject's stated race. Most subjects, whether transracially adopted or same-race adopted or of black, mixed, or undecided racial identity, showed good or very good self-esteem in a 90-minute interview. Vroegh also found that more than 90% of all subjects believed that they were doing as well or better in life than most of their peers. Only one of the 34 transracial adoptees reported concern about racial identity. Most subjects reported no racial incidents either at school or in the community; although of those that were reported, significantly more were experienced by transracially adopted children than same-race adoptees. Name-calling and avoidance were the most frequently reported incidents. Nearly two-thirds of the subjects in both groups reported that they saw transracial adoption as a good idea without reservation. The remainder thought that it was a good idea, providing that there was parental sensitivity to the needs of the child.

In the Vroegh (1997) study, of the transracial adoptees, 79%

reported getting along well with their mothers and 73% with their fathers. Of the same-race adoptees, 69% reported getting along well with their mothers, but only 50% reported getting along well with their fathers. More than 80% of both the same-race and transracial adoptees reported having white friends. While all of the same-race adoptees had black friends, 25% of the transracial adoptees did not, primarily because of a lack of opportunity to form such relationships. Most of the transracial adoptees reported that their closest friends were white, while most of the same-race adoptees reported that their closest friends were black. While 66% of the transracially adopted females reported dating blacks, only slightly more than a third of the transracially adopted males reported dating blacks. All same-race adoptees dated blacks. Dating patterns were predominantly determined by the racial makeup of the subject's school.

In generalizing these results to specific cases, it should be noted that the adoptive families of these adolescents have incomes of over $40,000. More significantly, 75% of the transracially adopted children had one black and one white birth parent, whereas nearly all (95%) of the same-race adoptees had two black birth parents. Regarding self-identification, 33% of the transracially adopted subjects labeled themselves as black, and 55% labeled themselves as mixed, with 12% undecided. Of the same-race adoptees, most of whom had two African American birth parents, 83% labeled themselves as black, and 17% as either mixed or undecided. Vroegh offers the following interpretations of this phase of the study:

> For the most part the TRAs [transracial adoptees] in this study have light complexions. In addition, the majority also have one black and one white birth parent, a fact not previously reported in studies of transracial adoption. Given their light skin color and birth parents of two races, these children might reasonably be expected to have identity problems, whether their adoptive parents were black or white. . . . The transracial adoptees studied here appeared to have developed identities with which they were comfortable and that opponents of transracial adoption might find acceptable. (pp. 573–574)

Vroegh concludes:

> No evidence was found in the present study . . . that everyday relationships with black people are key to the development of a black racial

> identity. The majority of the transracial adoptees lived in white neighborhoods and half of them attended white schools, yet they declared their identities to be black or mixed. They also preferred, as did the inracial adoptees, black friends and dates, and exercised this preference whenever possible. For both groups, friendships and dating choices appeared to be dictated by opportunity. . . . Research findings suggest that the placement of young black children in white homes can meet the best interests of children who would otherwise remain without permanent homes for far too long. (p. 574)

In contrast to the call in the 1994 Association of Black Social Workers position paper for review of every proposed transracial placement by representatives of the African American community, the current legislative climate dictates exactly the opposite approach. Howze (1996) cites the Howard Metzenbaum Multiethnic Placement Act of 1994 (MEPA), which is a law designed to prevent discrimination in the placement of children and to decrease the time that children spend waiting for adoption. The act also is intended to facilitate the identification and recruitment of foster and adoptive families.

The Molinari Bill (HR 3286), entitled "A Bill to Help Families Defray Adoption Costs and to Promote the Adoption of Minority Children," contains a section addressing the removal of barriers to "interethnic adoption." This section, Title II of the act, mandates that neither states nor any entity within a state that receives federal funds for adoption or foster care may "(A) deny to any person the opportunity to become an adoptive or foster parent, on the basis of race, color, or national origin of the person, or of the child, involved; or (B) delay or deny the placement of a child for adoption or into foster care, on the basis of race, color, or national origin of the adoptive or foster parent, or the child, involved" (HR-3286, Sec. 201). The Molinari Bill further states that noncompliance with the above is deemed a violation of Title VI of the Civil Rights Act of 1964. Noncompliance is also punishable under the act with a reduction in federal monies allocated to the state or other entity. It is of interest, however, that these provisions do not affect children who are the subject of the Indian Child Welfare act of 1978, which affords protection to Native Americans against assaults on their tribal identity. However, the exemption under the Indian Child Welfare Act does not apply to children born of Native American parents who do not maintain some form of affiliation with their tribe.

OPEN ADOPTION

"Open adoption" is a term that has come to signify a range of continuing contact between adopted children and their birth parents and a range of birth parents' direct involvement in these children's lives. Under most state statutes relating to adoption, and under all of the model legislation considered in Chapter 2, termination of the birth parents' rights is a prerequisite for adoption. This requirement precludes any legally enforceable open adoption contract between adoptive and birth parents. An approximation to such a contract is a "directed surrender" in which the birth parent surrenders his or her parental rights to the child under certain conditions specified in the surrender document. Although a birth parent may surrender his or her child contingent upon placement with an individual who the parent believes will provide opportunities for involvement with the child after adoption, a specific provision mandating continuing contact would probably not pass muster in the courts' review of such a document in most states.

Hardin and Lancour (1996) note that open adoption is an option available in at least 11 states, where parents retain limited rights to information, contacts, or visits after the child is adopted. Hardin and Lancour state that open adoption may be appropriate in cases in which there is (1) an older child who had close emotional ties to the birth parent, (2) no risk of abuse or neglect associated with the limited contacts under the agreement, and (3) an accord between the adoptive and biological parents on the arrangement. Hardin and Lancour note that 5 states have statutes that specifically permit postadoption visitation agreements and make the agreements enforceable by courts. These states include Indiana, Nebraska, New Mexico, Oregon, and Washington. Hardin and Lancour also note that Ohio has a statute authorizing the creation of open adoption agreements and makes these agreements enforceable. Six other states have case laws reflecting an acceptance of postadoption visitation agreements.

Lee and Twaite (1997) report that open adoption is a popular concept, although there are few hard data on the number of adoptions that are open. Lee and Twaite also note that, despite various theoretical positions asserting the pros and cons of open adoption, there is very little empirical research as to differences in outcomes. Prior to their own study, there had been only a handful of empirical studies of open adoption, most of which relied on impressionistic clinical data and employed extremely small samples. These studies generally yielded results favorable to open adoption, as measured by parental attitudes.

Lee and Twaite studied 238 middle- and upper-middle-class mothers of privately adopted children. All of the children had been adopted within 3 months of the child's birth and were under 18 years of age at the time of the study. The adoptive parents responded to a survey sent through the mail. It was found that most of the adoptive mothers in the study did not have fully open adoptions but rather "semi-open adoptions" in which the adoptive and birth mothers did not exchange names and addresses but did have contact by letter, by telephone, or in person prior to or shortly after the birth of the child. Adoptive mothers who have contact with the birth mother may realize by virtue of this contact that the birth mother is not an uneducated and unintelligent person but rather an intelligent young woman who has given up her baby after reflecting on the situation and deciding that adoption would be the best course. They also may realize that the birth mother cares about her child, who is not a "throwaway baby," thus leading to a perception that the child has an adequate genetic endowment and has had adequate prenatal care. Obviously, the results of this study have only limited relevance to the typical situation treated in the present volume, namely, the foster parent adopts an abused or neglected child. In such cases, "throwaway babies" are not uncommon.

Brodzinsky et al. (1998) reviewed the literature on open adoption. They conclude that the dire predictions of harm expressed by critics of the practice are unfounded and that openness in adoption generally has beneficial effects. The authors cite studies indicating that children in an open adoption arrangement either had fewer behavioral problems than did children in closed adoptions or else that there were no significant differences in adjustment between the two groups. The authors stress that because the needs of children in open adoption arrangements may change over time, owing to their developmental level and other circumstances, contact plans between birth parents and their adopted children may have to be modified to address individual needs.

Regarding practical experience with informal open adoption practices in cases in which the rights of an unfit birth parent have been terminated, the results are mixed. I have been involved in cases in which the foster parent has developed a relationship with the birth parent wherein boundaries were established early on and the birth parent was not so disturbed or character disordered as to violate these boundaries. These relationships have a tendency to carry over after adoption and to provide the child with the benefit of positive contact with a birth parent under the best possible circumstances, whereby the birth parent is experienced as a benevolent visiting relative who does not attempt to intrude on the adoptive parent–child relationship. It is not uncommon in such cases to find that the birth parent acknowledges in some form that the child has become profoundly attached to the adoptive parent and belongs in that home permanently. The case proceeds to a termination hearing only because the birth parent feels that the child would resent the fact that the birth parent had not fought to prevent the severing of rights or because the birth parent feels he or she owes it to the child to put up resistance to termination of rights rather than merely sign a surrender.

GAY/LESBIAN ADOPTION

As of the present writing, gay and lesbian adoptive parents continue to encounter legal challenges, although less so than was the case a decade ago. They also lack the guarantee of legislation that explicitly authorizes such unmarried pairs to serve as adoptive parents of foster children in every state except for New Jersey, which recently struck an agreement with the American Civil Liberties Union granting this recognition ("State Clears Adoption by Gay Couples," 1997). Under the New Jersey plan, the state will repeal its policy that, in the case of unmarried persons who are cohabitating, only one of two persons who are cohabitating can legally adopt a child. Other provisions of the settlement are that state officials must use the same rules that they apply to married couples when unmarried heterosexual and homosexual couples apply for adoption and that gay or lesbian couples who feel that they have been denied an adoption because of sexual orientation or marital status can appeal the decision in court.

In my clinical experience, the fact that a foster child is cared for by gay or lesbian foster parents occasionally introduces an additional element of conflict into the case, resulting in a more intense expression of the birth parents' psychopathology than would otherwise be the case. With disturbed birth parents who have deeply ingrained homophobic attitudes, the knowledge that their child is being cared for by homosexuals tends to exacerbate both their distrust of the child protective system and their preoccupation with the fantasy that the child is being physically or sexually abused in the foster home. Birth parents' and grandparents' distress over having a child in the custody of gay or lesbian foster parents has also occasionally resulted in death threats against child protective services workers and against the foster parents themselves. Understandably, in cases that reach the stage of a hearing for termination of parental rights, such birth parents pressure their attorneys to introduce the alleged unfitness of homosexual caretakers as an element of their defense in the termination action.

Recent case law has supported foster and adoptive parenting by individual gays and lesbians and by homosexual couples. In a case of a gay couple that applied to adopt a child, *In re M. M. D.* (1995), the District of Columbia Court of Appeals found that nothing in the adoption statute precluded unmarried couples from adopting a child. In another case, *In re Petition of K. M. and D. M. to Adopt Olivia M.* (1995) an Illinois appellate court stated explicitly that adoption by gays and lesbians is permitted in Illinois. A Massachusetts case, *In re Adoption of Tammy* (1993) also affirmed the rights of gay and lesbian couples to adopt children. In that case, the Massachusetts Supreme Court ruled that a woman and her lesbian partner may adopt the woman's biological daughter, who was conceived through artificial insemination, and that state statute permits adoptions regardless of sexual orientation.

The Wisconsin Supreme Court in *Holtzman v. Knott* (*In re H. S. H.-K,* 1995) ruled that a trial court has the authority to grant visitation with a child born to a former lesbian partner on the basis of that former partner's relationship with the child, which was similar to a parent–child relationship. In *A. C. v. C. B.* (1992), a New Mexico court stated that in custody matters a party's sexual activities should be considered only to the extent that they affect the child and that custody and visitation may not be denied on the basis of a party's sexual orientation alone. In *Bottoms v. Bottoms* (1994), a Virginia court of appeals found that an open lesbian relationship did not, in itself, constitute sufficient grounds to remove a child and to place that child with a nonparent. The trial court had held that the birth parent was unfit as a matter of law because she had admitted to living in a sexually active lesbian relationship with her lesbian partner and had engaged in illegal sexual acts, namely, oral sex in violation of Virginia's sodomy law. The appeals court, however, was persuaded by the psychological testimony that a parent's homosexual relationship alone does not harm a child and by social science evidence showing that sexual orientation is not strongly related to parental fitness.

Tasker and Golombok (1995) state that lesbians have been refused access to donor insemination and have been refused permission to adopt or serve as foster parents on the grounds that they would be less able than heterosexual parents to provide an optimal family environment. In a study of 25 young adults from lesbian families and 21 adults raised by heterosexual single mothers, Tasker and Golombok found that those raised by lesbian mothers functioned well in adulthood with respect to psychological well-being and family identity and relationships. The study did not support the commonly held assumption that lesbian mothers will have lesbian daughters and gay sons. The authors note that the findings may have somewhat limited generalizability because of the self-selected nature of the sample. Tasker and Golombok (1997) report the results of the British Longitudinal Study of Lesbian Mother Families. These authors cite positive outcomes with respect to the psychosocial adjustment of young adults raised by lesbian mothers.

Patterson (1995), in summarizing the research on children of gay and lesbian parents in an official American Psychological Association Public Interest Directorate publication on the subject, notes that occasionally courts have assumed that gay men and lesbians are mentally ill, that lesbians are less maternal than heterosexual women are, and that lesbians' and gay men's relationships with sexual partners leave little time for ongoing parent–child interactions. Patterson states that the results of research to date have failed to confirm any of these beliefs and that there is no reliable evidence that homosexual orientation per se impairs psychological functioning. Patterson cites the removal of homosexuality from the American Psychiatric Association's list of mental disorders more than 20 years ago and the adoption of the same position by the American Psychological Association in 1975. Patterson also cites a large number of studies that demonstrate that lesbian and heterosexual women do not differ in their overall mental health or in their approaches to child rearing, that lesbians' romantic relationships do not detract from their ability to care for their children, and that there is no reason to believe that gay men are unfit as parents.

Patterson (1995) notes that, in addition to judicial concerns about homosexual parents themselves, courts have had concerns about the effects on children of being reared by homosexual parents. First, courts have been concerned that the development of sexual identity will be impaired among children of gays or lesbians. Patterson discusses research that indicates that the children of lesbian parents have normal gender identity. There is no research reported in this area for children of gay fathers. Patterson also states that studies have found no difference between children of lesbian and heterosexual parents in gender role behavior as indicated by toy preferences, activities, or occupational choices. In one study, children of lesbian mothers did report greater psychological femininity on the Bem Sex Role Inventory than did children of heterosexual mothers. No data are available in this area for children of gay fathers.

Patterson (1995) further notes that other research has found no significant differences between children of heterosexual and lesbian mothers in television program preferences, favorite television characters, or favorite games or toys. While lesbian mothers reported that their daughters often participated in rough-and-tumble play and occasionally played with masculine toys such as trucks or guns, there were no such differences reported for sons. Furthermore, lesbian mothers were no more or less likely than heterosexual mothers to report that their children often played with feminine toys such as dolls. No data on these issues are available for children of gay fathers.

Patterson (1995) reports that in all 12 studies of sexual orientation that she reviewed, the great majority of offspring of both gay fathers and lesbian mothers described themselves as heterosexual. She concludes that these studies, in aggregate, do not suggest elevated rates of homosexuality among offspring of lesbian or gay parents.

Patterson (1995) summarizes the results of a number of studies of other dimensions of personal development, including separation/individuation, psychiatric assessment results, behavior problems, moral judgment, self-concept, and the personality of the children of gay and lesbian parents. As was the case for sexual identity, there were no major differences between children of lesbian and heterosexual mothers identified in any of the studies. The one statistically significant difference that emerged is that children of lesbian mothers reported greater symptoms of stress but also a greater sense of well-being than did children of heterosexual parents.

Patterson (1995) also notes that research on peer relationships does not disclose any differences between children of lesbian and heterosexual mothers and that both the researchers and the parents and children themselves described the quality of their peer relationships positively. No data are available on the peer relations of children of gay fathers. Patterson states that studies of children's relationships with adults indicate no significant differences in the quality of those relationships between children of homosexual and heterosexual parents. In fact, Patterson cites research demonstrating that self-esteem among daughters of lesbian mothers whose lesbian partners lived with them was higher than among daughters of lesbian mothers who did not live with a partner. In regard to the question of possible sexual abuse of children reared in a lesbian or gay household, Patterson states that the available evidence indicates that gay men are no more likely than heterosexual men to perpetrate child sexual abuse and that sexual abuse of children by adult women is extremely rare. Patterson states: "Fears that children in custody of gay or lesbian parents might be at heightened risk for sexual abuse are thus without basis in the research literature" (p. 6).

On the negative side, Patterson (1995) states that children's silence about the sexual orientation of their parents might add to their feelings of isolation from other children. She notes that a sample of 11 adolescents in one study exercised selectivity about when they disclosed information about their mothers' lesbian identities. In another study reviewed by Patterson, 29% of young adult respondents had never known anyone else with a gay, lesbian, or bisexual parent, "suggesting that the possibility of isolation is very real for some young people" (p. 7). Crawford (1987) states that children in a lesbian family will experience stress associated with being different. Crawford notes that, no matter what lesbian mothers do to protect their children in a homophobic society, these children will be faced with many decisions regarding who can and cannot be told about their parents' sexual orientation and other matters concerning the relationship that these families have with the world.

Taking all of the existing studies of gay and lesbian parenting into account, Patterson (1995) concludes: "Not a single study has found children of gay or lesbian parents to be disadvantaged in any significant respect relative to children of heterosexual parents.

Indeed, the evidence to date suggests that home environments provided by gay and lesbian parents are as likely as those provided by heterosexual parents to support and enable children's psychosocial growth" (p. 8).

EARLY TERMINATION OF PARENTAL RIGHTS

Hardin and Lancour (1996) note that, while diligent efforts toward family preservation are justified in many cases, there are other cases in which the circumstances are so extreme that they are either futile or hopeless. In the interest of properly allocating scarce social service resources, Hardin and Lancour recommend a triage system in which some cases are diverted from coercive state involvement, some are slated for family preservation services requiring court involvement, and some receive speedy action to free children for adoption.

Hardin and Lancour (1996) define early termination as follows:

> When adoption is the initial goal for the child and there should not be enforceable contacts between parent and child, the agency should seek "early" termination of parental rights. Early termination means that the agency seeks termination of parental rights soon after the child's removal from the home, instead of after a period of time during which the parent undergoes rehabilitative therapy. The agency's initial goal is to free the child for placement in an adoptive home, and as quickly as possible. The agency seeks termination of parental rights in a relatively short time, in order to provide stability and safety for the child. (p. 6)

Echoing the views expressed by Goldstein et al. (1979), Hardin and Lancour stress that the child's sense of time is a factor that aggravates the child's stress in foster care. Hardin and Lancour note that young children cannot experience placement in foster care as temporary because of this difference in time sense and that the perceived endlessness of the child's situation compounds the child's adjustment problems.

Hardin and Lancour (1996) list several grounds for pursuing termination of parental rights at an early stage in the case. These grounds include (1) a parent's failure to make the necessary improvements for the child's safe return; (2) a long-standing or extreme pattern of parental disinterest; (3) projected long-term parental incapacity to care for the child because of mental or emotional illness, retardation, or physical incapacity; (4) drug- or alcohol-related incapacity, with a history of repeated unsuccessful attempts at rehabilitation; (5) prior neglect or abuse of the child or siblings despite diligent efforts by the state to remedy the situation; (6) extreme neglect or abuse; (7) a child's deep aversion to or pathological fear of the parent as a result of abuse or neglect; and (8) a parent's imprisonment projected to last through an extended period of the child's minority.

Demonstration of failure to improve consists of three key elements: (1) a realistic case plan designed to correct the abuse or neglect, (2) demonstrated efforts at implementing the plan, and (3) concrete documentation of failure to improve in spite of these efforts.

In Chapter 2 it was noted that parental abandonment of a child is frequently cited in statutes as sufficient grounds for termination. Hardin and Lancour (1996) seek to expand this rationale to include a parent's disinterest as well. Hardin and Lancour state that "extreme parental disinterest" exists when the parent has shown the intent not to accept full parental responsibility for the child in question. This disinterest may be demonstrated by neglecting to visit or pay child support, by leaving the child with inappropriate caretakers, or by failing to return to take custody of the child as promised. Regarding the situations of newborns who are abandoned without identification, left with another adult, or not visited by the birth parent, some states have extended the concept of extreme parental disinterest to these situations, which lead to termination of rights within a shorter time than would abandonment of an older child. Hardin and Lancour also note that some states have added special grounds for termination of parental rights in cases of unwed fathers who do not display any interest in the child during the mother's pregnancy or shortly after the birth.

Projected long-term incapacity to care for the child depends very heavily on an expert diagnosis of the parent. Hardin and Lancour (1996) state that in such cases the expert must be prepared to testify that the parent cannot benefit from reunification services. Hardin and Lancour characterize such cases as "condition cases," in which the parent has a condition that is incapacitating and that is not likely to improve even with rehabilitative services. Hardin and Lancour note that such conditions are typically extreme, such as catatonic schizophrenia or persistent vegetative coma. They also note, however, that wherever special needs children are concerned a mild condition may be sufficient for termination. This would be the case in situations in which, for example, the child required vigilant monitoring of a potentially life-threatening medical problem with administration of precise dosages of medications that must be measured and administered in a prescribed manner. In such a case, a parent with mild mental retardation may be deemed unfit because of the combination of the parent's mild disability and the child's special needs.

Wherever neglect or abuse has been extreme, early termination is sometimes justifiable without a prior history of agency efforts to rehabilitate the family. This situation is discussed in the Adoption and Safe Families Act of 1997, which is analyzed in Chapter 3. The act specifies that in "aggravated circumstances," as when a parent has been convicted of murdering another child or a child has been tortured, abandoned, or chronically abused, reasonable efforts toward rehabilitation of the parent are not required and states are mandated to initiate termination proceedings without delay. Hardin and Lancour (1996) argue that some crimes, by their very nature, should disqualify a parent as the child's caretaker. Such crimes would include a parent's sexual abuse of a child or sibling that involves serious injury or a parent's child abuse or neglect that has caused the death of a sibling. Hardin and Lancour also argue that cases involving torture of children may demonstrate that the children should never be returned home. Hardin and Lancour state "The deep-seated character flaw in the parent leading to torture of the child is unlikely to be eliminated through rehabilitative services" (p. 18).

Regarding the last criterion for early termination set forth by Hardin and Lancour (1996), namely, a parent's prolonged imprisonment, the authors note that many states do not include such incarceration as a ground for termination of parental rights. The authors state that this policy reflects a concern that a parent is being punished twice for an offense; first, by incarceration, and second, by termination of parental rights. Hardin and Lancour observe that although this policy may be fair to the birth parent, it ignores the child's interests. The authors suggest the compromise of creating an exception to the termination of parental rights because of a parent's imprisonment if the parent did not abuse or neglect the child before entering prison and if there is a competent relative or close friend who is willing and able to care for the child until the birth parent's release from prison.

Hardin and Lancour (1996) feel that overly restrictive grounds for termination of parental rights has the paradoxical effect of defeating rather than enhancing efforts to achieve family reunification. The authors state that child protective service workers become demoralized by having to pursue obviously futile efforts with chronic abusers, chronic schizophrenic patients, and other cases with an extremely poor prognosis. They state: "By making a clearer distinction between cases where reasonable efforts are required and where they are not, social workers will find better results and fewer failures. More efforts will be provided for those families which have a chance to be reunited, and social workers will not feel worn down by the futility or working with families that are beyond help" (p. 68).

I feel that these arguments advanced by Hardin and Lancour have merit, but that policy makers should also take into account other factors. Any acceleration of the process to terminate parental rights carries with it the danger of depriving the birth parents, in subtle or obvious ways, of due process. Furthermore, in many cases, expert predictions early in the case to the effect that a birth parent cannot be rehabilitated, prior to any genuine attempts by social service personnel to work toward that end, may not withstand scrutiny under *Daubert*. Worse, the expert's predictions of incorrigibility may be accepted uncritically by a court only to be proven false within a short time after the termination of rights has been effected. Clearly, there are many cases in which early termination would spare children, caseworkers, and sometimes birth parents themselves, undue distress; however, early termination provisions of state and federal statues have a significant potential for misuse.

LONG-TERM FOSTER CARE AS AN ALTERNATIVE TO ADOPTION

A recent New Jersey appellate court decision, *In the Matter of the Guardianship of K. H. O.* (1998) raises the issue of long-term foster care as an alternative to adoption. This case involved the 4½-year-old daughter of a drug-addicted mother who had not been able to overcome her addiction to the satisfaction of the New Jersey Division of Youth and Family Services in spite of being offered extensive drug rehabilitation services. It was undisputed that the child had bonded with her foster caretakers, with whom the child had lived since she was a month old. The birth mother continued to register positive drug tests until a few weeks before the termination of parental rights hearing. While the appellate court stated that a "stable and permanent home" is always preferable to long-term foster care," it stressed the view of Johnson (1996) that "there are special psychological connections that children have with their parents of origin, regardless of whether the parents of origin are absent or present" (*In the Matter of the Guardianship of K. H. O.*, 1998, p. 13) and that severing these ties can result in psychological harm. The court also cited the views of Nitti (1994) that open adoption, which the court apparently considered in this case as being substantially equivalent to long-term foster care, was highly preferable to traditional adopting in which parental rights are severed.

In such cases, in which the birth parent may not ever be capable of caring independently for the child, defense attorneys argue that long-term foster care offers the best of both worlds. The child can remain with the caretakers to whom he or she has formed an attachment and yet retain a tie to the biological parent. Regarding traditional adoption, Johnson (1996) states: "It is during the ages of six through eighteen that adopted children are likely to become troubled by the adoption, grieve the loss of the family of origin, and may exhibit psychological, behavioral, and academic problems" (quoted in *In the Matter of the Guardianship of K. H. O.*, p. 19). The court went on to state that the status quo of preserving the child's tie with her mother and other members of her biological family through foster care rather than adoption represented an appropriate solution. The court states: "There is no doubt that the foster parents have provided K. O. with a positive and nurturing environment during her critical early years in life. She is obviously deeply attached to them, as well as to her foster family siblings—as they are to her. We are neither blind nor unfeeling to that. But we do not sense that if adoption is not a viable alternative, K. O.'s foster family will disappear" (p. 27). The appellate court therefore reversed a lower court's termination of the birth parents' rights and ordered a resumption of visits between the child and the biological family in the maternal grandmother's home.

Research cited by authorities in the field of foster care and adoption is informative with respect to consideration of long-term foster care as an alternative to adoption. Brodzinsky, Smith, and Brodzinsky (1998) cite a series of studies conducted in Sweden (Bohman, 1970; Bohman & Sigvardsson, 1978, 1979, 1980) that examined an age cohort of children from four different groups: (1) children raised in long-term foster care, (2) children raised by their biological mothers after the mothers reneged on their decision to place the children for adoption, (3) adopted children, and (4) children raised by their biological parents. The sample was studied from age 11 years until age 23 years. This research found "clear evidence of deterioration" in long-term foster care children between the ages of 11 and 15 years as compared to controls. At age 18 years, the long-term foster care children registered poorer psychological and social adjustment than the controls did, while adoptees fared significantly better than the long-term foster care subjects. Finally, when the subjects were reassessed at 23 years of age, males who had grown up in foster care were more likely to be registered for criminal behavior and alcohol abuse, or both, than were subjects in any other group.

Fanshel, Finch, and Grundy (1990) conducted an extensive analysis of the life experiences of 585 children in Casey foster care, a system of long-term foster homes. Fanshel et al. found that children who lost contact with their birth parents early appeared to be in better condition than those who were still involved with their birth parents. The authors state that children's entanglement in a relationship with their birth parents while in foster care causes the children to relate to their foster caretakers with a pervasive lack of trust and unreasonable expectations, thus hampering the children's attachment.

On the other hand, the research of Bush and Goldman (1982) indicates that the situation is different for older foster children. The authors report that for older children who have an ongoing, positively valued tie to birth parents who remain unable to care for them, adoption by foster caretakers is often perceived as a threat to that attachment. The authors also note that the older foster children surveyed in their study depended on their continuing contact with their birth parents to reinforce their sense of identity as a member of the biological family. This study is discussed in greater detail in Chapter 8.

In the case of younger children, there are several practical problems associated with maintaining them in long-term foster care as an alternative to adoption. To begin with, the children remain wards of the state for the balance of their childhood. In other words, the state functions as the parent for each child and there is no specific individual with full parental authority over a child's welfare. Eventually, children in foster care become aware of their foster status, and they may see other foster children coming and going from the foster home where they have formed an attachment. This can be extremely anxiety producing for some children. Additionally, the fact that a child realizes that the foster parents do not have full parental authority over him or her creates conflicts of loyalties and leads to manipulations such as resisting parental demands by retorting, "You're not my mother!" This situation may lead to a diminution of the foster parent's commitment to the child, which would otherwise be unequivocal.

There are identity concerns associated with foster care status that counterbalance the identity concerns associated for some children with a severing of ties with the birth family. The fact that many long-term foster children have to deal with state caseworkers and visits with birth parents throughout the balance of their childhood reinforces a feeling of second-class status as a "state kid," as opposed to children who have clearly identified individuals invested with ultimate parental responsibility for their welfare. Additionally, the normal adolescent search for identity that is exacerbated by adopted status can be offset to some extent by what has now come to be a common practice in many states, the creation of a "lifebook" in which children write their recollections of living with birth parents and record information about those parents, including photographs, prior to adoption.

CHAPTER 8

Theory Review

It is routine among state psychology board examiners, in states that require oral examinations of candidates for licensure, to ask candidates to frame their case presentations with respect to a specific theoretical orientation and to discuss the case from that perspective. Some examiners even require the candidate to reconceptualize the case from a theoretical viewpoint different from the one that the candidate has declared as his or her primary orientation. Many clinical psychology graduate school programs are explicitly organized along theoretical tracks, allowing students to concentrate on either behaviorist, cognitive, or psychoanalytically oriented courses. Myers (1997) points out that all expert opinion offered in courts of law is based upon some underlying theory or process (p. 474). It is theory, the posited network of cause-and-effect relationships among phenomena, that ties together our fragmented experimental and clinical observations and represents psychology's best attempts at a cohesive view of the operation of the human mind, or (for purists who eschew anything that smacks of mentalism) the determinants of human behavior.

Even in this era of *Daubert* challenges to the admissibility of expert testimony, mental health professionals should not shy away from offering testimony that conceptualizes the facts of a particular case in the context of well-accepted psychological theory. For it is only through theory that mental health experts can offer courts a complex and nuanced picture of the child in question—in particular, a view of how that child's psychological development has been affected by placement and a view of the events leading up to placement, as well as the probable effects of various permanency outcomes upon the child's future development and mental health. Psychological expert testimony must be more than a mere disjointed recitation of experimental results and test findings; ideally, such testimony represents an integration of clinical data with relevant empirical literature within the framework of some coherent theoretical view of personality and psychopathology and thus provides the court with a rich and comprehensive picture of the clinical situation.

This chapter will explore several theoretical issues in termination cases from the perspective of attachment theory, psychoanalysis, separation–individuation theory, behavior theory, and cognitive theory. Additionally, recent work on the relation between attachment phenomena and trauma, including physiological effects of trauma on children (James, 1994), will be reviewed.

Moving from clinical theory to psycholegal questions, I will discuss what have come to be known as the "psychological parent" and "permanency" principles, as elaborated by Anna Freud and her collaborators. Specific controversies associated with these theoretical principles, which are sometimes mistakenly described as "theories," will be examined in detail, especially with reference to issues that crop up in court testimony. Additionally, I will explore the concept of resilience, introduced by Rutter (1979) and often cited by defense experts in termination cases to rebut predictions of harm associated with removal of children from foster parents to whom the children are attached. This chapter will serve as a background for the discussion of empirical research findings relating to attachment, loss, and trauma presented in Chapter 9.

ATTACHMENT THEORY

Attachment theory was developed by Bowlby, a British psychiatrist who identified himself as an ethologist and who viewed his theory as being an extension of both the ethological and evolutionary theories of biology. He was appointed in 1950 to undertake a study of the needs of homeless children for the World Health Organization. This study resulted in the 1951 monograph *Maternal Care and Mental Health* (later published commercially as *Child Care and the Growth of Love*; Bowlby, 1953) in which Bowlby reviewed the evidence relating to adverse influences on personality development as a result of inadequate maternal care during early childhood (Bowlby, 1988). In 1958, Bowlby formally advanced what was at that time a radical proposition, namely, that attachment was an instinct in the same category as feeding and sex. He stated that, rather than being secondary to the gratification of primary drives, attachment is part of the instinctual programing of the human being that serves the purpose of survival. Bowlby (1977) defined attachment as an affectional tie with some other differentiated individual who is perceived as stronger or wiser.

Sperling and Berman (1994) note that Bowlby's theory rests on the concept of an attachment behavior system, which they describe as "a homeostatic process that regulates infant proximity-seeking and contact-maintaining behaviors with one or a few specific individuals who provide physical or psychological safety or security" (p. 5). Bowlby includes such phenomena as the baby's social smile and crying as manifestations of the attachment instinct. Once the infant has established a specific emotional tie to the mother, the infant uses the mother as a "secure base," a term that Bowlby (1988) attributes to Ainsworth. This concept involves a retreat to the mother when feelings of fear and anxiety threaten to overwhelm the infant upon straying too far away from the secure base of comfort. It also involves a turning to the mother for protection in the face of perceived danger, such as strangers, darkness, or other alarming perceptions. As a corollary to this, the infant experiences anxiety upon being separated from the mother. Bowlby conceived of the attachment system as continuing to develop in some form throughout the balance of childhood and into adolescence. While the attachment system continues to operate during adulthood, it remains relatively unchanged unless modified by psychotherapy.

Rothbard and Shaver (1994, p. 33) state that the development of a secure attachment relationship is contingent upon the caregiver's sensitivity and responsiveness and on the child's ability to trust in the caregiver's accessibility. When these elements are missing, or when the caregiver displays inconsistent accessibility, is excessively intrusive into the infant's activities, or rejects the infant's approaches for physical contact, then there emerge "secondary conditional strategies" such as anxious clinging, vigilance, or premature pseudo-independence. Rothbard and Shaver observe that these secondary strategies, while possibly adaptive in the short term in coping with the caregiver's failings, are likely to cause problems for the child in subsequent relationships later in the life cycle.

It is the later elaboration of attachment theory presented by Main, Kaplan, and Cassidy (1985, cited in Rothbard & Shaver, 1994) that is of greatest relevance to issues in termination of parental rights cases. Main et al. formulated the concept of internal working models of attachment (IWMs), whereby the child's early experiences with attachment figures serve as a template for that child's attitudes and behavior in subsequent relationships, particularly intimate relationships. Rothbard and Shaver (1994) note that, unlike simple cognitive schemata, IWMs are defined as including affective and defensive components in addition to cognitive ones. Rothbard and Shaver add that these mechanisms, which function largely outside the sphere of conscious awareness, provide a template for anticipating and interpreting the behavior and intentions of others. IWMs are particularly active in situations involving attachment figures, whether these are parent figures in childhood or intimate partners in adolescence and adulthood. In therapy, then, a disturbance or disruption of the attachment bond, or repeated disruptions of a child's attachment, will result in psychological damage through distortion of the child's IWMs. Furthermore, the theory predicts that this damage will be of a long-term nature since the IWMs determine the individual's pattern of behaving in intimate relationships throughout the life cycle.

The notion that disruption of a child's attachments can be completely offset by the child's forming of new attachments to subsequent figures is inconsistent with attachment theory, which stresses the specificity of the attachment relationship and the fact that such a relationship takes place with no more than a few significant individuals in the child's world. Indeed, Bowlby's original work on the subject of disrupted attachment, published in 1951, described what he termed "affectionless characters." These were delinquents who had experienced numerous changes in placement to the point where they did not appear to have any significant attachments to others. Bowlby noted that these delinquents seemed to lack the capacity for affectionate connection to other people and were singularly lacking in conscience. Attachment theory links this condition to the replacement of personal caretaking by impersonal and transient foster care environments during the period in which the inner template for attachment-related behaviors was in the process of development.

In studies spanning two decades, children's attachment styles have been categorized by a large number of researchers according to a typology established by Ainsworth and associates (Ainsworth, Blehar, Waters, & Wall, 1978) with a paradigm known as the Strange Situation. In this procedure, the attachment-related behaviors of an infant are elicited through repeated separations from an attachment figure and interactions with a stranger. Of particular interest in regard to children in foster care is a type of attachment behavior recently identified by Main and Hesse (1990) whereby infants show signs of disorganized and contradictory behaviors when reunited with a caregiver. Main et al. relate this phenomenon to the caregiver's unresolved attachment-related traumas and losses, as well as a history of abuse, neglect, or depression in the caregiver's own childhood. Rothbard and Shaver (1994) relate secure-versus-insecure attachment to children's vulnerabilty to stressors that produce psychopathology; the degree of distress associated with separations, relationship threats, and losses in romantic or intimate attachments as adults; and other psychological variables. The empirical evidence on which these theoretical propositions are based is reviewed in Chapter 9.

CLASSICAL PSYCHOANALYTIC THEORY

Psychoanalytic theory stresses the child's development of positively valued and realistic internal representations of parent figures as an essential element of healthy personality structure—in particular, the formation of the ego, or executive sector of the personality that is the basis of conscious awareness. Moore and Fine (1968) state that these inner representations of the parents, together with the child's representation of self, "provide the material and framework for all mentation, including the ego's adaptive and defensive functions" (p. 64). Furthermore, psychoanalytic theory lays heavy stress on love relations and positive identifications with parental objects during infancy and early childhood. Moore and Fine comment: "An indication of the major importance of progressive object relations in optimal functioning is the positive correlation between the development of the ego and the child's object relations" (p. 64).

The particular vulnerability of the child's immature ego to separation and loss experiences is also explained in classical psychoanalytic theory by the concept of the repetition compulsion. Moore and Fine (1968) explain the repetition compulsion as a general tendency to repeat painful experiences. This is particularly evident in individuals who go through a series of similar negative life experiences, which superficially appear to be the result of "bad luck" but are, on closer examination, seen to be unconsciously orchestrated by the individual to repeat a similar childhood dynamic. This self-created repetition of the same "configuration of the stress imposed and the adaptive response evoked" is also known by the now archaic term "fate neurosis." Moore and Fine cite other manifestations of the repetition compulsion such as children's stereotyped play that serves to master the experience of loss, and the self-defeating behaviors in adult patients with character disorders. Under this scenario, the child who has suffered the traumatic loss of a central parental love object during a critical period of development will be condemned to structure most future interpersonal interactions around the theme of experiencing and coping with this catastrophic loss, including the engineering of further losses of love objects. An example of this is the clinging, demanding, coercive behavior of borderline personality disorder patients toward their intimate partners that ultimately has the effect of driving the partners away, thus precipitating a psychological crisis in the patient.

Psychoanalytic theory also has a good deal to say concerning the development of conscience, or in jargon terms, the "superego." Jacobson (1964) describes in great detail the way in which the preschool child's selective identifications with the positively valued qualities of parents results in the formation of this psychic structure that provides an ideal toward which the child aspires in future personal development and that provides a behavior template in the form of internalized values and standards. The child who is deprived of suitable parental models during the period in which the superego is forming, usually at 4 to 5 years of age, or whose relationship with such figures is traumatically disrupted, will have a defective superego. The result is a conscience that is either oppressively punitive, leading to self-attack and chronic guilt, or one that is simply absent, leading to antisocial attitudes and behavior.

Hartmann (1964) notes that the process of healthy personality development is guided by repeated experiences of frustration and gratification. According to Hartmann, the principle of optimal frustration provides the ideal set of circumstances for ego development. Children who are never appropriately frustrated will be crippled in adulthood when confronted with the inevitable frustrations and disappointments of daily life. On the other hand, children who are exposed to levels of frustration that are beyond their developmental capacities to tolerate, especially when these levels reach the plane of traumatic experiences, are also crippled psychologically in adulthood. Such children do not develop a sense of themselves as capable of mastering challenges and are lacking in normal self-confidence and confident expectation of the world as a predictable place. Rather than instill resiliency, traumatic experiences create further vulnerability to stress because of the resulting deficits in ego strength in a child who has not even had an approximation of optimal frustration during crucial developmental periods.

SEPARATION–INDIVIDUATION THEORY

Separation–individuation theory, as elaborated by Mahler (Mahler, Pine, & Bergman, 1975), is an extension of classical psychoanalytic theory and examines in minute detail the processes by which the preschool child develops an adequate sense of his or her personal identity and the capacity to tolerate separations from attachment figures. Based on research that has employed direct observation of parent–child dyads and interaction among children in a nursery school setting, Mahler et al. have divided the psychological growth of the infant and toddler into discrete subphases, each with its own set of developmental tasks and specific vulnerabilities to the effects of trauma or deprivation.

The earliest period of infancy, lasting until approximately 3 months of age, is termed the "autistic period." It is thought that during this subphase the infant is primarily absorbed in processes of gratification that do not involve connection with parental love objects, except in a grossly physical way, as when a parent is assigned the role of soother to assist the child in overcoming tension states through holding and comforting. Spitz (1968) has shown that in the autistic subphase, infants will display a failure to thrive, also known as "marasmus," or "hospitalism," if they receive adequate physical care but are deprived of a consistent mothering person to provide soothing and emotional stimulation. This is a life-threatening condition that, in some of Spitz's subjects, resulted in the infant's death, in spite of the fact that the purely physical aspects of the child's care were adequate. The theoretical significance of this phenomenon is that it suggests a biologically based need in the human infant for nurturing behaviors from a mothering figure as a condition of survival prior to age 3 months. Spitz also describes the development of life-threatening depression in slightly older infants that resulted from separation from their mothers and relegation to standard nursery care after a period of being raised by their mothers following birth.

The symbiotic subphrase begins at approximately 3 months when the infant enters a shared ego experience with the mother in which there is little if any differentiation in the infant's experience between self and love object.

At approximately 6 months, according to separation–individuation theory, there occurs a psychological birth that is the mental counterpart of physical birth. The infant emerges from the symbiotic orbit with a rudimentary sense of "self" and "other" as separate beings. Acquisition of the mother as a specific parental love object is reflected in the phenomenon of stranger anxiety that accompanies this period. Earlier connections to adults in the infant's experience generally lack this specificity. While it is true that an infant in earlier developmental phases must attach to a specific adult in order to facilitate the development of the drives, it is not until the differentiation subphase that a true mental representation of the mother develops as a major component of psychic structure.

The practicing subphase begins when the child acquires mobility, typically at 11 months. At this point, the child begins a love affair with the world, and the dependency on the mother eases. The child seems to be more self-sufficient and confident in exploring the environment and returns to the mother only for brief periods of emotional refueling. The predominating affects of this period in the child's experience are an exuberance and confidence that permit exploration of the physical environment without a preoccupation about the mother's availability. Then the child delights in a sense of competence and exercise of the newly developed powers of mobility and other aspects of coordination. There is a sense of invulnerability.

The critical subphase known in Mahlerian terminology as "rapprochement" begins at approximately 18 months and lasts until about age 3 years. It is at this point that the child's powers of perception and mentation yield the conclusion that the world is not as safe and secure a place as it had appeared during the practicing subphase and that the comforting that only the mother can provide is necessary as an antidote to anxiety. It is at this stage that the child becomes clinging to the point of being unable to tolerate even brief separations from the mother, even when she goes to the bathroom and closes the door. Rapprochement is associated with a normal crisis in development when the child shadows the mother and uses coercion to manipulate her into giving in to the child's whims. It is common to see tantrums during which the child calls for the mother to come and give comfort, but pushes her away when she attempts to do so. The child's behavior tells the mother that she cannot do anything right, that gratifying is bad and not gratifying is equally bad. During the rapprochement phase, which coincides with the "terrible 2's," children normally fail to integrate their perceptions of the good parent with their perceptions of the bad parent. This phenomenon is termed "splitting."

The 2-year-old who is going through this rapprochement stage loses all sense of the mother as a good, nurturing, rewarding figure during tantrum states provoked by frustration. At that moment, the mother is virtually demonized by the child, and her comforting is not accepted. In the next moment, however, the child overcomes the frustrations and tantrums and experiences the mother as all good again. This experience is correlated with the desperate dependency that 2-year-olds display. Mahler held this period of development to be one of extreme vulnerability to trauma and deprivation to the point where even the mother's psychological unavailability produces harmful effects on the process of ego development. Indeed, according to the theory, if the young child is deprived of a consistent love object with whom to enact this drama, then the capacity to tolerate frustration, to view others realistically as an amalgam of both "good" and "bad" attributes, and to function as a separate individual with a solid sense of self, which should be the result of a successful resolution of this developmental subphase, are never fully achieved. The adult personality into which such a child grows ("matures" would hardly be the applicable term here) responds to intimate partners and to general life frustrations as though the person were a 2-year-old attempting to engage the unavailable parent figure in this primitive mode of interaction. Although this is developmentally normal for a 2-year-old, it is crippling for the adult fixated at this subphase.

THE IMPORTANCE OF INTERNALIZATIONS IN PERSONALITY DEVELOPMENT

In both classical psychoanalytic theory and separation–individuation theory, there is heavy stress on the young child's internalizing positively valued aspects of the parent and maintaining a positive emotional tie to the parent as precursors of the development of a healthy adult personality. Blanck and Blanck (1986) list seven functions of such internalizations in maintaining psychic equilibrium and enhancing the capacity of the ego to cope with the demands of interpersonal reality.

The first of these functions is the provision of the background feeling of safety. This feeling of safety, which is rarely the subject of conscious attention but suffuses all functioning of the intact ego, permits the ego's operations to go forward smoothly and without distraction. By contrast, persons who lack a background sense of safety are constantly preoccupied with anxiety, and occasionally panic, generated by the underlying sense of being in a hostile, unpredictable, and dangerous world where other people are potential betrayers, where pleasures abruptly turn into horrors, and where the immediate present is the only reliable basis for perspective.

These internalizations also perform regulatory functions and assist the individual in imposing limits on behavior. When such internal regulation is absent, a condition of imbalance exists in which the ego either is excessively passive, relying on direction from without, or is rebellious, resisting limits that are actually helpful in achieving a reasonable accommodation to the demands of reality.

Internalized parental objects serve the additional function of promoting ego autonomy. The popular view is that psychoanalytic theory is focused exclusively on the conflict between id urges, superego prohibitions, and the mediating activities of the ego. Modern refinements of the theory, however, stress the capacity of the ego to function autonomously in performing many functions. Rational thinking, perception, and control of physical motility, for example, are ego functions that take place in a conflict-free sphere. In the absence of positively valued, well-developed internalizations, psychic conflict is allowed to invade thought processes and other sectors of the conflict-free sphere of ego operations. Thinking, for example, becomes subservient to neurotic needs rather than guided by rationality and based on accurate perceptions of interpersonal events. If traumatic separations and losses distort the process of internalization, the adult's immature ego responds to the challenges of interpersonal adaptation with pseudologic and distorted perceptions.

Internalized parental love objects also serve as models for character formation. Character may be thought of as those attributes that we experience as part of ourselves, acquired through the process of identification with parental figures. That which we prize in ourselves has not come about by chance, but is the result of our internalizations, now long forgotten, of desired characteristics of our parents and other important figures. So thoroughly have we assimilated these characteristics that we experience them as parts the self, having taken them over entirely. In their totality they constitute our character.

Furthermore, it is through the process of positively toned interactions with reliable and accessible parental figures that the superego, or conscience, is formed. The superego serves as a template for our behavior, relieving us of having to make a conscious moral choice every time we have the least opportunity to break rules or laws. The superego is formed from internalizations of parental prohibitions, demands, and values. The importance of protecting this process from traumatic disruption is obvious.

This process is also responsible for the formation of the ego ideal. This ideal represents that to which we consciously or unconsciously aspire. Based on identifications and idealizations of the parents and other significant figures, this collection of ideals provides goal direction in many areas of life adjustment. The ego ideal is particularly important during adolescence when a satisfactorily developed ego ideal will provide a healthy basis for the altruistic and idealistic commitments typical of this age. On the other hand, a defective ego ideal will stimulate antisocial activity as a pathway to achieving a subjective sense of self-worth during the identity seeking of adolescence.

Finally, the process of internalization enables the child to overcome infantile conflicts and to proceed toward more mature modes of psychological functioning. Object representations assist the child in maturing to the point where the sexual wishes and raw aggressive fantasies associated with earlier developmental periods are repressed. This achievement sets the stage for entry into the relatively conflict-free period of latency when psychic energy is devoted to academic learning and acquisition of social skills. Without healthy object representations, the ego is burdened with the pressures of primitive drive material throughout latency and arrives at puberty ill equipped to handle that period's physiological upheavals and their accompanying psychic stresses.

CONSEQUENCES OF DEVELOPMENTAL PATHOLOGY IN OBJECT RELATIONS

In the clinical and theoretical literature of ego psychology, the following psychological characteristics are associated with defects in ego development. These defects are often encountered in individuals who have lacked stable object connections in childhood, either owing to physical separations in early periods or owing to the psychological unavailability of parents during periods of critical need.

Splitting

The term "splitting" refers to the tendency to view the self and others as either all good or all bad. Its behavioral manifestations include forming quick idealizations of others, only to have the idealized person fall off the pedestal abruptly into complete depreciation. Individuals in whom splitting primarily affects the representation of the self tend to alternate between (1) an abrasive or intimidating grandiosity and (2) bouts of depression in which the despised, weak, devalued self comes to the fore. Splitting is considered by ego psychological theorists to result from an inability to develop cohesive self and object representations in which both good and bad attributes are fused into a realistic whole.

Projection

Projection is the tendency to attribute undesirable traits, wishes, feelings, or impulses of one's own to other people is associated with defects in both the self and object representations. In projection, the boundary is weakened between the inner psychic world, on the one hand, and the realistic external cues of the objective interpersonal world, on the other. The individual's early interactions with parents were such that persecution and criticism are substituted for acceptance, approval, and love. In an adaptation strategy that reflects considerable impairment of the capacity for accurate perception of reality, the individual defends against forbidden impulses by attributing them to another with very little justification in the way of objective evidence for such an attribution.

This projection strategy is actually an attempt to replay early interactions with persecutory caretakers by acting out those interactions in the world of current interpersonal reality as though the original parental objects were present. In a variant of this, known as projective identification, the individual projects a despised portion of the self onto someone else and behaves as though the other person were this bad self, with the projecting individual in the role of the persecutory or abusive parent. This pathological identifying with the parent's aggression, while simultaneously disowning the painfully experienced victim-self, is the individual's only means of achieving positive self-esteem. In this situation, brittle, unstable self and object representations have coalesced around traumatic experiences of aggression, blame, rejection, and hostility.

Acting Out/Antisocial Tendencies

Individuals who have had the experience of being valued by their caretakers develop positively valued, stable internal images of those caretakers. This generalizes into a tendency to appreciate other people in the adult world as separate beings with needs and feelings that command respect and sensitivity. Conversely, individuals who suffer the degrading experience of being shifted from one placement to another, or of being cast off after a few years by indifferent foster parents to whom they may have formed a one-way attachment, cannot develop the capacity to truly experience themselves or others as having intrinsic value.

One possible manifestation of this impairment is for the individual to remain at the "need-gratifying" stage of interpersonal relations and to view other people as having value only in so far as they can gratify the individual's transient need of the moment—which in an extreme form is seen as a tendency to regard others as impersonal objects to be used and discarded, as the individual felt that he or she was treated by early caretakers. In cases of brutal crime in which the perpetrator seems to have no "human feeling" for the victim, this lack of valued inner objects is to some degree invariably present. Bowlby (1953) referred to these individuals as "affectionless characters," whose callousness is directly traceable to an early history of multiple separations from maternal figures. These are the types of characters who display no remorse when caught for a heinous crime, often attributing blame and responsibility to the victim with no comprehension of the suffering of the other person.

Self-Esteem Deficit

Another dimension of distorted ego development is that of faulty self-esteem. In the case of individuals who have had certain types of early childhood experiences centering on being devalued by others, a stable sense of self-worth is lacking in their personality makeup. It is unimaginably difficult for such individuals to view themselves as being endowed with the same rights and privileges as others are. They do not see themselves as having the same degree of entitlement that others do, and they are thus, in their own estimation, automatically placed on the outside of any social group and at a disadvantage in any social interaction.

A closely related phenomenon involves defects in the sense of personal identity. Individuals who have not had the experience of an interested caretaker who made observations about their feelings or behavior—for example, "There, there, Mommy knows that hurts," or "Look how far you ran!", or "You look so pretty today!"—have not got a clue as to how they are being perceived by others in the adult world and really have no idea as to how they should view themselves. In other words, their early childhood deprivations have left them without a basis for realistic assessment of their own assets. They may react to deficiencies in self-esteem and identity with an exaggerated aggressiveness or hostility, with depressed or fearful withdrawal, or with a hypervigilant suspiciousness in their interpersonal adaptation strategies. At the heart of all of these maladaptive patterns is an essential lack in ego functioning as a result of early wounds that have made the individual's experience of the world qualitatively different from that of someone with a healthy ego.

COMMON ELEMENTS OF VARIOUS PSYCHOANALYTIC SCHOOLS WITH RESPECT TO DEVELOPMENTAL DISRUPTION

In summary, psychoanalytic theory, and the various schools of psychological thought derived from it, view the development of the human personality as a complex and fragile process in which the goals are to develop the capacity to tame primitive impulses; to form a satisfactory, cohesive, stable, and positively valued sense of self; to establish stable emotional ties with others and to acquire an appreciation of their status as separate, feeling beings with their own needs and desires; to regulate behavior according to societal norms; to use aggression in a responsible and constructive manner; and to maintain a normally positive mood state. This process depends very heavily on events in the period of life prior to 6 years of age, especially the period from 6 months to 4 years of age. The necessary conditions for normal development include secure attachment to a stable parental figure or figures; identification with a parental figure or figures; and adequate rule setting, nurturance, and empathic understanding of the child by the parental figure or figures. In general, the earlier traumatic events occur, with 12 months as the lower age limit, the more severe the disruption of the psyche. Effects continue downward to 6 months as well, but with less severity between 6 and 12 months.

COGNITIVE THEORY

Cognitive theory forms the basis of a number of therapeutic schools, ranging from Ellis's (1977) rational emotive therapy to Beck's cognitive therapy (1972; Beck, Rush, Shaw, & Emery, 1979). This school of thought stresses the individual's cognitions as the major factor in determining psychopathology and also as the key to resolving such pathology. In brief, cognitive theory states that modification of an individual's dysfunctional cognitions will help that individual to overcome anxiety, depression, and even severe personality disorders. Rather than take an empathic listening approach or wait for the patient to approach insights through free association or other protracted therapeutic work, cognitive therapists attack the patient's dysfunctional thought patterns and assist the patient in replacing them with more reality-oriented, constructive cognitive schemata.

Cognitive theory is curiously silent on the subject of child development. Although psychoanalytically oriented systems place major emphasis on developmental topics, cognitive theorists prefer to work with the here and now, both in techniques employed with their patients and in their theoretical formulations. Cognitive theorists take the dysfunctional cognitions as a given, as it were, and do not feel that there is any purpose to examining their origins. Instead, the focus is on modifying the cognitions in a healthier direction. Therefore, the literature on cognitive therapy and theory generally has little light to shed upon the subject of children's reactions to loss from a developmental point of view. However, theorists outside the mainstream of cognitive therapy have employed cognitive concepts to address the subtleties in children's reactions to abuse, neglect, and perceived abandonment.

Briere (1992) employs cognitive therapy concepts to develop a cogent model of children's dysfunctional attempts to make sense of various forms of maltreatment. Briere concludes that because of children's developmentally normal egocentric cognitive processing of events and their relatively primitive cognitive processes generally, they tend to view themselves as having deserved any experienced abuse or abandonment and therefore come to see themselves as inherently bad. The specific formulation is as follows: I am being hurt by a parent or trusted adult. Based on how I perceive the world, this maltreatment means either that my parent is bad or that I am bad. Since I have been taught that parents are always right and that they do things for your own good, it must be the case that I am bad. It is my own fault, and I deserve this. Therefore, I am as bad as whatever is being done to me; if I am hurt quite often or quite deeply, I must be very bad.

Briere (1992) notes that the resulting passivity, self-blame, and low self-esteem associated with the experience of unfair treatment by another seems illogical but is a natural consequence of children's immature cognitive processes. He also states that the extent of self-hatred that these dynamics can produce is often startling and that such children often grow into adults or adolescents with a propensity for self-defeating behavior in order to perpetuate this childhood dynamic.

THE TRAUMA BOND AND RELATED CONCEPTS

James (1994) discusses attachment phenomena from the perspective of the impact of trauma on children's attachment-related behavior. The author notes that attachment may be defined as "a reciprocal, enduring, emotional, and physical affiliation between a child and a caregiver" (p. 2). James states that infants and very young children typically develop a primary attachment, and that this attachment is usually with the mother. The author describes the psychological mission of the infant's or young child's primary attachment figure as performing the roles of (1) protector, assuring the child of safety and responsible limits setting; (2) provider, furnishing physical support, love, shelter, and stimulation; and (3) guide, furnishing the child with a sense of "This is who you are and who I am. This is how the world works" (p. 2). James states that children who have undergone experiences of abuse and neglect in the birth parent's home may have difficulty in forming new ties to substitute caretakers. These children lack trust and also may not even know how to relate to another person in an intimate, reciprocal relationship. The author further states that intimacy may be intolerable to the abused or neglected child because it signals vulnerability and danger, owing to the egregious failures of the child's original attachment figures.

Regarding the notion of attachment-related trauma, James (1994) states: "Loss of the primary attachment figure represents a loss of everything to a child—loss of love, safety, protection, even life itself, and prolonged unavailability of the primary attachment is the same as total loss for a young child" (p. 7). And regarding the issue of the capacity of another adult to replace the primary attachment figures as though such figures were interchangeable in the child's mind, James states: "Other adults can provide some comfort when the child's worries are minor, but a child's deep fears can be alleviated only by the presence of an attachment relationship. The loss of the attachment figure evokes a fear that cannot be assuaged, depression and despair that are inconsolable, because the source of love and safety are gone" (p. 8).

Consistent with psychoanalytic formulations, James (1994) views trauma as occurring "when an actual or perceived threat of danger overwhelms a person's usual coping ability" (p. 9). The author views the results of trauma as affecting many aspects of children's psychological and behavioral functioning, including identity formation, cognitive processing, experience of bodily integrity, basic trust, and behavioral controls. James cites the work of Perry (1993) who found that trauma alters the brain and that the traumatized child's template for brain organization is the stress response. The result is a fight-flight-freeze pattern that produces regressive tantrums, aggression, dissociation, oppositional-defiant behavior, and other pathological manifestations.

Citing other neuropsychological work by van der Kolk and others, James (1994) discusses the common pattern in traumatized children as an oscillation between extreme arousal (in response to reminders of the traumatic situation) and numbing (in an attempt to manage the overwhelming arousal). James notes that children's numbing responses to suppress the excitement, anxiety, and somatic sensations associated with terror include dissociation, depression, withdrawal, and avoidance of tactile or emotional stimulation. If a child is unable to numb himself or herself in this manner, then the numbing response may extend to provocative behaviors that court the risk of severe punishment, self-harm, and harm to others. James states that work by van der Kolk demonstrates a physiological basis to much of these behaviors in that the provocative acts seek further trauma that is associated with endogenous opioid response that actually supplies self-medication in the form of an internally produced "narcotic" relief.

James (1994) cites a familiar example to illustrate this sequence:

> An exasperating and puzzling behavior often seen in children placed in out-of-home care is their extreme negative reaction to apparently positive experiences. Veteran professional caregivers can predict with incredible accuracy the length of time before a child damages a new item of clothing or gift he has received. They know that a child who has just had a good time on a family outing will be asking for punishment by the end of the day or they await with dread the predictable aftermath when the youngster played well on the soccer team. . . . Other puzzling behaviors are those which are dangerous and can result in harm to the child or to others. These behaviors include mutilating self, hurting animals, physically or sexually assaulting children, eating disorders, destroying property, and provoking abuse from others. (p. 18)

James (1994) describes the phenomenon of the "trauma bond," in which the child's attachment to the parent is based upon factors other than the usual nurturance, protection, limits setting, and comforting that make up the role of the attachment figure. The author states that the trauma bond is actually a relationship based on terror. It is difficult to understand the tendency of many children who cling to those who abuse them. James likens the situation of the chronically abused child to that of a hostage who bonds with captors because "the relief victims experience when not killed is often expressed as gratitude toward the perpetrator" (p. 24). The author states that the chronically abused child's responses of self-blame, numbing, and dissociation interfere with judgment and allow the child's need for attachment to overcome fear of the abusive parent.

James views such a situation as one of learned helplessness, supported by cognitive distortion.

The significance of the trauma bond for those who evaluate children is that it is possible to confuse attachment and trauma bonding. James (1994) cautions evaluators not to assess parent–child relationships solely on the strength of the connection but, additionally, to examine the quality of the attachment. In the trauma bond relationship, love has been superseded by terror; and the experience of the attachment figure as necessary for survival, which is also characteristic of normal attachments, is actually due to the fact that the abused child sees the attachment figure as a life-threatening person who must be appeased so that the child can live. In the distorted cognitive world of such a child, the indulgence of the abusive parent in permitting the child to live must be rewarded with gratitude on the child's part. James also notes that, in contrast to the normal attachment relationship in which the proximity of the attachment figure is associated with safety and pleasure, in the trauma bond such proximity is associated with conflict that triggers the alarm-numbing response. Thus, James concludes: "A trauma bond is potentially dangerous, and we should place no more reliance on a youngster's stated desire to remain in that situation than we would on a child's stated desire to be in any other dangerous situation" (p. 26).

Even trauma bonds, however, carry a danger for the young child in the form of separation trauma. James (1994) notes that this issue complicates the problem of removing young children from homes where they are chronically abused. The author states that separation from the abusive parent can in itself be traumatizing and that the resulting idealization of the absent abusive parent can interfere with the child's capacity to form another primary relationship. James advises providing supervised contact with the abusive parent in an environment that is emotionally and physically safe as a measure to mitigate the effects of separation from the child's abusive attachment figure.

THE CONCEPT OF RESILIENCE

The concept of "resiliency" appears frequently in termination hearing testimony in which the central issue involves the effects of removing a young child from foster or preadoptive caretakers with whom that child has bonded. Resiliency is sometimes discussed in court as though it were a theory unto itself; actually, it is more accurately considered as a focus of research. The central question in resiliency studies is why certain children develop competence when conditions are unfavorable or highly adverse (Masten & Coatsworth, 1998). A related question in resiliency research is whether there is something distinctive about resilient children that enables them to succeed, in spite of adversity, where other children have failed.

Frequently, defense experts will quote the views of Rutter (1979) indicating that there are factors within the individual child and heredity–environment interaction that make certain children "invulnerable" and that it is not separation experiences per se that cause psychological problems but rather the interaction of such experiences with other factors such as family discord. Milchman (1996) notes that the work of Anthony (1987) on resilience and invulnerability is also cited in this vein, and often simplistically as an assertion that "children are resilient." Milchman states that the idea that children can be "invulnerable to trauma" is a socially irresponsible myth. In fact, one of Anthony's (1987) cautions about resilience is that children who have lost an attachment figure tend to develop "pathological resilience" characterized by pervasive detachment and a resistance to forming future intimate relationships. Rutter (1979) cites research indicating that having one good relationship with a parental figure is a protective factor against pathological reactions to future stressors, but that this protective effect operates only in cases in which children are still residing with their attachment figures.

Masten and Coatsworth (1998) state that recent research on the question of resilience consistently identifies two major factors associated with this trait: "The two most widely reported predictors of resilience appear to be relationships with caring prosocial adults and good intellectual functioning" (p. 212). Masten and Coatsworth observe that these findings reflect the reality that the attachment relationships between caregivers and children are fundamental to human adaptation and development. The authors also state that resilient children tend to have caretakers who provide authoritative parenting that includes warmth, structure, and high expectations. In short, then, there is no research or mainstream theoretical support for the simplistic notion that "children are resilient" to stressors such as the loss of their central parental love objects. Indeed, the literature in this area gives rather strong support to the premise that it is the child's attachment to caretakers that makes the child resilient to stress, so long as the attachment figure remains available.

GOLDSTEIN, FREUD, AND SOLNIT'S CONTRIBUTIONS AND CONTROVERSIES

Arguably, the most important work in the area of child welfare relating to foster placement and adoption is *Beyond the Best Interests of the Child* by Goldstein et al. (1979). This work has had an enormous impact on both institutional policy and the law, introducing concepts such as bonding, psychological parent, and child's sense of time to social service personnel, judges, and legislators. The model termination of parental rights statute proposed by Goldstein et al. is reviewed in Chapter 2.

A central tenet of Goldstein et al.'s position is that the court should focus on protecting the child's relationship with his or her psychological parent, or primary attachment figure. The authors state that the child's early attachment relationships form the basis for all future human relationships and that the child's "demands for affection, companionship, and stimulating intimacy," when answered reliably and regularly, result in a firm parent–child relationship that has profound effects on development. Goldstein et al. caution that interruptions of this relationship have adverse effects: "Where there are changes of parental figure or other hurtful interruptions, the child's vulnerability and the fragility of the relationship become evident" (p. 18). The authors associate interruptions in the continuity of this relationship with regressions in emotional, cognitive, and social skills. Goldstein et al. further state that it is only after the child has achieved a degree of maturity that this vulnerability will be outgrown. The authors also relate these early relationships to the development of inner psychic structure, consistent with classical psychoanalytic theory.

Goldstein et al. seem to regard the status of psychological parent as a dichotomous variable rather than as a relationship that can have shades of intensity. They also ascribe a fragility to this relationship to such an extent that they fear the breaking of a parent–child bond even after a relatively short period of placement outside the home. The latter phenomenon is a logical extension of the authors' view that a child's sense of time determines the sustainability of that child's inner tie to caretakers and that a period of time that for an adult would be relatively brief could represent an unbearable eternity for a young child separated from attachment figures. In the case of a child under the age of 2 years, this interval, in the view of Goldstein et al., is a matter of only a few days: "During such an absence for the child under two years of age, the new adult who cares for the child's physical needs is latched onto 'quickly' as the potential psychological parent" (p. 41). Goldstein et al. consider any absence of greater than 2 months as beyond the comprehension of any child under the age of 5 years, and an absence of greater than 6 months as beyond the comprehension of the younger school-age child.

Bowlby (1953) notes that Anna Freud and Dorothy Burlingham, while operating a residential nursery in England during World War II, recorded detailed studies of children under the age of 5 years who displayed severe separation reactions that involved loss of emotional ties and regression in behavior. Bowlby quotes from a report by Burlingham and Freud that describes a 24-month-old boy who was well developed and had a good relationship with his mother. Bowlby notes that, despite being looked after by the same substitute mother and being visited by his mother during the first week of his stay, the child deteriorated when his mother reduced her visits to twice per week and regressed severely when she gave up visiting him altogether. Burlingham and Freud write:

> He became listless, often sat in a corner sucking and dreaming, at other times he was very aggressive. He almost completely stopped talking. He was dirty and wet continually, so that we had to put nappies on him. He sat in front of his plate eating very little, without pleasure, and started smearing his food over the table. At this time the nurse who had been looking after him fell ill, and Bobby did not make friends with anyone else, but let himself be handled by everyone without opposition. A few days later he had tonsillitis and went to the sickroom. In the quiet atmosphere there he seemed not quite so unhappy, played quietly, but generally gave the impression of a baby. He hardly ever said a word, had entirely lost his bladder and bowel control, sucked a great deal. On his return to the nursery he looked very pale and tired. He was very unhappy after rejoining the group, always in trouble and in need of help and comfort. He did not seem to recognize the nurse who had looked after him at first. (quoted in Bowlby, 1953, p. 30)

Robertson and Robertson (1989) report a number of intensive clinical studies of young children who evidenced the typical pattern of protest, despair, and resignation described by Bowlby while in foster care during periods in which the mother was ill or otherwise unavailable. The Robertsons chronicled the foster care experience of one of these children, Kate, age 2 years, 5 months, whom the Robertsons fostered for a period of 27 days while her mother was giving birth and then caring for the new infant.

Although Kate managed to hold together well during the first 2 weeks of the placement, with her adjustment reinforced by regular visits from her father who explained the situation to her and communicated his expectations of good behavior, there was a sharp deterioration around the 14th day of the placement. The Robertsons attributed this deterioration to the fact that Kate's father never responded to her requests to take her home. In fact, the change in Kate's attitude was so marked that her father actually refrained from visiting her for several days because she had been so cool to him and he was upset by this. Kate's coolness toward her biological father was matched by an increased interest in the foster father and constant invitations to the foster father to play with her. The Robertsons state that Kate was becoming less sure of her biological father and that she angrily told them, "Daddy don't want Kate. . . . Daddy don't love nice Kate."

On the 17th day, as Joyce Robertson was preparing Kate for a visit to her mother in the hospital, Kate became oppositional. When asked if she was ready to go to see her mother, Kate replied, "No, I not ready to go." She was persuaded to leave for the hospital, and, once there, she allowed herself to be hugged and kissed by her mother. However, after the visit, she refused to enter the car and screamed, kicked, and slapped her foster mother. Later that day, she smiled at a photograph of her mother and, then, with a puzzled expression, said, "That's not my mummy. Where is Kate's mummy?" She became angry and threw the photograph of her mother to the floor and stamped on it. She told the foster mother, "I don't like Kate's mummy. Kate's mummy is naughty."

By the end of the third week, Kate began to initiate intimate contact with her foster father, touching him affectionately and asking to sit on his knee. She showed off for him and pretended to be fearful so that she could run to him for protection. In the fourth week, she became possessive of her foster mother, picking quarrels with her foster parents' biological daughter and slapping her. When admonished by the foster mother about this behavior, Kate shrieked at the foster mother's daughter, "It's my mummy, not your mummy." On the 25th day of the placement, when the foster mother explained to Kate that she had her very own mummy and daddy and that she would soon be returning home to them, Kate shouted at her, "You are my mummy. You are my mummy."

During her first week home, Kate showed only minimal stress, sleeping restlessly and wetting the bed on two occasions. At 10 days after returning home, Kate became somewhat clingy with her biological mother and wanted to know where her biological mother was when she was out of sight. Kate was angry with her biological father and spoke crossly to her biological mother. Kate was stubborn and resistive at 10 days, but this behavior was gradually replaced by a pattern of running to a corner, burying her head in a chair, and crying. Kate was impatient and demanding. She avoided objects that were connected with the separation, such as favorite toys that she had played with while in foster care. She did not spontaneously mention either of the foster parents and would turn away when anyone else discussed them. The Robertsons note that Kate vomited on the last day of the placement and did not vomit again until 10 days after she was returned home, when Joyce Robertson visited the home. On the 16th day after returning home, Kate became ill with bronchial asthma, which was the first time she had been diagnosed with this condition. This followed a visit to a school where she would be enrolled in 2 years and where she knew the Robertsons' daughter was also enrolled. That night, Kate awoke screaming; and in the morning, she was acutely breathless and cried a great deal in a way that was so unusual for her that her biological parents took her to the doctor. The doctor diagnosed bronchial asthma and informed Kate's biological parents that it was probably a reaction to stress.

Data from both the Robertsons and Freud and Burlingham strongly support the Goldstein et al. position about the child's sense of time as being a critical factor affecting reactions to separation and placement. Even brief placements, although the child is told that he or she will be returning home in a specified period of time, are extremely stressful for young children. It is interesting to note that the Robertsons observed extreme distress relating to the lost attachment figure in the 2-year-olds whom they fostered but not in the 1-year-olds, who had not developed much object constancy and ego maturity and who were therefore able to accept the foster mother without loyalty conflicts. The Robertsons speculate that, in contrast to the severe separation conflicts that would have affected the 2-year-olds had they been placed permanently with the Robertsons, the two 1-year-old children whom the Robertson's cared for would have weathered a permanent transfer without major difficulty.

Goldstein et al. stress the immature quality of children's perceptions of events and caution child welfare professionals against mistaking children for "adults in miniature" in this regard. In addition to the drastically different time sense that young children posses, they are also egocentric in their view of cause-and-effect relationships. Goldstein et al. state that children may experience a move from one house to another as being a grievous loss imposed on them, or they may experience the birth of a sibling as an act of parental hostility. They may experience the emotional preoccupation or illness of a parent as a rejection and the death of a parent as an intentional abandonment. The corollary to this is that young children will experience the loss of a surrogate caretaker who has assumed the status of their psychological parent as being associated with some behavior or intrinsic quality of the child. The often quoted words of 3-year-old Baby Richard as he was being carried away from his adoptive parents by his birth father after having been awarded to the latter, "Please don't let me go! I'll be good!" reflect this immature mode of thinking.

Goldstein et al. predict varying degrees and types of psychological harm associated with removal of a child from his or her psychological parents at different developmental periods. The authors predict discomfort, distress, and delays in orientation resulting from disruptions of continuity of care in infants from birth to age 18 months. For older infants and toddlers, Goldstein et al. state that a change in caretakers affects the course of the child's emotional development, including setbacks in the quality of a child's next attachments, which will be less trustful. The authors warn that children of this age who are subjected to multiple changes in placement will grow up lacking warmth in their interpersonal relations, with emotional attachments during the childhood years becoming increasingly shallow and indiscriminate. (See discussion of more recent research on reactive attachment disorder in Chapter 9.) For any child under age 5 years, Goldstein et al. predict breakdowns in self-care and other developmental achievements, such as cleanliness and speech, resulting from changes in placement. For school age children, if a child is removed from psychological parents, especially if subjected to multiple changes in placement, the authors predict a breakdown in the internal system of values related to identifications with the standards of attachment figures. According to Goldstein et al., the resulting breakdown of a child's inner value system, related to what is popularly termed "conscience," results in antisocial, delinquent, or criminal tendencies especially if the child is subjected to multiple changes of caretakers.

Bush and Goldman (1982) have stated that the views of Goldstein et al. are overly mechanistic and draw attention away from child welfare professionals' alleged failure to provide adequate assistance in the direction of family observation. Bush and Goldman state that, unlike most social science variables, the "psychological parent" concept proposed by Goldstein et al. is presented in an unduly precise manner, well beyond any supportive evidence for such precision, and that it is a dichotomous rather than a continuous variable. Bush and Goldman point out that the notion that an individual either is or is not the child's psychological parent and that there are no gradations of psychological parenting is unrealistic and does not comport with practical experience in the field of child welfare casework. Bush and Goldman speculate that Goldstein et al. have ascribed this dichotomous status to psychological parenting in order to place the concept on a par with biological parenting, which does have this characteristic. Bush and Goldman also question the notion that children's attachment relationships as described by Goldstein et al. are fragile and that such relationships can be irrevocably ruptured by even a short absence from the biological parents or the mere exposure of a child to a period of time when the issue of who holds custody is in doubt. Bush and Goldman state further that Goldstein et al. do not elaborate on how the child's psychological parents are determined but offer the unqualified assumption that the process will be accomplished effectively if guided by their theory.

Bush and Goldman (1982) also fault Goldstein et al.'s insistence on its being the case a priori that when a child has lived with surrogate caretakers for a certain period of time—say, a period of 1 year or more in the case of a child placed at 3 years of age or younger—the surrogate parents are automatically to be considered the child's psychological parents. Bush and Goldman also vigorously object to the notion that children's stated preferences are too unstable and fickle to be of any value in determining their best interests. The authors state that their own research with large numbers of children in placement indicates that the children were able to describe their situations and prospects in ways that were consistent with the reports of the adults who were familiar with them and that any differences of opinion between these children and the adults stemmed from differences in interests and perspectives that were readily understandable. In their study, Bush and Goldman found that older foster children in particular who had spent significant time in the care of the birth parents felt a continuing tie to those birth parents and resisted the idea of being adopted by foster parents even though it was clear that the children would not be able to return to the birth parents owing to the birth parents' lack of rehabilitation.

In their critique of the psychological parenting and permanency principles, Bush and Goldman (1982) stress that reversible adverse circumstances, not parental abandonment, are what lead to the placement of most children into foster care. The authors state:

> The majority of families who come to the attention of child welfare agencies do not come because parents have suddenly conceived the notion that they no longer wish to care for their children. They come because physical ill health, unemployment, poverty, divorce, poor living conditions, and mental ill health have reduced the parents to circumstances in which they think, or state officials think, that they are no longer capable of looking after their children. (p. 226)

Bush and Goldman (1982) assert that some of these situations could be resolved through measures such as extra financial aid and temporary in-home care. While this might have been the case at the time of the publication of Bush and Goldman's article, the present child welfare situation is entirely different. It is not families with temporary medical or financial problems who come to the attention of state child protective services; it is individuals who are character disordered and have severe drug and alcohol problems who constitute a significant segment of workers' caseloads. In a Florida study of social services to families in which there was abuse or neglect of a child, fully 58% of the client families were involved with cocaine (Metro-Dade, 1989). Court systems are being inundated with expanding numbers of child abuse and neglect cases related to parental drug abuse (Kusserow, 1990), and in some cases courts have been overwhelmed to the point where juvenile court judges feel unable to address all of the necessary issues in such cases (Select Committee on Children, Youth, and Families, 1989).

State agencies typically do not rush to terminate parental rights; instead, many child protective services, and family courts as well, bend over backward to accommodate birth parents who present very severe personal and community adjustment problems. It is almost routine in many big-city hospitals to allow infants born with drugs in their system to go home with the birth mother, so long as the birth mother presents some slight prospects for caring for the baby at least marginally well. Furthermore, solutions such as providing extra financial aid, while appropriate in the past, would be considered naive today. An extremely frequent behavior of today's typical drug-addicted client is spending the welfare grant on drugs and cashing in food stamps at the store of an unscrupulous grocer for a 75% cash discount to obtain more drug money. It is my understanding that these patterns, stemming from the drug epidemic in inner cities and in some other areas as well, have provided the impetus for the present national legislative mandate to speed up adoptions of children in foster care rather than allocate vast resources to family reunification efforts that frequently prove futile.

I agree in part with the criticisms of Bush and Goldman (1982) regarding Goldstein et al.'s position. Clinical experience indicates that children are able to attach to more than one or two parental figures, although the greater the number of such figures, the more diffuse, less specific, and less intense the child's attachment to any one of them. Furthermore, there are certainly gradations of attachment rather than a mysteriously dichotomous process. It is more accurate to conceptualize these degrees of attachment as involving the degree of centrality that any one parental figure occupies in the emotional life of the child. In the event of the loss of the central parental attachment figures, it is exceedingly difficult for someone at the periphery to become an equally significant attachment figure; however, it is possible for another adult who has an ongoing relationship with the child and a degree of importance in that child's life to serve as a new attachment figure if the child has not been so traumatized and previously frustrated and confused by multiple changes in placement that he or she has developed a reactive attachment disorder.

Regarding the question of time guidelines, I believe that such rigid formulations should not be mechanically applied to situations that are by their very nature extremely complex. One must take into account the frequency and nature of the child's contacts with birth parents subsequent to placement into foster care, how the placement is explained to the child, and what the child's own feelings are toward the birth parents and surrogate caretakers. There are profound differences between a foster child's experience of placement with a surrogate parent who sees herself as a temporary caretaker and has three or four other short-term foster children in the home and that of placement with a surrogate parent who is actively seeking to adopt and has no other children in the home. There are profound differences in the placement experiences of a child who has been in foster care for a year with no contact with the birth parents and the child whose year in foster care has seen consistent weekly or biweekly visitation with the parents supplemented with presents, letters, photographs of the birth parents and other family members, and telephone calls. There are profound differences as well between the placement experiences of a child whose foster mother discourages any reference to the birth parents and that of the child whose foster mother reinforces the expectation that the child will be returning home once the parents' situation improves.

Rather than rely in a mechanical fashion on rigid time guidelines, it is the practice of virtually all mental health experts who consult in termination cases to evaluate each child's unique situation clinically. Factors such as the age of the child at placement, special needs, history of contact with the birth parent, observed degree of attachment to the foster parent, and numerous other factors need to be assessed in order to formulate appropriate recommendations for child protective services and the court.

CHAPTER 9

Empirical Research and Clinical Studies

An essential component of adequate expert testimony in a great number of contexts, including termination of parental rights cases, is the witness's familiarity with the empirical literature in the area and the application of findings to the specifics of the case at hand. Elsewhere, I (Dyer, 1993) have noted that the forensic psychologist is held to a higher standard of validity than is the clinician, who is actually encouraged to explore speculative conclusions that may lead to fruitful hypotheses in treating patients. The forensic psychologist is forbidden to offer speculation on the witness stand, unless the speculation is clearly labeled in such a way that it cannot be mistaken for solid expert opinion. The conclusions offered by psychologists as expert witnesses must convey, or give the impression of, reasonable psychological certainty or reasonable scientific certainty. This concept is defined in the New Jersey Board of Psychological Examiners' guidelines for child custody and visitation evaluations as conclusions that are based on empirical research, substantive clinical observation, or well-accepted theoretical propositions and that are clearly not speculative in nature.

One of the central questions in termination hearings is the impact of removing a child from foster or parafoster caretakers to whom the child may have formed an attachment. This determination entails a prediction that must be based on something more substantial than the witness's individual clinical experience. Ideally, such testimony should rely on experimental evidence that shows a specific level of harm associated with removal of children at various developmental stages with various lengths of time in placement. Regarding the question of long-term irreversible effects on children resulting from separation from caretakers to whom they are bonded, the following would constitute the optimal experimental design, from the point of view of scientific rigor. We start by randomly selecting infants at various stages of development to be assigned to new caretakers. We randomly allow various degrees of contact between these infants/toddlers and the biological parents. We then randomly return the children to the biological parents at various ages. We include assessments of the biological parents to determine genetic contributions to psychopathology, and we include assessments of the substitute caretakers to determine parental adequacy in order to evaluate the contribution of environment prior to the separation. Furthermore, after randomly exposing the sample of infants to several further separations and placements with the original caretakers and strangers, returning some to the birth parents, and so forth, we analyze the children's personality patterns by using psychometric testing and rating methods. We then wait until the children reach adolescence and conduct further testing, and then we conduct a final assessment in adulthood.

If we conduct a comprehensive multivariate analysis of these data, we will then be able to specify the relative contributions of and interactions among (1) the child's innate psychic apparatus; (2) the genetic characteristics of the birth parents; (3) the psychological characteristics of the surrogate parents; (4) the parenting skills of the surrogate parents; (5) the impact of separation trauma, both single insult and repeated; and (6) the attitude of the birth parent toward a biological child returned to that parent's care (e.g., acceptance of the validity of the previous attachment to the surrogate caretaker vs. denial of that relationship and blaming of the child for alleged disloyalty).

Needless to say, as ethical psychological researchers, we do not wish to add any more misery to a world that abounds with suffering. Therefore, rather than conduct this optimal, though Nazi-like, experiment that would once and for all resolve any controversy as to the relative contribution of various factors, children's resiliency, and other issues, we must content ourselves with studying the existing misery that attends the shifting of children from one placement to another. Of course, this research strategy will hardly satisfy those attorneys who on cross-examination demand that the witness produce studies (preferably longitudinal) that demonstrate a highly specific effect, such as whether a 4-year-old child who has been in placement since birth but has had some visits with the birth parents will inevitably suffer harm and be completely unable to bond with the biological parents if removed from the placement and returned to their care. It is ironic that some attorneys who make an art out of contorting legal theories and precedents to achieve a procrustean fit to the facts of a particular case vociferously object to psychologists' and other mental health experts' generalizations from theory and related research.

Psychologists who work in all but the most rigorously experimental fields, such as neuropsychology, human factors, or perceptual studies, rely on a combination of clinical observation, reasoning according to theory, and reliance on fundamental experimental evidence to formulate conclusions regarding a specific and unique set of circumstances. (See Chapter 10 for a discussion of these issues in connection with the *Daubert* standard for scientific evidence.) In many cases, the phenomena that child welfare experts deal with are so extreme that demanding to have a certain conclusion buttressed by an experimental study conducted on children in identical circumstances is rather like refusing to accept an expert's opinion that water heated to 250 degrees Fahrenheit will boil because the only prior evidence introduced in the case was that water boils at 212 degrees. In other cases, the situation of the child is so unique that there is simply no suitable comparison group from which to draw general conclusions as to that category of early life experiences.

In the instant matter, there is an enormous amount of evidence to demonstrate that the loss of a central parental attachment figure produces substantial psychological harm. The harm is found in several areas of functioning, primarily in the subsequent capacity to regulate (1) mood and anxiety, (2) serve adequately in the role of parent for the next generation, (3) form new attachments, (4) feel empathy, (5) develop delinquent behavior, and (6) develop personality disorders. This evidence comes from three distinct sources: (1) clinical studies of adults undergoing psychoanalytic psychotherapy; (2) empirical studies of adults that assess causal effects from a retrospective paradigm; and (3) observational studies of children, some with a longitudinal component. These studies will be discussed by topic.

Research on general issues involving children in foster care is also reviewed.

CHILDREN'S REACTIONS TO SEPARATION

In termination of parental rights cases, the focus of the expert testimony is often on the consequences of the loss of the child's central parental love object. It is therefore instructive to study the psychological impact on children of temporary separations, a much less severe but much more researched stressor, from which it is possible to extrapolate about the impact of separations after which there is no reunion and no possibility of reunion with the lost parental figure. Although much more impressionistic and less scientifically rigorous than large-scale studies that employ standardized measurement and assessment instruments and statistical procedures, the clinical study of children has certain advantages. Contacts are typically more extended in time and are much more intensive. One studies fewer subjects, but learns a great deal about them.

This approach characterizes a series of clinical studies of hospitalized children conducted by James Robertson in the early 1950s (see Robertson & Robertson, 1989). The Robertsons note that it was common knowledge in the late 1940s and early 1950s that young children could be "changed" by a stay in the hospital under the then-prevailing system in which parental visitation was forbidden and children were not given more than minimal individual attention by hospital staff. While older children seemed to fare well, or at least without undue distress in institutions following this policy, Robertson noted that younger children seemed to be overwhelmed and sat in their cots desolate and tearful or silent. Robertson documented on film the experience of one such toddler, Laura, a girl who was 2 years and 5 months old and who was hospitalized for eight days for surgery for an umbilical hernia. Robertson's notes on the child's emotional states and behavior in the hospital, accompanied by stills from the film, are presented in Robertson and Robertson (1989).

The myth of the "happy children's ward" among nursing staffs dictated that after a brief period of crying, children eventually "settled" and remained quietly, but happily, adjusted to the hospital environment, unless disturbed by a nurse who offered individual attention, which would then "cause" the child to begin crying again. This phenomenon provided a rationale for placing severe limits on parental visitation, if it was allowed at all, since the ward nurses felt that the sight of the parents upset the "settled" children. Robertson's observations of hospitalized children indicate that, rather than causing distress, a friendly nurse was in fact discovering it, and that the child was not settled at all but profoundly unsettled and in a state of despair, as described by Bowlby. Laura's reactions of protest, despair, and detachment at various phases of her hospital stay, both alone and during visits with her parents, were recorded on film as part of the research. Robertson describes in detail how the emotional state of this initially happy and well-adjusted toddler deteriorated into what may be described as a clinical level of depression in response to the impersonal behavior of the ward staff and the absence of her mother. The film also captures similar reactions of other toddlers who were hospitalized on the same pediatric ward.

Robertson describes the follow-up observations of this child at 48 hours after discharge, 6 months later, 9 months after discharge, and at age 16 years when Robertson showed the subject the film that he had made of her at age 2. Robertson states that he was struck by the change in the child's expression 2 days after she left the hospital and that "it was as though a lamp had lit up inside her." This change was followed by a period of irritability, temper tantrums, regression in bowel and bladder control, and sleep disturbance. Laura became extremely clingy with her mother and became very upset if her mother was momentarily out of her sight. The child also displayed a pattern of hugging her mother and then suddenly punching and scratching her.

Although Laura refused to discuss her stay in the hospital and turned a deaf ear to anyone who brought it up, she displayed anxiety upon seeing shop assistants wearing the same kind of white uniforms that her nurses had worn. This behavior gradually lessened; however, approximately 6 months after discharge Laura accidentally saw a few scenes from the movie about her that was being edited. The child immediately began to cry and angrily asked her mother, "Where was you all that time?" Three months after that incident, the family attended an exhibition at which there was an area where children could be left while parents toured the exhibits. Laura accepted being left there without protest, even though the attendants were wearing white. As the child's parents were leaving the building, however, they heard her scream and returned to the children's area. The child was "hysterical," and it was more than an hour before she regained her composure. The parents were informed that an official photographer had pointed his camera at the child, which triggered the "hysterical" state. Robertson notes that the camera reminded Laura of his daily filming sessions with her in the hospital ward.

Robertson also reports that when Laura was 16 years old he took the film to her home to show at a family gathering. After the showing of the film, while the child's relatives were recovering from the experience of seeing this profoundly distressed 2-year-old, Laura stood up and announced, "That meant nothing to me." Robertson continues:

> But she could not maintain the cover-up and reached out and took hold of her father's tie. The relatives were much amused. I was told that when Laura was unhappy she had a habit of clutching her father's tie. Now they understood that this went back to the scene in the hospital where in her unhappiness she seeks to detain her father by holding his tie and saying "Don't go, Daddy." (Robertson & Robertson, 1989, p. 42)

Laura's upset upon exposure to stimuli associated with her hospital stay suggests that the experience had a genuinely traumatic quality for her and that the observed behaviors after her return home were indicative of a posttraumatic reaction similar to posttraumatic stress disorder. These behaviors reflect several of the criteria for posttraumatic stress disorder, including (1) intense physiological distress at exposure to events that symbolize or resemble an aspect of the traumatic event, (2) efforts to avoid activities or situations that arouse recollections of the trauma (Laura's refusing to discuss her hospital stay or even listen to anyone who mentioned it), (3) irritability or outbursts of anger, (4) difficulty falling or staying asleep, and (5) loss of recently acquired developmental skills such as toilet training. This is of interest in light of recent findings that patients' reactions to stress, even traumatic stressors, are shaped to a substantial degree by their cognitions (Everly, 1993). In this case, the subject was constantly reassured that her parents would return to visit her and that in a specified period of time she would be taken home from the hospital. Despite the inculcation of this cognitive framework to process the experience, Laura still displayed significant emotional and behavioral sequelae when being discharged from the hospital after a relatively brief separation from her parents.

EARLY LOSS OF PARENTAL OBJECT RELATED TO DEPRESSION

Clinical Studies

Blanck and Blanck (1974, p. 274) discuss a clinical case in which a woman in her early 30s had at age 4 years suffered the loss through death of her psychotic mother. The patient awoke depressed one morning and thought that if she held her breath long enough she could die. She was able to interrupt her thoughts of smothering herself with a pillow by concentrating on the idea that her therapist wanted her to continue living. The Blancks attribute the patient's depression to her aggression directed at the internal object representation of the dead mother, insufficiently differentiated from the self representation.

The Blancks (1974, p. 272) cite a second case involving a young adult female patient who had been reared by a somewhat distant stepmother after her birth mother died when the patient was 2 years old. The Blancks discuss themes of loss of part of the self, as well as disillusionment, aggression, and reduced self-esteem arising from the 2-year-old's experience of the failure of the mother's omnipotence. The Blancks characterize such early losses as "an early life situation that predisposes to depression" (p. 273).

Jacobson (1971, pp. 185–203) presents three cases of pathological response to early object loss. The author identifies as a common thread in these cases the belief that the loss of the parent through death or desertion was not the fault of the lost parent but was attributable to the surviving parent's "intolerable character or moral worthlessness" (p. 186). Jacobson further comments (p. 203) that the young child's inability to go through a true mourning process predisposes such children to depressive states. The author states that these children attempt to resolve their injured narcissism and their ambivalence conflicts with a parental surrogate or with a surviving parent by means of unrealistic fantasy, thus impairing the child's relationship with that parental figure.

Adam and Adam (1978) report a number of clinical cases in

which the behavior of suicide attempters displayed striking parallels to the behavior of children following separations from their attachment figures as described by Bowlby. Adam (1994) notes that the common denominator in these cases is a history of traumatic loss of a parent in early life followed by the failure of alternative care and persistent conflicts over dependency, jealousy, and concerns about being loved.

Bowlby (1988) cites a psychoanalytic case, reported by C. Winnicott (1980), involving a patient, a 41-year-old professional woman, who had been self-sufficient emotionally until the sudden onset of a number of psychosomatic symptoms. The therapy disclosed that the patient had been exposed to separation experiences, including one for which she had not been given any preparation or warning. The patient had been cared for by a nanny from birth to age 2½ while her mother worked full time. The nanny left suddenly; and after a period of 6 months, when the patient was around 3 years old, she was taken by her mother to have tea with a friend. The patient later discovered that her mother had disappeared and that she was alone in a strange bed. The next day, the patient was taken to a boarding school where her mother's friend worked as a matron, and the patient remained there until she was 9 years old, usually spending holidays there as well. Winnicott reports that from that time forward the patient's emotional life had dried up.

Pedder (1976) reports a case, also cited in Bowlby (1988), in which a patient, a teacher in her mid-20s, manifested symptoms that included somatic complaints, anxiety, and emotional constriction. Treatment disclosed that at the age of 18 months, the patient had been sent to live with an aunt during her mother's next pregnancy. After 6 months there, the patient came to feel that her aunt was more of a mother to her than her birth mother was. Returning home was a painful experience; and until the age of 10 years, the patient experienced chronic terror whenever she thought she would be subjected to another separation. At age 10, the patient found that she could "turn off her anxiety like a tap," which resulted in a suppression of most of her emotional life.

Retrospective Empirical Studies of Adults

Several researchers have conducted studies of the effects of separations during childhood and adolescence on adult personality by examining the histories of adult subjects. Bowlby (1988) cites four studies conducted by Brown and Harris with representative female samples in London and in the Scottish Highlands. Brown and Harris (1978) found that a female's loss of her mother because of death or prolonged separation prior to the female's 11th birthday was very strongly related to adult depressive disorders. This finding was replicated in studies of two other large samples (Brown, Harris, & Bifulco, 1985; Bifulco, 1985; Bifulco, Brown, & Harris, 1987, cited in Bowlby, 1988).

The extensive review of the literature on attachment theory by Patterson and Moran (1988) cites a number of studies that have found early separation from parents to be predictive of depression (Frommer & O'Shea, 1973; Lindeman, 1960), suicidal ideation (Lindeman, 1960; Adam, 1982) , and suicide attempts (Adam, 1982).

Adam (1994) reviewed the literature on early parental loss or unavailability as it relates specifically to suicidal behavior. He found that all 17 studies published on this subject since 1941 found a higher incidence of parental loss in clinical cases than in controls. Of 5 studies of completed suicide, 3 found excesses of parental death or permanent separation in suicides, and 2 found no such excess. Adam, Bouckoms, and Streiner (1982) studied 98 hospitalized patients following suicide attempts and 102 controls from general practice who had never attempted suicide. More than 50% of the suicide attempters had experienced parental loss, while only 22% of the controls had experienced such a loss; 92% of suicide attempters were rated as having had unstable or chaotic early family life as opposed to 40% of the controls.

Tennant, Hurry, and Bebbington (1982) conducted a retrospective study of 800 South London adults to examine the relationship between childhood separation experiences and adult depression and anxiety. Although Tennant et al. found that the incidence of depression and anxiety was not significantly greater in subjects separated between birth and age 4 years, there were strong trends that are of interest. Those separated some time between birth and age 4 years because of war evacuation had nearly twice the incidence of depression as the comparison group, and those separated because of marital discord had nearly twice the incidence of depression and anxiety as the control group. A statistically significant finding emerged for the group that experienced separation between 5 and 10 years of age. In that group, separations caused by parental illness and marital discord were related to pathological conditions. In the case of those separated because of marital discord, the separation was more likely to result in depression than anxiety. It should be noted that in the birth-to-four-years group, the substitute caretaker in cases of marital discord was the other parent in 75% of cases and relatives in 25% of cases. For those 4-years-or-under children separated by war evacuation, the substitute caretaker in 85% of the cases was the mother and in 15% of the cases were other relatives. Thus, the Tennant et al. study does not address the type of catastrophic loss that is the subject of this chapter. Yet it is of considerable interest that even these types of separations from one parent, often with the other parent as the substitute caretaker, are related to adult psychopathology.

Studies of Children

Adam (1994) cites a study by Rosenthal and Rosenthal (1984) in which 16 preschool children who exhibited serious suicidal behavior were compared with a group of 16 nonsuicidal preschoolers with serious behavior problems. The suicidal children expressed profound feelings of abandonment and despair, a yearning for reunion, and a lack of hope of remedying their lot, while none of the nonsuicidal behavior-problem children expressed these sentiments. Additionally, Rosenthal and Rosenthal classified all 16 suicidal children as having disturbed attachment behavior.

OBJECT LOSS AND PERSONALITY DISORDER

Clinical Studies

Many psychoanalytic authors have noted the destructive effects of early object loss on the developing personality, with differential effects depending upon the specific developmental phase in which the loss occurs. Rochlin (1953) draws the clinical conclusion that early object loss affects the developing ego and that the specific effect depends on the developmental phase in which the object loss occurs. The child cathects an inanimate object as a substitute. This is an unhealthy strategy that provides gratification at the expense of reality testing. Wolfenstein (1969) discusses a pathological response to object loss in children that is characterized by the use of the primitive defenses of undoing, splitting, denial, and derealization. In the recent literature on lower-level ego structures, splitting has been identified as a typical feature of the borderline personality and as a defense that does not appear in the adaptive repertoire of the more structured ego. Dietrich (1989) concurs with Rochlin's conclusion that specific effects of object loss depend upon the child's developmental stage at the time of the loss. Dietrich lists oedipal complex resolution, drive fusion, superego structuralization, object relations, ego development, and defenses as areas that are vulnerable to disruption as a result of loss of the parental love object.

Mintz (1976; cited in Bowlby, 1988) reports a case in which a young woman came for psychoanalysis because of feelings of irritability, depression, being "filled with hate and evil," and emotional detachment. The patient's parents divorced when she was 3 years old, and her mother, who was forced to work full time, had little time for the patient. At age 4, the patient was placed in an orphanage by her mother, where she remained for 18 months. The patient left home during her teens; and by the time she was 21 years old, the patient had been married and divorced twice. The patient's anxiety and depression were activated by situations involving separation and loss even at 5 years after the conclusion of her treatment.

Bowlby (1988), in commenting on this case, states that the patient presented aspects of schizoid personality disorder. His analysis of the dynamics of her condition is that as a result of the intense emotional pain that this patient experienced during her preschool years, associated with separations and losses, the behavioral system governing her attachment behavior had become deactivated. As a result of this process, desires, thoughts, and feelings related to attachment were absent from her awareness. In Bowlby's view, this process produced the schizoid features noted in the personality, serving to protect the patient from reactivation of the attachment system, which had been associated with such trauma early in her life.

West and Keller (1994) report a case that can be classified as either schizoid personality disorder or avoidant personality disorder in which the loss of a parent affected the patient's (David's) subsequent ability to form new intimate attachments in adulthood. The authors state:

> In his psychotherapy, David's withdrawal from personal relationships was developed around the childhood loss of a loving parental relationship. . . . Eventually his work led him to an attempt at intimacy. He met

> and dated a woman from a small liberal arts college where both of them taught. Although this opportunity for closeness resurrected the old danger of feared loss, which had first of all led to David's compensatory self-sufficiency, it was also evident that the almost overwhelming anxiety he experienced derived from the reality of the woman's emotional availability. For someone who had turned away from others, and who lacked a belief in himself as worthy of caring, the hope or expectation of attaining a meaningful attachment was indeed a frightening feeling. . . . Clearly the possibility of an intimate relationship had repercussions for David's defensive attachment pattern. (pp. 318–319)

In commenting on the case, West and Keller note that for the insecurely attached individual the possibility of losing an attachment relationship constitutes a chronic stressor. Their feelings of possessiveness, aggression, despair, and other loss-triggered emotions lie dormant, threatening to be mobilized by the loss of the other. For many of these individuals, it becomes almost a self-fulfilling prophecy, as they unleash these affects on their partners in response to suspected or fantasized abandonment to the point where they then actually succeed in driving the partner away.

Empirical Research

In their review of attachment theory research, Patterson and Moran (1988) conclude that the evidence suggests that parental loss, especially if it occurs at an early age, may lead to maladaptive patterns of attachment such as anxious attachment and compulsive self-reliance. The authors relate these maladaptive patterns to the development in the adult of borderline personality disorder, dependent personality disorder (anxious clinging), and schizoid personality disorder (compulsive self-reliance). Patterson and Moran further state: "If loss can lead to subsequent disorder, as attachment theory suggests, then loss in childhood is likely to be particularly damaging" (p. 617). The authors also note that children's avoidance of grief, or failure to progress through the normal stages of the grief process, can lead to "unusually prolonged disturbances of functioning" and that the experience of loss "could make the anxiously attached person even more conscious of the precariousness of attachments, and the compulsively self-reliant individual yet more reluctant to engage in them" (p. 617).

West and Keller (1994) review the empirical research linking attachment issues to personality disorders. Sheldon and West (1990) found that the criterion of desire for an attachment relationship with simultaneous fear of such a relationship is characteristic of individuals without an attachment figure who are diagnosed with avoidant personality disorder. Livesley, Schroeder, and Jackson (1990) found that insecure attachment is central to the style of relating of individuals with dependent personality disorder. West and Keller cite a number of studies (Melges & Schwartz, 1989; Livesley & Schroeder, 1991; West, Keller, Links, & Patrick, 1993; Sperling, Sharp, & Fishler, 1991) indicating that individuals with borderline personality disorder direct both care-seeking and angry behaviors toward their attachment figures as a result of fear of abandonment or fear of failure to meet the needs of the other. Regarding the etiology of these conditions, West and Keller state: "The developing child is more or less hurt by a lack of empathic care. . . . Things do not go well, either in childhood or in later life, when this basic provision is lacking. Subsequent relational efforts are hampered by the individual's glum and pessimistic beliefs, which predict that attachment needs will be unmet, current attachment figures will be unresponsive, and security will be lost and not restored" (p. 317).

PARENTS' REPETITION OF CHILDHOOD DEPRIVATION WITH THEIR OWN CHILDREN

Early experiences of loss or even of inadequate or insensitive parenting have well-documented ramifications for the next generation. In several studies conducted retrospectively, mothers' reports of their own early family relations predicted the quality of their relationships with their infants (Main et al., 1985; Morris, 1980; Ricks, 1985, cited in Sameroff & Emde, 1989). Presumably, those infants will be influenced by the quality and nature of care they received from their own mothers and will replay the same interactions with their future offspring.

Scott (1980) reviewed a number of social history indicators in samples of mothers of abused and nonabused children. Scott found significant differences between the experimental and comparison groups on 14 of 20 indicators, including separation from one or both parents during childhood, foster home placement during adolescence, and temporary or long-term separation from one or more of the subject's children prior to the abuse incident. Scott concluded that mothers of abused children have significantly more negative childhood experiences relating to the development of attachment, poorer affiliative behavior in adolescence and adulthood, and poorer overall parental behavior.

Patterson and Moran's (1988) review found that mothers who had been separated from either parent during childhood exhibited depression, marital problems, and difficulties in parenting their own children (Frommer & O'Shea, 1973). Patterson and Moran cite a study by Main et al. (1985) indicating that parents with a history of secure attachments as children tended to produce securely attached children of their own and that parents who had experienced the death of an attachment figure and had not successfully resolved this loss were frequently parents of insecure, disorganized infants.

Rutter (1979) cites a number of studies relating childhood experiences of deprivation or loss to later parenting behavior. Rutter and Mudge (1976) found that people who were raised in unhappy or disruptive homes were more likely to have illegitimate children, to become teenage mothers, to have unhappy marriages, and to divorce. Meier (1965, 1966) showed that former foster children had a rate of marital breakdown several times that of the general population. Spinetta and Rigler (1972) found that parents who abuse their children tend to have experienced neglect, rejection, or violence in their own family of origin. Frommer and O'Shea (1973) found that women raised in disrupted homes were more likely to prop up their 2-month-old babies to feed themselves and more likely to become pregnant again during the year after delivery than women who were raised in intact homes. Wolkind, Hall, and Pawlby (1977) found that women from broken families interacted less with their 4-month-olds and were less likely to see them as individuals in their own right. Later studies, Rutter, Quinton, and Liddle (1983) and Quinton and Rutter (1985) found that mothers whose children had been placed into foster care were more than three times as likely to have been in government care themselves during childhood. These mothers were also far more likely than a comparison group to have been separated from their parents owing to apparent conflict or rejection. Jones and Moses (1984) obtained a similar finding by studying a large sample of former foster children in West Virginia who had not been adopted but who had aged out of the system. Nineteen percent of the children of the adult individuals in the sample either were or had been in foster care. Jones and Moses also found a 20% rate of alcoholism in this sample.

DEVELOPMENTAL DELAY, SOCIAL COMPETENCY, AND DISORDERS OF ATTACHMENT

The effects of disturbances in children's attachment relationships, on the one hand, and developmental delay, on the other, have been the subject of research since the 1940s. Spitz (1945) studied 91 infants raised in a foundling home. During their first 3 months, the infants were breast-fed by their mothers or by a surrogate mother if the birth mother was unavailable. At that time, the infants appeared, and also registered on psychometric testing, average in development. After the third month, mother and child were separated. The infants remained in the home, where they were adequately cared for with respect to every purely physical need, including food, hygiene, and medical care. One nurse was assigned to the care of 8 infants, and occasionally the case load reached as high as 12 infants per nurse in a shift. Spitz estimated that, as a consequence, the infants received approximately one-tenth the emotional supplies provided in the usual mother–child relationship.

Upon being separated from their mothers, the infants typically went through a stage in which they became depressed. After 3 months, the infants began to present symptoms of general developmental arrest, well beyond ordinary depression associated with object loss. They displayed motor retardation, passivity, defective eye coordination, spasms, and autistic self-stimulation. Psychometric testing showed a progressive decline on the developmental quotient until, at the end of the second year at the foundling home, the average infant's score was 45% of normal, or in the severely retarded range. Nearly one-third of the sample died within their first year, and another 8% died within their second year. Spitz attributes the infants' developmental delay and high mortality to maternal deprivation, despite the adequate physical care that the infants received in the facility.

A second study by Spitz (1946) followed 123 infants who were raised in a women's prison nursery. After delivering their children at a nearby maternity hospital, the mothers were allowed to rear their children in the nursery. Some of the birth mothers, however, were only allowed to be with their children during the first 6 to 8 months, after which (for unspecified "administrative reasons") the mothers were not allowed to visit the nursery for an unbroken period of 3 months, and the children remained in the nursery under the care of the general staff. Spitz noted a syndrome that he labeled "anaclitic depression" that was universal among children who experienced this 3-month separation from the birth mother.

This syndrome consists of excessive crying, demandingness, and clinginess during the first month. During the second month, the weepiness becomes wailing, and there is weight loss and a lowering of the developmental quotient. During the third month, the child refuses contact and lies prone in the cot most of the time. There is continued weight loss, and insomnia sets in. There is motor retardation and a susceptibility to disease. Facial rigidity sets in and becomes firmly established after the third month.

There was a significant difference between the developmental quotients of children who were suffering from this syndrome and children who were reared by their mothers, with the magnitude of the discrepancy increasing with the length of time that the child was separated from the birth mother. Interestingly, Spitz noted anaclitic depression only among children who, prior to separation, had had a good relationship with their mothers. Those children who had a poor relationship with their birth mother developed other types of disturbances upon separation, but not anaclitic depression. Spitz attributes the phenomenon of anaclitic depression solely to the child's undergoing an intolerably long period of separation from the birth mother. Unlike hospitalism, in which there is virtually total maternal deprivation, anaclitic depression is not associated with a significant increase in mortality.

Longitudinal Studies of Children

Tizard (Tizard & Joseph, 1970; Tizard & Rees, 1974) followed institutionalized children from infancy to age 8 years. While there were apparently no harmful effects on the children's intellectual level from institutional rearing (average Wechsler IQ = 99), there were marked effects on psychosocial development. Tizard and Rees (1975) and Tizard and Tizard (1971) found that children at age 2 years who had been reared in institutions were more clinging and were more diffuse in their attachments than children who had been reared in conventional families. At age 4 years, the institutional children were more clinging and less likely to develop deep attachments. The children also tended to be overly friendly with strangers and to seek attention. At age 8 years, these children had still not formed a close attachment to their house mothers and sought attention more than other children did (Tizard & Hodges, 1978; Tizard, 1977). These children were more attention seeking, disobedient, restless, and unpopular at school, with the difference between these children and a comparison group characterized as striking (Rutter, 1979). Rutter notes that the Tizard research demonstrates a continuity between clinging and diffuse attachment behavior in infancy, attention seeking and indiscriminate friendliness at age 4 years, and impaired relationships with adults and other children at age 8 years. Dixon (1978, cited in Rutter, 1979) obtained closely comparable findings to those of Tizard. In studying children reared in institutions for the first year of life, Dixon found more disruptive and attention-seeking behavior and rejection by peers as compared to children of similarly disadvantaged biological parents who were personally fostered from infancy. In a carefully designed time-sampled observation procedure, Dixon found the institutional children to be inept in their social interactions and inappropriate in their attention-seeking behaviors as compared with the comparison group of children who received personal foster care from infancy onwards.

Concurrent Studies of Children

In current diagnostic terminology, "attachment disorder" is sometimes called "reactive attachment disorder," stressing the role of environmental deprivation or trauma in its etiology. Zeanah, Mammen, and Lieberman (1993) propose several types of attachment disorders, each with its own specific symptoms and etiology. In their Type I attachment disorder, there is a failure to develop a preferred attachment figure. The authors view this failure as resulting from extremes of neglect or multiple changes in primary caregivers. Zeanah et al. cite studies by Skeels (1966) and Tizard and Rees (1974) in support of this etiological formulation. Zeanah et al. cite the case of a 20-month-old boy whose foster mother thought that he was either depressed or autistic. This child had been removed from his biological mother at age 11 months and was placed with a foster family. The foster mother described him as a "vegetable," unresponsive to social interaction except for aggressive acting out with other foster children in the home, including his twin sister. Before an intensive outpatient intervention program could be implemented, the child's foster parents gave him up, and he was transferred to a shelter. Within 2 weeks, he improved dramatically, acquiring expressive language skills and becoming more responsive to people. Zeanah et al. attribute this to the fact that he was the youngest, and favored, child at the shelter and that he had developed a preferred attachment to a caretaker.

Zeanah et al.'s Type II, or indiscriminate attachment disorder is characterized by a failure to check back with the caretaker in unfamiliar situations and by failure to retreat to the caregiver when frightened or threatened. The authors attribute this phenomenon to a history of disrupted early attachment histories, such as multiple foster placements. With this disorder, there is an indiscriminate and promiscuous use of others for comfort and nurturance. It has been my experience that foster parents of such children are extremely concerned with protecting them from sexual abuse, since this type of child "goes to anyone." Zeanah et al. present the case of a 14-month-old girl whose foster mother, with whom she had been for 3 months, suspected that the child was depressed. The child sat for long periods of time by herself and rarely smiled or vocalized. The authors note this girl's history of multiple placements away from her biological mother, with transfers among foster homes occurring within the span of 1 or 2 months. History from both the foster mother and birth mother indicated that the child had no preferred attachment figure and consistently demonstrated indiscriminate sociability.

Zeanah et al. describe Type III, or inhibited attachment disorder as a condition in which there is an unwillingness to venture away from the attachment figure in order to engage in age-appropriate exploration. The authors note two subtypes: excessive clinging and compulsive compliance. They cite the case of a 30-month-old boy who was referred because of extreme negative behavioral reactions whenever he was picked up by his caseworker for weekly visits with his birth mother. He had been removed from his foster mother at age 20 months and had spent 10 months in the same foster home. When the clinician conducting the evaluation observed the boy in his foster home, the boy was happy and relaxed. However, when the caseworker arrived to transport the boy for a visit with his mother, the boy screamed, appeared terrified, attempted to hide, and had to be carried, kicking and screaming, into the caseworker's car.

Upon arriving at the birth mother's apartment, the boy did not greet his mother and became low-key. He complied passively with his mother's instructions and did not move from a spot unless his mother directed him to do so. He did not speak at all during the entire 45-minute observation. He watched his birth mother continuously throughout the session, maintaining a vigilant and anxious expression on his face.

It should be noted that, while Zeanah et al. classify this case as an attachment disorder, the theoretical perspective of the present work would also allow the view that this child was employing passive–aggressive means to protest the threat to his new attachment posed by forced contact with the birth mother.

Zeanah et al.'s Type IV, aggressive attachment disorder is characterized by aggression that is directed either toward the self, by head banging or scratching, or toward the attachment figure, by biting, kicking, or other physical means. The authors relate this type of attachment disorder to children's witnessing domestic violence or being physically abused. The authors cite the case of a 26-month-old boy who was described by his parents as "a holy terror." He threw tantrums constantly, hit his mother when she tried to contain him, and lashed out at his father when the father attempted to discipline him. The family history involved considerable domestic violence and parental threats to abandon each other and the child. This boy was cared for inconsistently by a large number of family members, friends, and even casual acquaintances.

Patterson and Moran (1988) cite a number of studies that have yielded parallel findings to those above. Regarding the question of whether reactive attachment disorder is associated with an inadequate level of general stimulation—or, specifically, to the absence of a unique attachment to a single caretaker—the authors note that Provence and Lipton (1962) found that institutionalized infants who were given toys and other sensory stimulation, but only limited attention by caretakers, were as impaired as other institutionalized infants who were not given such stimulation. Regarding the question of reversibility of this disorder, Patterson and Moran cite research demonstrating that individualized caretaking can reverse the symptoms, provided that care is initiated prior to age 3 years (Clark & Hanisee, 1982; Dennis, 1973; Rutter, 1979).

DEVELOPMENT OF EMPATHY VERSUS DELINQUENCY

In general, early relationships are internalized by the child and become the template for the future actions of the adult. For example, Olweus (1980) and Troy and Sroufe (1987) found that adults who exploit others had parents who rejected them punitively or who were emotionally unavailable during their childhood. On the other hand, children who have experienced responsive parental care are able to relate to their peers in an empathic, concerned manner and with "commitment" (Pancake, 1985; Sroufe, 1983). Children with histories of avoidant attachment, which is associated with insensitive care and rejection, tend to exploit the vulnerable and to engage in devious behaviors, including stealing, lying, and cheating (Sroufe, 1983).

Marshall, Hudson, and Hodkinson (1993) cite research indicating that a family breakup prior to age 5 years is more likely than a later breakup to produce juvenile delinquency and that prolonged separation from the mother between age 6 months and 3 years is followed by behavioral problems. The authors also cite a study by Misra (1977) indicating that separation from parents and neglect by parents contribute to the development of juvenile delinquency. Marshall et al. state: "Although many children are exposed to various negative experiences, only a few develop inappropriate behaviors as a consequence. It is our view that the quality of home life significantly prepares the growing child to be resilient or vulnerable to such influences. The crucial aspect of the quality of home life in this regard is the development of secure or insecure attachment bonds" (pp. 170–171).

Witt and Dyer (1997) review the literature on the role of attachment in the development of juvenile delinquency. They note that several researchers view attachment bonds to prosocial figures as a protective factor that can assist the juvenile in resisting negative factors that are predictive of delinquent behavior.

Block and Block (1980) found that children with histories of secure attachment (i.e., responsive parenting) had higher scores on a measure of empathy than did children with histories of avoidant attachment. Rosenberg (1984) found that children with avoidant attachment histories tended to have much less elaborate play than did securely attached children with approximately the same IQ. The avoidant children's play and fantasy material was almost completely devoid of themes concerning people. LeFreniere and Sroufe (1985) found that children with avoidant attachment histories engaged in more unprovoked aggression and hostility toward other children than did securely attached children.

This tendency toward aggression and lack of empathy has important ramifications for future behavior in adolescence and adulthood. Fonagy et al. (1997) propose that crimes, at least in adolescence, are often committed by individuals who do not have adequate "mentalizing" capacities. This concept refers to an individual's capacity for appreciating the mental states of others, which is an outgrowth of satisfactory attachment experiences. Fonagy et al. state: "We assume that crimes against people are normally inhibited by the painful psychic consequences of identifying with the victim's mental state and the equally uncomfortable awareness of the beliefs and feelings of important others" (p. 256).

Levinson and Fonagy (submitted, cited in Fonagy et al., 1997) using the Adult Attachment Interview, conducted a study of 22 prison inmates with a diagnosable psychiatric disorder and comparison groups of psychiatric inpatients and normal controls recruited from a medical outpatient department. Levinson and Fonagy found that there were significantly more secure attachment histories among the normal controls than in either clinical group. Current anger with attachment figures was dominant in the psychiatric patients, but relatively more intense in the inmate group. Inmates had significantly lower scores on a measure of reflective function (capacity for empathy) than did normals or psychiatric patients. Furthermore, when the inmate group was split into those who had committed violent versus nonviolent offenses, the violent group had significantly lower empathic capacity, as measured by the reflective function instrument, than did the nonviolent offenders.

Weber, Meloy, and Gacono (1992) compared adolescents with conduct disorders to a group of dysthymic inpatients. The authors found that the conduct-disordered adolescents showed very weak desire for relationships as compared with the depressed adolescents and manifested emotional detachment and devaluation of other people to a much greater degree than did the depressed group.

Fonagy et al. (1997) view these phenomena as resulting from early experiences of separation and abandonment, as described in Bowlby's attachment theory, and they state:

> Most pertinent, from our viewpoint, is Bowlby's third state, detachment, which is thought to follow prolonged separation. Detachment

> represents an apparent recovery from protest and despair, but there is no resumption of normal attachment behavior following the refinding of the object. The infant is apathetic and may totally inhibit bonding. There is an intensification of interest in physical objects and a self-absorption which is only thinly disguised by superficial sociability. (p. 229)

Bowlby's seminal work on the relationship between early maternal care and later personality functioning, published originally as a report (*Maternal Care and Mental Health*) to the World Health Organization and later commercially under the title *Child Care and the Growth of Love* (1953), cites retrospective studies of delinquents, prostitutes, and other deviant individuals. Bowlby (1944) compared 44 juveniles with a history of theft whom he treated at a guidance clinic to a matched comparison sample from the same guidance clinic similar in age and gender, but without a history of theft. Bowlby found that the experience of complete and prolonged separation from the birth mother or established foster mother during the first 5 years of life was overwhelmingly more frequent among the thieves than among the clinical comparison group.

Furthermore, Bowlby found that there were 14 "affectionless characters" among the thieves and none in the comparison group. Bowlby defines "affectionless character" as a child or adolescent who has no real feeling, no emotional response to situations where it would be normal to have such a response, no capacity to care for others or to make true friends; such a person is psychologically inaccessible, is devious and evasive, and has problems in school. Bowlby also found that the affectionless characters among the thieves almost always had a history of separation and were far more delinquent than any of the others. Bowlby concludes that adults whose relationships with their mothers have been severely disturbed are at great risk for gross impairments of their capacity to appreciate the humanity of others.

Meloy (1992) cites a great deal of clinical and psychometric data in support of the premise that violent behavior is related to repeated experiences of intolerable separations, losses, or parental unavailability during infancy and early childhood. Meloy relates disturbed childhood attachment history to pathological adult phenomena, including stalking, catathymic violence, sexual homicide, erotomania, and psychopathic behavior.

SEXUAL ACTING OUT

A number of authors relate attachment difficulties to aggressive sexual behavior from childhood to adulthood. Esquilin (1995) states that children whose sexual behavior is motivated by more chronic developmentally disruptive issues such as attachment difficulties may be at risk for long-term problems with sexual behavior than are children who are reacting to abuse without deeper personality involvement.

Marshall et al. (1993) cite research indicating that disrupted attachments play a significant role in the development of sexual acting out. Awad, Saunders, and Levene (1984) found that a high percentage of juvenile sex offenders had experienced separation from their parents for prolonged periods. Almost half the subjects in this sample were described as loners. Saunders, Awad, and White (1986) found that in a sample of 63 sexually assaultive adolescent boys, those who had sexually attacked peer-aged or older victims had experienced long-term separation from parents.

Marshall et al. (1993) relate disturbed or insecure attachments to specifically sexual, as opposed to general delinquent, acting out through a process by which the attachment difficulties produce low self-esteem and diminished social skills. Adolescent boys who have those characteristics tend to avoid conventional sexual interactions in which self-esteem and social skills lead to success because they fear rejection in such situations. Instead, such adolescent boys focus upon impersonal, nonaffectionate scenarios in which they can achieve a sense of masculinity and power through aggressive sexual acting out against others. Marshall et al. state: "Responding to those scenarios will tend to entrench a set of beliefs and attitudes that are self-centered, oblivious to the needs or desires of a partner, and show a preoccupation with physical gratification; not the type of disposition that might lead to intimate loving relations but, unfortunately, one that would fail to inhibit tendencies to offend sexually" (p. 175).

RESILIENCY

As noted on Chapter 11, predictions concerning psychological harm to young children removed from caretakers to whom they have become attached are countered with the argument that children "are resilient" and thus able to overcome such losses with little difficulty. Research in the attachment theory tradition addresses the issue of children's resiliency in relation to that quality of their prior attachment experiences. Lewis and Fiering (1991, cited in Rothbard & Shaver, 1994) examined the relationship between early attachment patterns and later psychopathology by using two attachment-by-environment models that were labeled "vulnerable child" and "invulnerable child" models. Infants were classified as securely or insecurely attached at age 12 months by using a modification of the Strange Situation (Ainsworth et al., 1978). Mothers of the subjects completed rating scales covering school competence, peer behavior, and social activities when the children were 6 years old. Lewis and Fiering found that significantly more insecurely attached children showed psychopathology at age 6 years than did securely attached children. There was also a significant interaction between attachment security and family discord, with poor environmental conditions contributing to pathology in insecurely attached children and securely attached children remaining relatively unaffected by future environmental stress.

Elicker at al. (1992, cited in Rothbard & Shaver, 1994) studied 47 high-risk children at age 10 and 11 years who had been classified into attachment groups at age 12 and 18 months. The authors found that children with secure attachment histories were rated as more emotionally healthy, self-assured, and competent, spending more time with their peers and less time with adults. The least securely attached children showed more negative bias and less interpersonal sensitivity and understanding in rating the behavior of their peers. Grossmann and Grossmann (1991, cited in Rothbard & Shaver, 1994) studied a sample of German children over a period from infancy to age 10 years. The authors found that the least securely attached children, based on ratings taken in infancy, had the fewest number of friends and were most likely to describe themselves as exploited or ridiculed by their peers and excluded from group activities. Using a definition of "resiliency" as the ability to respond to problem situations with flexibility, persistence, and resourcefulness, and remaining organized even when under stress, Arend, Gove, and Sroufe (1979, cited in Rothbard & Shaver, 1994) found that securely attached infants were more ego-resilient than two groups rated by teachers as insecure.

Thus, consistent with the conclusions of Rutter (1979) the

research literature provides strong support for the notion that, although many children are "resilient" under a number of definitions, this resiliency is founded upon a history of good early relationships in which as an infant and toddler the child received responsive and consistent care and was spared traumatic separations and losses. For instance, Rutter (1971) found that a good relationship with one parent serves to protect a child brought up in an otherwise discordant, unhappy home. Rutter does conclude, however, that maternal deprivation, while being a significant stress factor, is not typically the sole determinant of psychological problems. Rutter notes that many of the studies that he reviewed involved subjects with a number of risk factors and that the real contribution of maternal deprivation shows up as an interaction with other risk factors, such as family discord, in causing emotional or personality problems.

Regarding depression specifically, Parker (1994) states that the results and methodologies of numerous studies on parental loss are lacking in consistency. Parker notes that these studies have paid little attention to the quality of the support system before and after loss and that when these factors are considered the loss itself tends to have a negligible effect on pathology. Parker states that recent reviews of the literature in this area "consistently point to the possibility that any determining variable may emerge primarily from parental psychopathology (or bond distortions) before and after the separation, rather than from bond disruption per se" (p. 301).

CHILDREN IN FOSTER CARE

Children in foster care have, virtually without exception, suffered some sort of traumatic life experience, whether it be neglect; separation from or complete loss of birth parents to whom the children were attached; or physical, sexual, and emotional abuse. Kates, Johnson, Rader, and Strieder (1991) note that foster children in clinical settings have been described as lacking the capacity to form relationships of any depth, having deficient internalizations of parental love objects, either idealized or deidealized, and being confused about their personal identities. Fein (1991), however, states that many studies have demonstrated equal or better developmental outcomes for children who remain in foster care than for those who are returned home. These measures include IQ, adjustment, self-esteem, and academic achievement. Barth and Berry (1987) also state that children who are returned home have inferior measurable developmental outcomes compared to children who remain in foster care. A return to a rehabilitated birth parent does not by any means ensure a successful outcome, even though services have been provided and casework personnel deem a transfer of the child back to the parental home appropriate.

Family maintenance programs, in which abused or neglected children are allowed to remain in the home with supportive services, have had a spotty track record and have been shown in several studies to be clearly inferior to foster care in various outcome measures. In a 5-year study of 389 families receiving this type of service, Jones (1983) found that among families receiving standard services, there was a reabuse rate of fully 22%. Provision of a more intensive program of services managed to reduce this to 17% in another group of families in this study. Jones notes that at the time of case closing only a third of these families were functioning adequately. Wald, Carlsmith, and Leiderman (1988) studied a sample of 5- to 10-year-old at-risk white children who were maintained at home with supportive services and a matched sample placed into foster care. Wald et al. found that reabuse and neglect rates were high for the children maintained at home.

Barth and Berry (1987) cite a large sample study by Runyan and Gould (1985) comparing abused children ages 11 to 18 years who were either moved into foster care or who received in-home services. Of the 114 children who received services at home, the reabuse rate was 25%, whereas only 11% of the 106 children who had been placed into foster care were abused. Half of the abuse of the foster children was perpetrated by the birth parents during reunification visits. Barth and Berry state that most studies of adoptive families find extremely low rates of abuse in that group, and the authors cite research indicating that adoptive parents are the alleged perpetrators in approximately 1% of all reports.

For many children, placement into foster care is an experience that disrupts their lives repeatedly. Nearly one in three children who entered foster care in 1985 had been in foster care previously (Mech, 1988). Ooms (1990; cited in Fein, 1991) indicates that 20% to 33% of foster children entering care have been in placement previously. Barth and Berry (1987) report that fully 25% of children who entered foster care in 1985 had been in foster care within the preceding 12 months and that 26% of children in foster care in 1985 had experienced three or more placements during the preceding 3 years. The authors state that, just as children were moved from foster home to foster home during the 1970s, children may now be moving from foster care back home and then back into foster care. Barth and Berry also cite some pessimistic results from reunification projects in various studies that reported rates of return to foster care from 20 to 32% after reunification with birth parents.

One of the most detailed and exhaustive studies of foster children published to date is Fanshel et al.'s (1990) analysis of the life experiences of 585 children in Casey foster care, a system of long-term foster homes with a centralized social service component by which a child has a single caseworker for his or her entire stay in the program. Of these children, 72% were white, 7% African American, 3% Latino, and 8% mixed racial background; 57.5% were male, and 42.5% female; 60% of these children were separated from their mothers permanently, and 75% were separated from their fathers permanently; 20% of the birth mothers in this study were deceased, and 20% of the children had birth mothers who were described as alcoholic.

The Fanshel et al. (1990) research produced a number of important findings about the role of attachment in the children's adjustment. The authors found that those children who were more attached to the foster family needed less extensive psychological or psychiatric services from the Casey program. Children who had spent more time in Casey care reported a closer attachment to their last Casey foster family. Interestingly, those children whose mothers visited them more while the children were in Casey care reported a closer measure of attachment to the last Casey foster family. Furthermore, children who were more attached to their foster parents had better adult employment with greater job stability and job satisfaction. Boys who were more attached to their last Casey foster parents were less extensively involved in serious crime as adults.

Fanshel et al. (1990) found that the number of placements that a child had was related to a variety of psychological and behavioral outcomes. The authors report that a child who had more Casey placements engaged in a greater extent of sexual acting out while in Casey care and was more likely to have been evaluated psychologically or psychiatrically. Fanshel et al. also found that a child who had spent a greater percentage of pre-Casey program time away from both parents had a greater chance of adoption disruption and also had a lesser attachment to the natural family. The authors also found that a child who was older when first separated from the birth parents was more attached to the natural family and more likely to be returned to the natural family. Children who had had a large number of living arrangements before entering Casey care had a large number of returns to the birth parents and a large number of total living arrangements away from the birth parents. Such children tended to be more hostile and negativistic when first placed in Casey care. Fanshel et al. note that, although these children's problems originally stemmed from the failure of the dysfunctional birth parents, the children developed dysfunctional defenses against rejection and developed associated obnoxious personality traits that then became a factor in the further disruption of their living arrangements. The authors note that a study of 10,000 foster children in California observed a pattern of conditions leading to placement that shifted from "things happening to children" to "things the children are doing" and that the presenting problems shifted to the child's psychological problems and impulsive behavior. (This pattern is illustrated by the case of Dee-Dee presented in Chapter 12.) Fanshel et al. also state that some children, particularly older foster children, have had so many unsuccessful placement experiences that they have problems in trusting parental figures and are therefore unadoptable.

One particularly difficult issue explored by Fanshel et al. (1990) is that of the influence of the child's involvement with birth parents during foster care. The authors cite a prior Columbia University study (Fanshel & Shinn, 1978) that found that loss of contact with the birth parents was associated with exacerbation of a child's developmental problems. Fanshel and Shinn found that children who were not visited by their birth parents while in foster care suffered a decline in nonverbal IQ scores, as compared to children who were visited by their birth parents. Children who were not visited by their birth parents also displayed more personality and behavior problems than did children whose birth parents visited them. Fanshel et al., however, came up with contradictory findings in their 1990 study, namely, children who lost their parents early appeared to be in better condition than those who were still involved with their birth parents. The authors attempt to reconcile these findings in terms of the child's degree of previous enmeshment with the parent. Fanshel et al. state that in cases in which parental behavior toward the child is not grievously assaultive, it is better for the child to work through the problems in reality with a dysfunctional parent than to have to deal with these conflicts through fantasizing about a missing parent. The authors note that the records from the Casey program contain instances in which children sought reunion with a birth parent often on a very unrealistic basis. The authors further state that children's entanglement in a mutually hostile relationship with their birth parents while in foster care causes the children to relate to their foster caretakers with a pervasive lack of trust and with unreasonable expectations. Fanshel et al. view children's anguish about the birth family's original failure to protect them as interfering with the children's ability to accept the better circumstances of the foster home. Furthermore, the authors point out that after a child has lived in many homes it is not clear whether the internal struggles over rejection and maltreatment involve the birth parents exclusively or whether there comes to be an amalgam of several frustrating parental figures in the child's mind.

The current research in the area of foster care leads to a number of conclusions regarding permanency planning. To begin with, the typical in-home services to prevent foster placement frequently fail to reverse the situations and result in high rates of reabuse and in eventual foster placement. Foster children fare better on a number of developmental measures than do children who are allowed to remain with the abusive or neglectful parent who has supportive services. There is a pattern in the current foster care system of children's bouncing back and forth between the birth parents and foster care parents, with a shockingly high percentage of children having multiple placements. This repeated placement of children into foster care, especially if the children are subjected to multiple moves to different foster homes, results in an eventual impairment of the children's capacity to attach and to trust. This experience leads to negativism, hostility, and pseudo-self-sufficiency that prevent the children from adjusting to any foster home. Children who undergo this assault upon their capacity to attach are at greatly increased risk for emotional and behavioral problems in comparison to children who have stabilized in a foster home and experience continuity of care. Those children who enter placement at a young age and are not involved in protracted contacts with birth parents, with whom they are enmeshed in a conflicted relationship, stand the best chance of emerging from the foster care experience without major psychological and behavioral problems. For many children, continued contact with the birth parents has the sole effect of interfering with their forming a stable attachment to the new caretakers. The experience of temporary foster care rather than adoption also creates problems that extend to the next generation in that former foster children are much more likely than the population at large to have their own children placed into foster care at some point.

CHAPTER 10

Standards for Expert Testimony

Psychological assessment in child welfare matters differs from ordinary clinical work in that there is often a substantial likelihood that the evaluator will be called as an expert witness at trial. This fact necessitates a change in approach that stresses the defensibility and admissibility of the end-product expert report, perhaps as long as a year or more down the road, over the immediate problems of clinical intervention. This requirement imposes a substantial burden on the forensic evaluator since these referrals often require specific interventions at the time of the examination; for example, whether a child should be moved from one placement to another or whether a birth parent should be referred for a psychiatric evaluation to determine the need for psychotropic medication. These short-term clinical issues may require assessment that employs speculative, intuitive, or highly subjective methods of test interpretation to address these referral questions.

Although these methods may be desirable in clinical assessments that are meant to generate hypotheses for exploration in subsequent therapy with the examinee, that situation differs dramatically from courtroom testimony based on the psychological report. Elsewhere, I (Dyer, 1997) have noted that, while such clinical hypotheses can be tested and modified as treatment progresses, the words of an expert are etched in stone, as it were, which means that one must refrain from expressing opinions that are formulated to a degree other than reasonable psychological certainty. I therefore stress that the guiding principle behind preparation of the psychological report in such cases be that of forensic acceptability, with the immediate clinical considerations having secondary priority.

In contrast to the expectations of what a standard clinical assessment can provide in the way of an in-depth understanding of the subject's personality and specific elements of psychopathology, the forensic report must adhere to scientific conservatism. Speculative interpretations should not be included in a forensic report, even though they may be of value otherwise. Experts should restrict interpretive statements to what can be supported with some level of external validity evidence that goes beyond the evaluator's intuitive understanding of what mental processes in the subject underlie the obtained results. The same is true of predictions made in forensic psychological reports. These should be related in a clear and rational manner to some external source of support for the validity of the prediction, given the specific circumstances of the case.

The current emphasis on scientific support for experts' conclusions is rooted, in part, in recent developments in standards for admissibility of scientific evidence in federal courts. Under the Federal Rules of Evidence, expert witnesses are permitted to testify on matters requiring scientific, technical, or other specialized knowledge. At the present time, all scientific evidence is subject to two standards in courts: (1) the *Frye v. United States* general acceptance test, based on a 1923 decision, and (2) the standards formulated by the United States Supreme Court in *Daubert v. Merrell-Dow Pharmaceuticals* (1993). Although *Daubert* appears to be emerging as the predominant paradigm, several states have explicitly chosen to retain the *Frye* standard.

Several state statutes discuss the scientific reliability of expert testimony in language that resembles *Daubert*. New Jersey, for example, requires that testimony must have a sufficient scientific basis to produce reasonably reliable results such that the testimony assists the court in determining the truth (Wulach, 1998). Wulach also notes that a 1991 New Jersey Supreme Court case (*Rubanik v. Witco Chemical Corp.*) found that novel scientific theories may be considered reliable if they are based on sound methodology of the type reasonably relied on by experts in that field and if they are proffered by a qualified expert who is capable of assessing the validity of the data. Referring to the *Rubanik* case, Wulach states: "The admission of expert testimony should be determined by sound reasoning and methodology to support the testimony rather than on general acceptance in the scientific community" (p. 320).

It is of interest that, although Wulach states that this is a recent case, it is nevertheless pre-*Daubert*, reflecting the fact that state supreme courts often grapple with complex issues of the same type as those considered by the United States Supreme Court. Additionally, some states, notably Texas, have published higher-court decisions that amplify the requirements of *Daubert*, resulting in even higher hurdles that affect not only hard-science testimony but also standard medical testimony (Wilkerson & Brown, 1998).

The role of the trial court in exercising a gatekeeping function for scientific evidence under *Daubert* was strengthened by another United States Supreme Court decision in *G. E. v. Joiner* (1997). In *Joiner*, the Court held that the trial judge did not err in rejecting scientific evidence because he drew different conclusions from the data than did the experts. Although the plaintiff had argued that the proper focus of the trial judge in assessing the reliability of such evidence should be restricted to "the principles and methodology, not on the conclusions that they generate," Justice Rehnquist held that "a court may conclude that there is simply too great an analytical gap between the data and the opinion proffered." The upshot of this amplification of *Daubert*'s emphasis on the trial judge as gatekeeper is that experts whose testimony rests heavily on experimental data must be particularly attentive to presenting their data, scientific reasoning, and conclusions in as accessible a form as possible in order to facilitate correct interpretation of the scientific evidence by a trial judge who may not possess sophistication in scientific or quantitative methodology.

The *Frye* test had its genesis in a District of Columbia appellate court case (1923) involving the admissibility into evidence of a precursor of the modern polygraph. The opinion set up the test of general acceptance in the relevant scientific community as the hurdle for admissibility of any novel scientific procedure. This federal test was adopted by numerous federal and state courts. At the present time, *Frye* has been explicitly retained by courts in New York, Arizona, Nebraska, California, and Florida. Critics of this standard question whether it can be determined when evidence is scientific or what the relevant scientific community for acceptance of the novel procedure might be. A further criticism is that there does not exist a well-articulated standard for proving "general acceptance."

Despite the overall tendency for *Frye* to be implemented as a conservative test that excludes evidence that could be helpful to juries, Clifford (1997) notes that there have been some egregious lapses under this standard and that "substantial and unfair verdicts have been rendered based on expert testimony that has no valid scientific basis" (p. 3:65). Clifford cites the case of *Carrol v. Otis Elevator* in which a clinical psychologist was permitted to testify as an "elevator button expert" that red elevator buttons attract children.

The United States Supreme Court's opinion in *Daubert v. Merrell-Dow Pharmaceuticals* was intended to remedy situations such as the above by articulating precise standards under which trial court judges were to assess the admissibility of novel scientific testimony. *Daubert* involved two infant plaintiffs whose mothers took the antinausea medication Bendectin manufactured by the defendant company while the mothers were pregnant with the children. The plaintiffs argued that their severe birth defects were causally related to their mothers' ingestion of this medication. The district court granted the defendant company summary judgment after the company's expert submitted an affidavit stating that there was no health hazard associated with taking Bendectin during pregnancy. The plaintiffs introduced eight well-credentialed experts who stated that Bendectin caused birth defects in animal studies. The plaintiffs' experts also introduced evidence based on analysis of chemical structure and a reanalysis of previously unpublished statistical studies of human subjects. The lower court ruled, however, that the plaintiffs' analyses did not meet the *Frye* general acceptance standard, and this finding was affirmed by the appeals court. The United States Supreme Court reversed these rulings, stressing that the Federal Rules of Evidence and not the *Frye* standard of admissibility was the appropriate criterion for admissibility of scientific evidence in a federal trial.

In its decision in *Daubert*, the Supreme Court noted that the Federal Rules of Evidence, especially Rule 702, assign to the judge the role of determining whether experts' testimony rests upon a reliable foundation and is relevant to the specific issue before the court. *Reliability* refers to the scientific acceptability of the procedure, which is to be assessed according to several criteria, listed in the *Daubert* decision. First, the trial judge is to determine whether the procedure has been tested and subjected to peer review and publication in appropriate scientific journals. Second, the known or potential error rate must be determined. Third, the party who proposes to introduce this evidence must demonstrate the existence of standards controlling the operation of the technique. With respect to psychological practice, this certification would correspond to the involvement of organizations such as the American Psychological Association (APA), National Council on Measurement in Education (NCME), or American Educational Research Association (AERA) in establishing standards for psychometric procedures. Fourth, the trial judge is to determine whether the technique is accepted in the relevant scientific community (basically a restatement of the *Frye* test, but relegated to the status of being only a single component of the complex *Daubert* criteria). The Supreme Court also noted that the technique or procedure must be derived by the scientific method and must undergo appropriate "validation." It is of interest to psychologists that the Court used the term "validation" here in the same way that it is generally understood in the field of psychological testing.

According to *Daubert*, the scientific evidence must also have the quality of *helpfulness*, which is defined by Clifford (1997) as the quality that characterizes evidence that "logically advances a material aspect of the proposing party's case." In other words, the evidence must be directly related to the ultimate legal issue before the court. Furthermore, the evidence must not be more prejudicial than probative. The *Daubert* decision addressed this concern in its recognition that abandoning the *Frye* standard would lead to "a free for all in which befuddled juries are confounded by absurd and irrational and pseudoscientific assertions." This is an implicit acknowledgment that experts, especially "well-credentialed" ones, are inordinately persuasive, sometimes to a degree that goes well beyond the scientific integrity of their data.

Finally, the Supreme Court addressed what it viewed as the more liberal admissibility standard that would result from the *Daubert* criteria. The Court stated in this decision that the relaxation of admissibility criteria would be counteracted by a number of factors that included vigorous cross-examination, the presentation of contrary evidence, and careful instruction to juries on the burden of proof.

A number of commentators have reacted to the *Daubert* decision with respect to its impact upon psychological experts. Goodman-Delahunty (1997) notes that, in addition to the above counterbalancing factors cited by the Supreme Court, *Daubert* will result in a greater incidence of pretrial hearings to determine admissibility. Goodman-Delahunty also states that it is necessary to conduct further investigation into the suitability of the *Daubert* standards to various forms of psychological expertise. Myers (1997) echoes this concern, noting that there is a question as to whether disciplines such as medicine, clinical social work, and psychology are "scientific" in the *Daubert* sense. Myers states that both medical and psychological evidence run the gamut from strictly empirical "science" to the subjective and clinical and that psychological testimony often rests on a mixture of clinical judgment and scientific research.

A recent federal Fifth Circuit appellate court decision (*Moore v. Ashland Chemical*, 1997) supports Myers's view on this matter. The case involved a truck driver who was exposed to dangerous chemicals while making a delivery and who subsequently brought suit against the company that received his cargo after the company required him to clean up a chemical spill. The plaintiff alleged that as a result of this exposure he contracted reactive airways disease. The defendant moved to strike the testimony of two physicians whom the plaintiff had consulted. The South District of Texas judge ruled that, while one of the physicians could testify as to the diagnosis and prognosis, the expert's opinion in regard to causation did not have a reliable basis under Federal Evidence Rule 702 and that under Evidence Rule 403 such testimony would have been more prejudicial than probative because of the expert's highly impressive qualifications. Interestingly, the same court admitted the opinion of the other physician with respect to both diagnosis and causation as scientifically reliable in spite of the fact that this second expert relied heavily on the first expert's opinion and based his own opinion on essentially the same data.

In this case, the appeals court noted: "Although clinical medicine utilizes parts of some hard sciences, clinical medicine and many of its subsidiary fields are not hard sciences. The purposes, criteria, values, and methods of hard or Newtonian science and clinical medicine are far from identical." The court also stated that *Daubert* factors, which are relevant to issues involving hard science, are not appropriate for assessing the admissibility of clinical medical testimony. The court recommended that "the trial court as gatekeeper should determine whether the doctor's proposed testimony as a clinical physician is soundly grounded in the principles and methodology of his [*sic*] field of clinical medicine."

Myers (1997), however, is not in favor of allowing all medical or psychological testimony in without scrutiny simply because much of it falls below the level of rigor of hard science and rests on clinical judgment. Noting that California courts do make this distinction, applying *Frye* or *Daubert* to scientific evidence but not to the personal opinion of experts, Myers states that this distinction ignores that fact that all medical and psychological testimony is based on some underlying theory or process. Myers states that, although *Daubert* is silent in regard to social science applications, lower courts do apply this test to social science evidence. He points out that even if, strictly speaking, it is not scientific, most psychological testimony falls under the rubric of technical or other specialized knowledge mentioned in Rule 702 and should be subjected to *Daubert* scrutiny if it involves a novel principle.

This view is reflected in the United States Supreme Court decision in *Kumho Tire v. Carmichael* (1999) in which the scope of judicial scrutiny of expert testimony under *Daubert* was clarified. In this case, which concerned the admissibility of expert testimony by an automotive engineer regarding the cause of a tire failure, the court stated that *Daubert* factors may apply to experts who are not scientists. The court observed that the Federal Rules of Evidence do not distinguish between scientific knowledge and technical other specialized knowledge and that it is the term "knowledge," not its modifiers, that establishes the standard of evidentiary reliability. Thus, the court continued, the trial judge may consider one or more of the *Daubert* factors (testability, publication/peer review, error rate, and general acceptance) in evaluating the admissibility of any expert testimony. The court cautioned, however, that the *Daubert* factors are not to be applied in checklist fashion, but that the admissibility inquiry should be guided by the nature of the issue before the court, the expert's particular expertise, and the subject of the testimony. The court ruled that trial judges have broad latitude in determining which specific *Daubert* factors should be applied to test the admissibility of expert testimony in a particular case. In practical terms, this decision suggests the likelihood that experts' testimony in termination of parental rights cases will come under more intense scrutiny in regard to its scientific basis, even where the particular opinion is essentially a clinical rather than a scientific one.

Although courts have traditionally defined "novel" scientific evidence as a new technique that has not yet gained general acceptance, per the *Frye* test, Myers (1997) offers an alternative definition. According to Myers, "novelty" should be equated with "reliability." In other words, any procedure should be considered "novel" if there are substantial questions concerning its scientific "reliability." He cites the example of the battered child syndrome, which was vigorously attacked when it was first proposed by Kempe in 1962. The concept very rapidly gained acceptance, and within a comparatively brief time courts, were taking judicial notice of the syndrome. Thus, while it was still "novel" in the length of time since its original publication, it was no longer considered "novel" in its scientific "reliability."

Myers (1997) states that a central concern of courts in assessing the admissibility of scientific evidence is whether the evidence is more prejudicial than probative. Thus, the task before the judge is to balance the probative value of the proffered evidence against the likelihood that the testimony will overawe, confuse, or mislead the jury. Clifford (1997) cites a case in which this standard was applied to the proffered testimony of a psychologist in a bank robbery trial. In *U.S. v. Rincon* (1994), a defendant convicted of bank robbery proffered expert testimony by a psychologist who proposed to explain various aspects of eyewitness identification, including perceiving encoding, storage, retention, retrieval of information, and the effects of stress in these faculties. The court ruled that such testimony was not helpful and would only serve to confuse or mislead the jury. The appeals court held that, even if the proffered testimony was found to be reliable under *Daubert*, it must also be helpful in resolving the ultimate legal issue before the court. It should be noted that in termination of parental rights hearings there is no jury present; the ultimate issue is decided by a family court judge. There is no issue of judicial scrutiny as to whether admission of a particular piece of scientific evidence at the time of trial would mislead jurors; nevertheless, the "more prejudicial than probative" objection is certainly one that can be raised on appeal, and is therefore of vital concern.

Along the same lines, Goodman-Delahunty (1997) notes that experts must demonstrate a relationship between the scientific evidence and the facts of the particular case under the requirements of *Daubert*. Goodman-Delahunty cites the case of a defendant who was charged with the statutory rape of his daughter and who sought to introduce evidence demonstrating that he did not share the characteristics of a group composed of 40% of incest abusers (fixated pedophiles). The defense wished to employ this evidence to support their argument that because the defendant was not a fixated pedophile, he was unlikely to have committed the offenses charged. This testimony was rejected by the court as falling short of the *Daubert* helpfulness standard. Conte (1991) states that it is still quite common for mental health experts to argue that a defendant either does or does not fit the profile of a sexual offender, even though reviews of the empirical literature have consistently failed to identify a psychological profile that reliably discriminates between such offenders and others. Conte notes that this type of testimony can have a powerful effect on the trier of fact since it comes from a witness with expert credentials and carries the apparent power of science.

My own practice supplies a further example of testimony that would have benefited from *Daubert* scrutiny as to scientific (and psychometric) reliability and helpfulness under the "more-prejudicial-than-probative" principle of the Federal Rules of Evidence. In a case involving a decorated African American police officer who was seeking reinstatement on the force subsequent to having been terminated after a protracted period in which he claimed that he was racially harassed, the plaintiff had been given a negative psychological assessment by the department's expert. That expert's conclusions were based in part upon an MMPI, on which the plaintiff registered a high *T*-score on the Psychopathic Deviate scale. At trial, the department's expert testified that the plaintiff was unfit for duty and that the high score on a scale that measures the construct "psychopathic deviate" indicates that the officer was psychopathic or antisocial. The labeling of this individual as a psychopathic deviate was, of course, quite prejudicial regarding the question of his reinstatement as a police officer.

My colleague and I have noted (McCann & Dyer, 1996; Dyer, 1997) that the MMPI-2 has very low internal consistency on certain scales. In fact, this was a criticism of the original MMPI (Graham, 1987) which the MMPI-2 was supposed to remedy. It was the original version of the test that had been administered to the plaintiff. Low internal consistency means that the content of the scale, instead of being homogeneous, is rather a hodgepodge. Graham indicates that it is possible for an individual to register a high score on the Psychopathic Deviate scale just by being an assertive individual with strongly held opinions, without having antisocial traits. I requested the raw response data for the test and found that the item endorsements driving the elevation of the Psychopathic Deviate scale were precisely of this latter type—in other words, reflecting an assertiveness and willingness to defend one's opinions and not anything even suggesting psychopathy or antisocial traits.

Clearly, then, the introduction of this high-scale score with such a flagrantly pathological label was prejudicial to the court and did not prove anything valid about the individual in question. The blame may be shared between the shoddy psychometric procedures behind the development of the original MMPI (a fault that, in my opinion, the MMPI-2 failed to correct in the least) and the opposing expert's failure to check the specific item content, or at least the supplementary content scales on the test, to determine whether the subject's responses were genuinely reflective of psychopathy. Thus, the "psychopathic deviate" finding not only was unreliable, in the *Daubert* sense, but also was far more prejudicial than probative. The author's testimony addressed the psychometric issues only; any testimony concerning *Daubert* and the Federal Rules of Evidence would, of course, be outside the scope of expertise of any witness who is qualified by the court as a mental health, rather than a legal, expert.

In my opinion, there are facets of typical mental health expert testimony in termination of parental rights cases that should clearly be subjected to *Daubert* scrutiny and others that may be more appropriately assessed by means of the standard rational legal criteria for weighing the validity of professional opinion. In the field of termination of parental rights and child welfare litigation generally, concepts such as attachment theory and predictions based on the theory and related empirical research are at this point arguably no longer novel owing to their wide acceptance. On other hand, concepts such as those advanced by Goldstein et al. (1979), although widely disseminated over a lengthy period of time, are nonetheless still arguably "novel" according to the criterion of demonstrated scientific reliability. The problems with Goldstein et al.'s formulations, especially regarding their scientific adequacy, are reviewed in Bush and Goldman (1982). This debate is summarized in Chapter 8.

OBJECTIVE AND PROJECTIVE TESTS IN COURT

Psychological tests used to support expert opinions on diagnosis and prognosis should have demonstrated reliability and validity with respect to the constructs that the testimony is to address. Objective psychological tests of the pencil-and-paper self-report inventory variety, in my opinion, should be subjected to *Daubert* standards for scientific evidence, including error rate, which in psychometrics is expressed as sensitivity, specificity, positive predictive power, negative predictive power, and overall classification efficiency. Heilbrun (1992) lists a number of standards for qualification of psychometric tests for forensic use. These standards include commercial availability, an adequate technical manual, review by the profession in mainstream publications such as *Mental Measurements Yearbooks* or *Test Critiques*, minimum reliability of .80, relevance to the ultimate legal issue, appropriate standardization, reliance on actuarial over intuitive/rational methods of interpretation, and assessment of response style as a feature of the instrument. Cicchetti (1994) states that psychometric measures with internal consistency reliability below .70 are unacceptable for clinical purposes but that an internal consistency level of .70 and .79 may be considered as fair, a level of .80 to .89 as good, and a level of .90 and above as excellent. Instruments that possess all of the above characteristics and that are employed in an appropriately conservative manner, should have little difficulty passing muster under the *Daubert* standards.

Although courts have justifiably begun to apply *Daubert* scrutiny to objective psychometric tests, recognizing them as scientific devices that measure a particular set of characteristics, projective methods are more problematic. As discussed in Chapter 5, projective techniques do not actually reach the level of scientific precision characteristic of a psychological test but are regarded by many in the profession of psychology as being more like a structured interview. Under that rubric, experts' use of projective techniques would be considered to be technical or other specialized knowledge rather than strictly scientific knowledge. Projective techniques should properly be placed in the same category as interview methods. The interview employs questions and other verbal techniques to elicit responses that reflect certain forms of pathology, while projective techniques employ unstructured visual stimuli to accomplish the same purpose. For example, looseness of associations can be assessed either by questions that elicit disconnected and bizarre responses or by inkblots that elicit a fusion of percepts (contamination) or bizarre confabulations that are rarely encountered in records other than those of subjects with a thought disorder.

Regarding predictions about risk of harm to the child and birth parents' prognosis for adequate functioning in a caregiving role that experts offer in termination cases, we have the blend of scientific knowledge and clinical judgment noted by Myers (1997).

This type of testimony entails the application of research findings to the specific case. The expert brings to bear on the facts of the case an extensive knowledge of the applicable literature and uses rational processes to formulate opinions about a specific individual. In such a situation, it is extraordinarily rare to encounter a research study that exactly conforms to the facts, and consequently there can be no satisfying a standard that demands exact experimental validation for clinical predictions. The reasonableness of the expert's opinion about the child is tested through cross-examination that exposes the specific reasoning processes leading to the conclusions. Although it would be enormously helpful for experts in these cases to have the benefit of an extensive data bank with information on, for example, the degree of disruption of personality development of 4-year-olds who have had two prior placements and have been in current placement 1½ years with monthly contact with birth parents for the last 6 months and sporadic contact before that, this must necessarily remain a question left to informed clinical judgment. Experts can generalize research results to individual cases with the help of clinical theory and careful observation of the parties involved in the litigation.

There are limits to the extent that clinical opinion should be allowed in child custody/termination of parental rights cases, however. The adoptive parents in the *Baby M.* case (*In the Matter of Baby M.*, 1988) presented psychiatric testimony that was roundly criticized in both professional circles and in the popular press. In that case, a surrogate mother reneged on her contract with the donor father and his wife and absconded with the donor father's baby. The expert psychiatrist for the adoptive mother and donor father in *Baby M.* observed a visit between the birth mother, Mary Beth Whitehead, and the infant. The expert testified that Whitehead was playing with the child by using pots and that she should have been engaged in more constructive and sophisticated play activities with the child. The consensus among experts following that case was that such testimony was not helpful to the court in deciding whether to terminate the rights of the birth mother. Understandably, the testimony as to the unstimulating quality of the birth mother's play interaction with the baby was not supported by any empirical literature.

VOIR DIRE

Stern (1997)' notes that an expert witness is "someone with specialized knowledge, skill, experience, training, or education who is able to explain to jurors something important about the litigation that they might not otherwise understand" (p. 21). In order to be qualified as an expert witness by the court, the individual must first go through a process known as *voir dire*, which is an examination of the witness's credentials regarding his or her proposed field of expertise, which may be followed by cross-examination by opposing counsel concerning the legitimacy or relevance of those credentials. Stern states that this presentation of the expert's credentials may sometimes be extensive. He cites a case in which the expert's testimony covered 53 pages of transcript and consumed an hour and a half of court time. The court ruled that such a lengthy presentation was appropriate since it served to anchor the witness's opinions.

The curriculum vitae of an expert must be provided to the other side prior to trial in order for opposing counsel to be able to prepare for *voir dire*. Stern (1997) recommends that the expert's curriculum vitae be thorough and complete. He cautions that it must, above all, be accurate, adding that there is no quicker way to be discredited as an expert than to include items on one's curriculum vitae that are inaccurate. Stern cites the example of an expert whose membership in a professional organization listed in the curriculum vitae has lapsed. It is an easy matter for opposing counsel to check whether an individual is on the membership rolls of a professional organization; and if a witness who claims membership in such an organization at the time of the trial is confronted on cross-examination with the fact that his or her membership has lapsed, this diminishes the witness's credibility in general. The witness may not be attempting to deceive and the listing of the lapsed membership on the curriculum vitae may be a harmless oversight. Furthermore, the particular membership may not be of crucial importance in establishing the expert as qualified to offer the specific opinions in the proffered area. Nevertheless, this omission can have a negative impact, and it is therefore incumbent upon experts to avoid being surprised in this manner when testifying about their credentials.

Stern (1997) lists the following, among others, as areas that should be covered in presenting the credentials of a proffered expert witness: education; dissertation papers; internships, if relevant; specialized training; academic awards; professional affiliations; board memberships; board certifications; licenses; employment experience; papers published; book chapters written; peer review of professional articles; workshops and other training provided; faculty positions held; prior qualification as an expert witness. My colleague and I (McCann & Dyer, 1996) note that experts should avoid listing those credentials that, while sounding impressive, do not actually have much substance to them. We cite the example of "fellow" status in the American Orthopsychiatric Association. Although a "fellow" of the American Orthopsychiatric Association sounds more impressive than "member," the only qualifications for "fellow" status in that organization are having been a member for 5 years and paying a higher annual membership fee. We note that stressing this particular credential on *voir dire* invites the following type of attack: "So you don't have to do anything but hang around the organization for 5 years and pay more money in order to be able to bill yourself as a 'Fellow,' do you, Doctor?" (p. 175).

We (McCann & Dyer, 1996) also caution experts against including lengthy lists of publications in the curriculum vitae if the majority of them are in journals that are not very rigorous in their acceptance policies. Especially to be avoided are lengthy lists of "publications" that are actually geared for a lay audience. Psychologists are frequently asked by school systems, clinics, and other institutions or groups to prepare something for newsletters and similar publications that are distributed for purposes of educating the public or to provide brief overviews of important issues for other professionals. While this type of writing is a valuable professional activity, it should not be offered during the process of *voir dire* as an indication of the witness's professional expertise. On the other hand, there is no harm in mentioning such writing as collateral evidence of the witness's involvement in professional activities apart from practice so long as there is no implication that this constitutes scientific or scholarly work. To misrepresent such professional activity or experience as scientific or scholarly, either through commission or omission, and then to have the cross-examining attorney show convincingly that it does not conform to a rigorous standard is a sure way to have one's credibility marred from the outset.

PREPARATION FOR TESTIFYING

Psychological consultation in termination of parental rights cases, and in forensic cases generally, requires special attention to record keeping and other matters, as outlined in the Forensic Specialty

Guidelines (Committee on Ethical Guidelines, 1991) formulated by the American Psychology–Law Society, or Division 41 of the American Psychological Association. The guidelines state that the standard for record keeping for forensic cases is higher than that required for general clinical practice. The guidelines note that psychologists practicing in a forensic capacity have an obligation to make available, subject to court order or the rules of evidence, all data that form the basis of their conclusions.

In practical terms, this requirement entails keeping detailed notes of contacts with the parties who are being assessed and documenting any unusual applications of psychometric instruments, such as using a test for a subject out of the usual age range, adapting the instructions in some form, or omitting a portion of an instrument that is usually administered. One is not barred from these departures from standard practice by the guidelines, but one is held accountable to document such departures. The higher standard of record keeping for forensic practice also implies the desirability, or perhaps necessity, of listing in the process notes the exact beginning and ending times of interviews, testing sessions, observations, and other client contacts. Psychological experts are routinely asked in the witness stand for the amounts of time consumed by the various components of testing and interviews. If there are no beginning and ending times listed in the process notes, then, unless one has actually recorded the sessions, the question cannot be answered except by speculative recourse to memory or to one's usual amounts of time spent in various types of client contacts.

Thoroughness in documentation should also apply to the expert's access to collateral materials that are relied upon to formulate conclusions. In child welfare matters that involve case reports and field notes prepared by lower-level workers without formal social case management training, the documentation is likely to be spotty, or even erroneous. I once consulted in a case where a 25-year-old birth mother developed Guillain–Barré syndrome (GBS) and as a result was paralyzed. The case report, prepared by a caseworker with a bachelor's degree, stated that the birth mother suffered from a chronic degenerative neurological disease. This report implied a very poor prognosis for the birth mother's ever becoming mobile enough to provide adequate care for her children and was very damaging to her at the outset of the case, when that report was accepted as true. In actual fact, GBS, while causing such total paralysis in some cases that the patient must be placed on a respirator in order to avoid suffocation because of paralysis of the lungs, is *not* a chronic degenerative condition. Patients typically regain most, and sometimes all, of their premorbid level of physical functioning over the natural course of the disease, and it is actually rare for a GBS patient to lose so much physical functioning that he or she would not be able to perform routine child care tasks without assistance. The 25-year-old patient about whom the above report was filed, regained total mobility and coordination spontaneously as the GBS ran its course. Her other severe problems, of a psychosocial nature, were not given their due attention, having been overshadowed by the concern over the patient's presumed "degenerative" neurological disease.

Stern (1997) recommends that experts review the most primary documents available. One should not rely exclusively on summaries of prior history contained in the reports of previous evaluators but should endeavor to obtain the same documents on which those evaluators relied. Stern also advises experts to pay special attention to seeing that their copies of documents are complete. The 2 pages missing from a 50-page record may contain material of critical importance. This omission can be particularly disconcerting if the expert first learns of the material contained in the missing pages while he or she is being cross-examined.

My colleague and I (McCann & Dyer, 1996) stress that one of the principles of preparing to give useful expert testimony is "Know the facts of the case." This not only allows the expert to respond appropriately, and with some forethought, to fact-based cross-examination questions but also facilitates tailoring the psychological report to the specifics of the case in such a way as to maximize relevance to the ultimate legal issue. This relates to another principle cited by McCann and Dyer (1996), namely, "Know the legal issues involved." As interesting as it may be clinically, and as familiar a theme as it may have been in one's original clinical training, a comprehensive picture of the examinee's psychic life is not going to be as helpful to the court as a focused report that addresses the specific psycholegal referral questions. In court, the comprehensive psychological portrait of the client that is common in clinical reports may actually prove to be prejudicial to the client by placing the focus upon characteristics such as sexual proclivities, learning disabilities, or unconscious mental processes that may have absolutely no relevance to the decision that the court is called upon to render in the case.

DIRECT AND CROSS-EXAMINATION

Stern (1997) discusses pitfalls that experts encounter when they are called to testify on the basis of their examination results. To begin with, Stern cautions the expert to not under any circumstances try to be the lawyer but to refrain from any sort of legal interpretation on the stand. In particular, Stern advises against the witness's making evidentiary rulings while testifying. Stern says that statements such as "I can't answer that; it calls for hearsay" should never be uttered by experts. He points out that in such a situation the attorney may have tactical reasons for refraining from any objection to the question, in which case the expert's demurral would have the effect of undermining the attorney's strategy. Stern further cautions that experts should not volunteer information that the attorney has not included in a question. In addition, witnesses should not attempt to answer questions that they feel should have been asked but were not. Such behavior may run counter to the attorney's tactical decisions, or may result in a mistrial if the disclosure violates a prior court order. In practice, experts are usually given a specific warning about any sensitive material that has been excluded from the trial and that the expert must not mention at the cost of provoking a mistrial. It has been my experience in testifying in such situations that it feels as though a tremendously distracting burden has been imposed. Telling an expert to refrain from any mention of a specific fact is rather like telling someone not to think of a giant polar bear sitting on a block of ice. The response potential increases rather than decreases.

A common source of confusion affecting even seasoned experts involves the degree of certainty that is demanded in giving an opinion. Where exactly along the continuum from pure informed speculation to hard-science hypothesis-testing certainty should be required of an expert? Stern (1997) offers a quotation from *People v. Mendible* (1988): "Diagnosis need not be based upon certainty, but may be based upon probability; the lack of absolute scientific certainty does not deprive the opinion of evidentiary value" (p. 562). In fact, Stern notes that expert testimony that contains qualifiers such as "possible" or "could have" is routinely admitted at trial; however, the lack of certainty detracts from the weight to be given the testimony. Stern states that experts should be guided by the principle that they are there in order to provide quality education to the jury.

My colleague and I (McCann & Dyer, 1996) note that in many

venues the higher standard of certainty to which the forensic expert is held accountable is termed "reasonable psychological certainty" or "reasonable psychological probability." It is routine in many courts for attorneys and judges to inquire of experts as to whether their conclusions are offered to a reasonable degree of psychological certainty; however, this term has been variously defined by attorneys as "99% certain" and as "more often than not." We note that these definitions parallel the "beyond a reasonable doubt" and "preponderance of evidence" standards. One useful definition of reasonable psychological certainty cited by McCann and Dyer (1996) comes from the New Jersey Board of Psychological Examiners. In its *Specialty Guidelines for Psychologists in Custody/Visitation Evaluations*, the New Jersey Board defines reasonable psychological certainty as requiring that expert conclusions be based on "substantive clinical observations, empirical research findings, well-accepted theoretical propositions, or an integration of these; moreover the conclusions must not be speculative" (McCann & Dyer, 1996, p. 37).

I (Dyer, 1996) have noted that the days in which experts delivered conclusory pronouncements based solely upon their individual authority are over and that witnesses are called on to justify their opinions in two fundamental ways. First, they are seen increasingly as representatives of a scientific or professional discipline and of the research results and mainstream theories generated by that discipline. Thus, experts are expected to base their opinions directly or indirectly on empirical research results whenever this is feasible. Second, experts are required to state explicitly the reasoning process by which they proceed from observation, to analysis and evaluation, and to conclusions. Saunders (1997) notes that inexperienced experts are sometimes shocked when their conclusions are not simply accepted at face value by judges and attorneys. Attorneys routinely ask for the bases upon which professional opinions are formulated, which would include the reasoning processes or interpretive process used to arrive at the conclusion, as well as the materials that the expert relied on in arriving at the opinion. Experts may expect to be questioned as to why they found certain facts to be credible and not others, why some materials were reviewed and not others, why one individual in the case was believed and another disbelieved, what scientific studies support the opinion, and how the expert reconciles his or her opinion with studies that appear to contradict it. Saunders also stresses the importance of being able to explain the reasons for an expert's rejection of competing opinions after considering several options in developing their conclusions.

Finally, Saunders (1997) advises that experts present themselves as unbiased, neutral educators of the court rather than as caught up in the adversarial nature of the proceedings. The attorneys are the advocates, not the experts. Saunders notes that it is easy for an expert to become caught up in the emotion of a case and to want to help to win the case for the attorney with whom the expert is working. In termination of parental rights cases, this emotional involvement may be somewhat of a greater pitfall than in other cases since many mental health experts who testify in termination hearings define themselves professionally as child advocates. The critical point to bear in mind, however, is that a witness who gives the impression of being an advocate loses credibility in the eyes of the court. Witnesses appear in court for the sole purpose of providing information for the trier of fact in order to assist in the determination of the ultimate legal issue. Witnesses may vigorously advocate for their opinions, by providing the data on which the opinions are based, stating their reasons for rejecting competing conclusions, explicating the process of reasoning that resulted in the opinions, and so forth; however, witnesses should be dispassionate in regard to the outcome of the case. Saunders states that a useful guideline to follow in achieving this type of neutrality is that the expert's report should be the same regardless of which side has engaged that expert.

CHAPTER 11

Cross-Examination Questions and Answers

In this chapter we consider some frequent cross-examination questions posed to the expert witness who testifies in regard to issues of children's attachment to foster caretakers and the harmful consequences of removing children who have formed such an attachment.

ALL CHILDREN IN PLACEMENT ARE TRAUMATIZED ANYWAY

Attorneys frequently attempt to gloss over the effects of trauma on an individual child by painting all children in the system as having been traumatized. Thus, if the expert's theory were true, there would be universal personality and behavior problems of an obvious nature among children in the foster care system. A sample question might be:

> "You testified that removal of this child will inflict a separation trauma. Is it not true that all children in foster care have been traumatized by the initial separation from their parents?"

The expert must concede that for the majority of children above age 6 months who do not display failure to thrive, separation from birth parents will produce negative psychological effects. As noted above, this depends on several factors, including the child's age at placement and the nature of the preexisting attachment to the birth parent. As far as can be determined at the present stage of our knowledge of such matters, children placed below the age of 6 months do not appear to suffer trauma as a result of placement (Bowlby, 1953). Furthermore, there are many cases of older children who have undergone significant emotional, cognitive, and physical deprivation in infancy and are placed because of failure to thrive. Such children are typically listless and unresponsive upon their arrival at the foster home but then "wake up" in response to the stimulation of a loving, nurturing, competent caretaker. In other words, there was no significant previous attachment to be broken, and the child's internal attachment system had not been activated. This observation is based on anecdotal evidence; however, there is more substantial support for the existence of this phenomenon—supporting evidence that may even be considered, in a sense, as reaching the level of a true experiment.

Although the empirical psychological literature is overwhelmingly correlational rather than experimental in nature—that is, researchers study naturally occurring situations rather than engage in any direct manipulation of variables—the Spitz study of anaclitic depression (reviewed in Chapter 9) comes as close as possible to a true experimental design. In that situation, mothers were removed from their babies for administrative reasons that were independent of such factors as the mother's degree of parenting ability or relationship with the child. Thus, for all practical purposes, the separations may be considered as randomly assigned. Spitz found that it was only those children who had had a good relationship with their mother who developed anaclitic depression. Those children who had not related well to their mothers did not suffer such depression, triggered by the loss of an attachment figure. This is persuasive experimental evidence that an infant's attachment system can remain relatively dormant in the absence of a good relationship with a parent, thus providing a rebuttal to the proposition that all foster children are traumatized to begin with by the very act of placing them.

ERRONEOUS CONCEPTUALIZATION OF CHILD'S SITUATION AS ONE OF FORMING BONDS, BREAKING BONDS, AND "REBONDING"

Many attorneys seem to have latched on to the notion of "bonding" as being, in a very literal sense, the deciding factor in these cases. These attorneys tend to view the psychological dynamics that of "forming a bond," "breaking a bond," and "rebonding." Often experts are pressured to give opinions on such questions as, "How long would it take him to form a new bond with the birth parents?" as though the formation of a new object tie after a grievous object loss were an absolute guarantee of mental health. Furthermore, the notion of "breaking the bond" becomes interpreted in a literal manner as referring solely to the physical act of removing the child. Again, it is emphasized that it is the deprivation and trauma resulting from the loss of the central parental love object that is the true focus of concern. The danger to the young child is that of impaired ego development as a result of the permanent loss of central love objects from whom the child below age 4 years is not yet psychically separate. It is not the loss of the foster parents per se that constitutes the harm, although such a loss is a terrible burden for the child. Rather, it is the ego damage, the disruption of delicate psychic developmental processes provoked by the loss, that is cause for concern.

On the other hand, in cases in which the child's original tie to the birth parent is protected by regular, positively experienced visitation and reinforcement of the primacy of the birth parent by the foster caretakers through showing the child pictures, encouraging the child to discuss the birth parent, and so forth, that relationship will serve to mitigate the effects of a separation from foster parents to whom the child has become attached. There is also a differential effect based on the developmental stage of the child at the time of the loss, with varying processes affected and varying degrees of overall vulnerability to ego modification.

This leads to an extremely vexing question concerning the timing of a removal if the court has decided that under the legal criteria of the particular state the rights of the birth parents should not be severed and the child should be returned. Attorneys may well ask about the feasibility of allowing a 3- or 4-year-old child to remain with the foster parents until age 5 or 6, supporting the tie to the biological parents through the measures discussed above. Would this not avert the dire psychic consequences associated with a removal at a younger age?

As children age they become more resistant to ego injury owing to the acquisition of basic personality structure by age 6 years (or by age 5 years, according to some authors). This maturation assumes continuing adequate development in a stable placement with loving, competent foster parents without the implicit, or explicit, threat of summary removal generated by inappropriate communications from the birth parents during visits. On the other hand, the longer children remain in one placement, the more profound will be their connection to those caretakers, relating to the caretakers as objects of love and as fellow family members and identifying with their values, lifestyle, and other characteristics. All of these factors make the loss of the foster parents even more devastating. Yet, it would be a loss inflicted on a relatively mature, intact ego rather than a developing one. To date, there has been no experimental or clinical evidence to guide such decisions with respect to the specific question of which course of action would produce more suffering for the child. Psychologists can only specify the contingencies in a rough fashion. Judges must supply the wisdom.

CAN'T COUNSELING FIX THE SEPARATION REACTION?

In cases in which the expert has made a convincing case for separation trauma if the child were to be removed, the defense attorney may attempt damage control by implicitly downgrading the damage to a separation "reaction" through a subtle shift in terminology. There may also be an attempt to capitalize on the expert's role as a therapist and endorsement of the value of psychotherapy by maneuvering the expert into position of conceding that therapy can completely heal the damage. After all, it is painful for some psychologists to admit that psychology cannot fix everything, especially after their excellent credentials have been paraded before the judge and opposing counsel during the *voir dire*. A sample question of this type would be:

> "Can the separation reaction that you describe [if the child is removed from caretakers to whom he or she has bonded] be mitigated in any way? Can it not be addressed through counseling?"

It is essential to clarify terms here. "Separation reaction" refers to a gamut of problems ranging from children who do not like to be left with a babysitter to school phobia, reaction to brief hospitalizations, and related problems. The harm predicted for the child in question is not a "reaction" but severe impairment of ego development resulting from a trauma. "Trauma" is a term that is reserved for situations in which there is such an enormous emotional shock that the individual's system of psychological defenses and adaptations is overwhelmed and a more or less permanent scar is inflicted. In the case of the immature ego of the preschool child, the trauma of losing central parental love objects results in permanent damage to the development of the personality.

Given this distinction, it is clear that we are discussing a psychological blow of catastrophic proportions. It is true, however, that in such situations there are mitigating factors that consist of the child's preexisting relationship with the birth parent and the birth parent's skill and empathic attunement in responding to such traumatization. We may infer the existence of a preexisting positive emotional tie to the birth parent through the child's ready acceptance of physical affection from the birth parent, the child's displaying physical affection toward the birth parent, the child's positive verbalizations concerning the birth parent, and the child's expressed wish to return to live with the birth parent.

If the birth parent is capable of recognizing that, at least for the present, he or she is not the central figure in the child's emotional world, then the birth parent will be able to appreciate the situation of a child who has suffered the loss of his or her psychological parents and is in a state of grieving. If the birth parent is able to acknowledge verbally to the child that there has been a loss of very important figures in that child's life, then this empathic understanding will help the child to cope with the loss. Unfortunately, the more usual case is for the birth parent to perceive the foster parents as a threat and to make the child feel guilty and bad for expressing any allegiance to them. It is not at all unusual to hear a birth parent respond to a child's request "Where's Mommy?" with "She's not your mommy. I'm your mommy." Most of the time, a birth parent will engage in this behavior, not as a malicious attack on the child, but rather as a way of expressing feelings of inadequacy and insecurity. The birth parent may also perceive the child as attacking the former whenever the child is pining for or expressing any allegiance whatsoever to the lost foster parents. Whatever the motive, such behavior severely compounds the child's trauma and grief.

As for the effects of counseling on a traumatized child, it is possible that counseling may alleviate some of the child's emotional pain, especially if there were collateral sessions with the birth parent to model appropriate responses to the child's behavior and verbalizations. However, if we wish to ensure that a child's arm grows healthy and straight after a healed fracture, it makes much more sense therapeutically to leave it alone rather than break it and then attempt to reset it. According to the present state of our knowledge of therapeutic outcomes, there is no reason to believe that counseling will have more than a palliative effect on a trauma of this magnitude inflicted upon the immature ego of a child.

IMPEACHING THE WITNESS BY PORTRAYING THE LATTER AS FAVORING THE MORE ADVANTAGED SIDE IN A "PARENTING CONTEST"

An essential difference between termination cases and divorce/custody cases is that the former is not a "parenting contest." Attorneys can discredit the expert psychologist by presenting the expert as formulating conclusions as to the child's best interests on the basis of which home would provide more material advantages, better schooling, greater security of extended family members, higher social status, and so forth. Even race can enter the picture in such situations. Consider the case of a sexually abused female child who was temporarily placed with a distant relative of the biological father who had molested her. The child's maternal aunt was also interested in caring for her and would allow some limited supervised contact with the severely dysfunctional mother who had neglected her daughter to the point where the child had been removed from the mother by the state and placed with the father. The father was Caucasian and the mother Latina, while the child could be taken either for a dark complected Caucasian or for Latina. One of the experts appearing on behalf of the paternal relatives argued that it would be much better for the child in the long run if she "were allowed to make it as a white child in the suburbs rather than as a Hispanic in the city." Needless to say, this recommendation caused the judge to invalidate the expert's entire testimony as biased.

Experts in termination cases should avoid even the appearance that a recommendation for permanent placement with foster parents is based on the perceived greater material or cultural advantages associated with the foster placement. A sample question and answer would be:

> "How much weight do you give the relative capacity of the birth parent and foster parent to provide advantages for the child in arriving at your recommendation for adoption?"

> "Unlike a divorce/custody case, the present case is not going to be decided as a parenting contest. I have already conceded that the birth parent has been rehabilitated to the point where she is able to provide at least marginally adequate parenting for this child. Therefore, the relative abilities of the foster parents and birth parents to rear this child with advantages do not receive any weight in my conclusions."

Of course, if the birth parent has not been rehabilitated to the point where there is a negligible risk for a recurrence of the neglect or abuse that occasioned the original placement, then the expert should argue the "parenting contest" issue vigorously, but from the point of view that placing the child with the birth parent would expose the child to further risk of harm, not merely to a relatively lower standard of parental care. In coming to such conclusions about birth parents, care must be taken to address only realistic situations of potential harm.

In the literature, there are some egregious examples of experts whose testimony has strayed from the scientifically, or clinically, defensible to the absurd. One such example is that of a psychiatric expert who testified in the well-known *Baby M.* case in which a working-class surrogate mother reneged on her agreement to surrender the child she bore for an infertile upper-middle-class New Jersey couple. The witness testified that, although the birth mother did play affectionately with the child, she allowed the child to play with pots and pans rather than give her educational toys or engage in structured activity with her and had therefore demonstrated an inferior parenting style to that of the contracting parents. The expert also criticized the birth mother's manner of playing patty-cake with the baby.

Clearly, such testimony does not rest on a firm scientific, or even clinical, basis; and expert witnesses of whatever mental health discipline would do well to avoid the appearance of judging the best interests of the child on the basis of their own personal lifestyle preferences. Testimony should be based on substantive issues involving parental competency, that is, whether a birth parent falls above or below the minimum acceptable standards of parenting adequacy, and the child's attachment profile. The fact that the foster/preadoptive parents may offer wonderful advantages that the birth parent could scarcely hope to achieve may be nice, but it is not an appropriate criterion for evaluating the case. Witnesses who rely on those factors will find themselves rather easily impeached by opposing counsel.

A RETURN TO THE BIRTH PARENTS WOULD AVERT FUTURE "ADOPTION KNOWLEDGE TRAUMA"

An attorney may attempt to minimize the significance of the separation trauma by introducing the issue of "adoption knowledge trauma," capitalizing on the attention given in the popular press to stories of adopted children who undergo psychological distress upon reaching adolescence. Such adoptees sometimes embark on a search for the birth parent and report that they feel different or incomplete without knowledge of the birth parent or a relationship with that person. By equating the two "traumas," an attorney may then argue that avoiding the trauma of losing the foster parents merely sets the child up for a traumatic reaction later in life when adoption issues surface. If counsel succeeds in equating these two noxious psychic events in the eyes of the trier of fact, then the separation/loss trauma argument fails as justification for allowing the child to remain permanently with the foster or preadoptive caretakers. Thus, it may be argued, if the child is to suffer trauma either way, the best course of action would be to get it over with now and at least spare the birth parents a major loss. A sample question of this type would be:

> "Aren't you just recommending the substitution of one trauma for another by testifying on behalf of adoption? Won't the child become damaged in adolescence when adoptees go through a crisis period and search for their birth parents?"

There are a number of studies and scholarly papers that describe pathological situations in adolescence connected with a self-perceived deficiency or inadequacy that often impels the individual to undertake a search for the birth parents as a means of healing this psychic lesion. However, there are three principal reasons that the "adolescent crisis" of many adoptees cannot be equated with the trauma of loss of the central parental love objects.

In the first place, the phenomena associated with adolescent adoptees' birth parent fantasies, reunion quests, identity issues, and so forth, are not traumatic in nature. Trauma refers to an emotional experience of such magnitude that the ego's coping mechanisms are overwhelmed and there is at least a very severe short-term reaction, typically accompanied by permanent psychic scars (Dyer, 1993; Moore & Fine, 1968). An adolescent's adopted status can certainly complicate the normal adolescent turmoil, identity crisis, and conflicts between mature striving for autonomy and regressive wishes for infantile reunion; however, these processes do not qualify as a trauma. Any additional turbulence caused by the adolescent's painful awareness of the fact of adoption will have been more than offset by the highly positive, therapeutic impact of a nurturing, stimulating environment with mature, competent, loving adoptive parents.

Second, the birth parent romance of adolescent adoptees is a variant of a more or less normal phenomenon in nonadopted adolescents. This period of development is typically one of great intrapsychic stress, as it is here that many infantile conflicts become remobilized (Blos, 1962). Of particular importance is the task of abandoning the incestuous tie to the parents and achieving a measure of separation and estrangement from them as a necessary step in psychic development (Moore & Fine, 1968).

Rosenberg and Horner (1991), in an article on birth parent "romances" in adopted children, note that the psychoanalytic literature abounds with references to the "family romance" in which children and adolescents develop fantasies of having been adopted by their birth parents and of actually being the child of another set of parents, usually of higher social status than the actual parents. These fantasized parents are imbued with the idealized characteristics that had previously been projected onto the birth parents, whose failure to live up to the child's idealized image of them provoked a disappointment reaction. Thus, this type of fantasy is a normal means of facilitating an adolescent's push for separation from parents and the search for nonincestuous objects. Rosenberg and Horner point out that adolescent adoptees may develop fantasies of having been the birth child of a third set of parents, other than the real birth parents and the adoptive parents, in order to be able to invest those figures with sufficient status and grandiosity to fulfill intrapsychic needs.

Finally, there is evidence that adolescent adoptees, contrary to popular belief, are no more likely to suffer from mental health or identity problems than are nonadopted adolescents. A study of 715 adoptive families reported in *The New York Times* ("Adopted Youths," 1994) found that the 12- to 18-year-old adoptees studied did not differ from nonadopted peers in self-esteem or identity development. The adopted adolescents reported slightly fewer signs of high-risk behavior, such as binge drinking and theft, and scored better on 16 indicators of well-being, such as friendships and academic achievement, than did a national sample of nonadopted adolescents.

This study contrasts with the findings of an older study (Kotsopoulos et al., 1988) that adopted children do present more often for psychological treatment than do nonadopted children. However, that study found that the adoptees did not present for therapy because they were troubled with anxiety or obsessive rumination concerning their adopted status but rather because of conduct disorders. The reasons for this are not clear, although the authors hypothesize that there are significant differences in the genetic backgrounds of adopted children as opposed to nonadopted children and that a variety of environmental factors, such as circumstances that facilitate or impede the development of affectionate bonds prior to and after adoption, identity issues, having two sets of parents, and disclosure of adoption, may contribute to the difference in treatment rates.

Triseliotis and Russell (1984) report that there are no differences between the mental health of older adoptees and that of the general population. A longitudinal study of adoptees by Elonen and Schwartz (1969) employing interviews with children, interviews with adoptive parents, and psychometric testing of children, all performed periodically through the child's 6th birthday and then after the child's 16th birthday, found that the adoptees did not have any poorer self-esteem or any greater incidence of psychological problems or delinquency than a matched group of nonadopted children.

"REBONDING" AS A PROPOSED STRATEGY

Some experts who testify on behalf of the birth parents recommend a process, sometimes informally termed "rebonding" but never identified as such in the professional literature, in which the child who is completely alienated from the birth parent is gradually exposed to greater and greater contact in the hope that an attachment to the birth parent will form. There is no clinical or empirical research evidence that such a procedure has any positive effect on a child.

One of the purposes of visitation between a child in foster care and the birth parents is to preserve the emotional tie between them. In many cases that reach the point of termination hearings, the tie has been completely severed, not through any fault of the child, but as a result of the failure of the birth parents to visit the child consistently during the critical preschool period. At that point, the child knows only that the foster parents are "Mommy and Daddy" and does not have any real conception of the status of the defendants as biological parents. In such a case, any protracted process of visitation with increasing frequency that progresses to home visits will merely increase the child's anxiety and insecurity over the permanency of the present foster placement.

It is also frequently argued that because a young child does not display anxiety, upset, or hostility during contacts with the birth parents, which typically increase in the months prior to trial, the child is "bonding" to them. It is essential to point out that there is no reason for the child to react negatively to birth parents so long as there are no memories of traumatic experiences during the time that the child resided with them and so long as the birth parents behave appropriately toward the child during visits. The child perceives the birth parents as interested, benign adults who come to share playtime and bring presents. As long as the visits proceed in this manner, they can be an enjoyable experience for the child.

However, as soon as the birth parents indicate to the child that they and not the foster parents are "Mommy and Daddy" and that the purpose of the contacts is to prepare the child to live with them permanently, each visit will become agony for the child. There will be endless questions such as, "Why are Mommy and Daddy going to give me away?", or "Will I be able to go home again after the caseworker takes me downtown for this visit?", or "What did I do to make Mommy and Daddy not want me anymore?" A child in such circumstances typically lives in a state of fear and apprehension. The child's sense of basic trust and normal optimism and enthusiasm very quickly erode; and instead of forming a new attachment to the birth parents, the child suffers a generalized impairment of the capacity to trust adults. These opinions are based on clinical experience with a few cases in which such measures have been inflicted on children.

THE EXPERT'S CONCLUSIONS REST ON A NARROW AND BIASED THEORETICAL BASE CONTRADICTED BY OTHER THEORIES

Attorneys who have not acquainted themselves with the state of theory in this area, especially those who are vaguely aware that the "psychological parenting theory" of Goldstein et al. (1979) has its detractors, may attempt to elicit a concession that there are other valid, competing theories that contradict attachment theory. In actual fact, there is no other well-articulated theory or systematized body of thought that refutes attachment theory. Nor is attachment theory a narrow psychoanalytically biased school of thought, as attorneys often like to portray it. A sample question of this type might be:

> "Isn't attachment theory, or bonding theory, only one school of thought among many conflicting views and doesn't it have a psychoanalytic bias?"

In the first place, John Bowlby, the founder of attachment theory, considered himself to be an ethologist and not a psychoanalyst. In the second place, conclusions as to psychic harm associated with removal of young children from caretakers to whom they are attached do not rest exclusively on attachment theory but are also based on ego psychological theory and substantial empirical support from both statistical and clinical studies. Finally, there is no psychological school of thought that refutes the conclusion that a preschool child's loss of the central parental love objects will cause severe harm to that child's ego development. Behavioral theories would predict severe harm associated with the precipitous loss of major reinforcement systems that result in a breakdown of the child's capacity for adaptive responding. Furthermore, loss of reinforcement is associated with the anhedonia and hopelessness of depression. It should be noted that behavioral or learning theories are silent on the question of intrapsychic dynamics.

Cognitive theories, with their stress on information processing and rational "self-talk" as determinants of behavior and emotional states, would predict severe harm to result from the young child's cognitive processing of events. As noted previously, young children have a tendency to interpret reality in egocentric terms. This is illustrated by the nearly universal phenomenon in divorce situations in which children attribute the breakup of the parents' marriage to their own misbehavior. Thus, cognitive theories would focus on the way in which children incorrectly attribute the loss of loved parental figures to their own unworthiness, misbehavior, or intrinsic unloveability. Because cognitive patterns determine emotion and behavior, such theories would view children with these eroneous or negative ideas as being crippled in their processing of information concerning future intimate relationships and in their expectations as to whether they will be valued and accepted by others in future interactions in many spheres of life. Finally, the cognition that any form of security can be abruptly withdrawn predisposes children to anxious rumination and a sense of hopelessness and powerlessness. (Theoretical issues relating to separation and loss are reviewed in Chapter 8.)

COMPARISON WITH THE SITUATION OF CHILDREN IN DIVORCE/CHILD CUSTODY CASES

Not all attorneys who represent birth parents are lacking in experience in family court matters. Occasionally, birth parents in termination actions will secure private representation by a matrimonial attorney, or a matrimonial attorney will happen to be assigned as pro bono counsel in the case. Attorneys experienced in child custody matters in the context of divorce actions may attempt to undermine the credibility of experts' prediction of harm associated with a removal by citing the common occurrence in family court of the ordering of a change of custody from one birth parent to another. Often, apart from minor adjustment difficulties, the child who has experienced such a transfer appears to have weathered it well. This can be an extremely powerful argument, especially in the case of family court judges whose caseload is predominantly matrimonial matters and who do not have extensive experience with termination of parental rights. An element of cognitive dissonance enters in here because judges may naively equate the situation of (1) removing a long-term foster child from caretakers to whom that child has bonded with the situation of (2) transferring a child from the residence of one divorced parent to the other, and judges will therefore tend to minimize the prospect of harm associated with the former because they have ordered the latter on so many occasions without apparent ill effect.

QUESTION: "You have described truly horrifying consequences allegedly flowing from the act of separating a young child from caretakers to whom that child has become attached. Yet, we see every day in this Family Court instances of children who are moved by order of the Court from one parent to another in the course of divorce/custody litigation without the children's suffering the dire consequences that you confidently predict. To be sure, any child of divorce will suffer the typical conflicts reported in the literature; but in dealing with hundreds upon hundreds of instances in which young children are separated from their custodial parents because the court orders a custody transfer, divorce attorneys and family part judges do not see the type of severe damage that you predict."

ANSWER: "This is merely another instance in which confusion arises from the indiscriminate lumping together of events that are dramatically different in their impact on young children's development. Once again, when a child is removed from foster parents to whom that child has become attached and when there is not a prior relationship with the birth parents to whom that child is being returned, the child suffers an absolute loss of the central parental love objects, which relationship, to foster parents, is the primary factor in the development of the sense of self; basic trust of others; capacity for emotional intimacy; regulation of mood, impulse, and behavior; and the background feeling of safety that makes the world a reasonably manageable place rather than a hostile, fear-provoking gauntlet through which a burdened ego must pass. This situation is entirely different from that of the young child who has formed an attachment to both parents and suffers the disruption of being transferred from one home to the other, but with continuing contact with the former custodial parent. A child of divorce who is bounced between Mommy and Daddy still has either Mommy or Daddy at any given time; and in the typical situation, the separation from the former custodial parent is not a loss of that parent because there is still visitation."

Goldstein et al. (1979) did the field an enormous disservice by equating a child's separation from foster parents, with whom the child has bonded, with a child's separation from a birth parent in a custody case, thereby provoking a backlash against any suggestion that separations inflict profound psychological damage on children. Witnesses need to be alert to attempts to discredit findings regarding the loss of the central parental love objects by equating that situation with divorce/custody studies, general judicial experience with divorce/custody cases, or brief separations. Sometimes the work of Robertson (1989), as cited in Bowlby (1988), on children's reactions to hospitalizations of brief stays in foster care, while an intact and competent parent undergoes some hospital procedure, is cited as proving that the effects of any loss are only short term. Occasionally expert psychologist witnesses will disingenuously mix up all these situations and come up with a general conclusion that there will be no long-term harm.

THE RESILIENT CHILD

Some experts in termination cases tend to seize upon the terms "resilient child" and "invulnerable child" that have appeared in the developmental literature, offering the simplistic opinion that "children are resilient." This impression creates the delusion that if a child suffers the loss of his or her central parental love objects at a critical developmental stage, the child "will get over it." The reaction of many judges at all levels of the judicial system to this type of testimony is that it demonstrates that there are two schools of thought on the matter, with some experts predicting severe harm and other experts predicting that the child will suffer only a short-term reaction and will then rebound into psychological health, perhaps with the assistance of counseling. Rarely do written opinions in termination of parental rights cases even acknowledge the enormous scientific and clinical literature supporting the prediction of long-term harm to a child who undergoes this type of traumatic loss, and even less frequently do written opinions note that predictions of "resilience" do not find any significant support in the psychological and psychiatric literature. Indeed, it is somewhat common to encounter citations of legal articles that claim that experts rely to an excessive degree on "bonding theory" in making predictions of harm; however, the legal articles cited do not contain any references to empirical studies in support of the "resiliency" position (see, e.g., Davis, 1987). (The literature on resiliency and invulnerability is reviewed in Chapter 9.)

QUESTION: "You have encountered the terms 'resilient child' and 'invulnerable child' in the literature. Is it not true that the child in this case may indeed be resilient to the effects of separation and thus be spared the dire consequences that you predict?"

ANSWER: "There has been an unfortunate confusion regarding the terms 'invulnerable child' and 'resilient child.' This confusion is found primarily in courtrooms and does not seem to exist in the original studies that are frequently misquoted in support of the no-harm theory. Attachment security has been found to be the basis for children's resilience. Traumatic loss is the most reliable way to insure that a particular child will not have psychological resiliency."

CHAPTER 12

Illustrative Cases I

CASE 1: FAILED ADOPTION OF A PSEUDO-SELF-SUFFICIENT OLDER FOSTER CHILD

Dee-Dee's early memories of her chaotic parental home are a jumble of images, many of them associated with fear, upset, and infantile rage. Indeed, her home life during the brief period in which she resided with her birth parents was not the type of experience that would form the kind of treasured early childhood memories that most persons can recall. Dee-Dee's father, a hardworking but borderline retarded mason's helper, was a passive and ineffectual figure in the home. He was dominated by Dee-Dee's psychotic mother, who intimidated the entire family into submission by her periodic rages. She often attacked her much larger husband and physically and emotionally abused her five preschool children, of whom Dee-Dee was the eldest girl.

For a long time, the birth parents demonstrated just enough pseudocompliance with the rehabilitative efforts of caseworkers that the parents were deemed viable caretakers for their children, who were allowed to remain in the home. But at age 3 years, Dee-Dee presented at a hospital emergency room with a spiral fracture of the arm and a high temperature. She was diagnosed as having battered child syndrome, and at that point Dee-Dee and her siblings were rescued from a dangerous home environment by the state. The children were kept in placement for 6 months, after which time the birth parents were judged to have displayed enough progress that they could resume caring for their children again.

But when Dee-Dee returned home to her birth parents, they noticed that her behavior toward them had changed significantly. Whereas she had affectionately called them "Mommy" and Daddy" before her removal, she now addressed them as "Hey you" and had to be told by her younger sister that they were her mother and father. She had also developed eating and sleeping problems and regressed to bedwetting, which she had not displayed prior to that, even with the chronic abuse she was undergoing at home. The parents expressed concern as to whether Dee-Dee might have been brainwashed or given some medication in the foster home that would cause her to behave this way.

Prior to her removal and placement in foster care there had been one other separation, a hospital stay of several days at age 2 years and 8 months for treatment of a medical condition unrelated to abuse. It had not been possible for her mother to spend much time with Dee-Dee during that period because her mother had to care for the younger children at home and preschool visitors were not allowed on the children's ward. (See Chapter 9 for a discussion of the Robertsons' research on children admitted to British hospitals.)

A brief course of therapy involving both parents and Dee-Dee was unsuccessful, and the pathological family interaction continued. Eventually, the children were removed again and placed into foster care because of neglect. Dee-Dee was reunited with her former foster mother and was never to return home.

Originally, family reunification had been the case goal for this second placement as well. However, after her children were taken away from her a second time, the birth mother deteriorated to the point where she flatly refused to cooperate and threatened workers with physical harm unless her children were immediately restored to her. She refused to visit any of the children, who had been placed in three separate foster homes, and prevented her husband from doing so. Five years after the second removal, the birth parents' rights to all of the children were terminated, freeing them for adoption.

Dee-Dee, now age 8, was placed with a preadoptive parent who began her relationship with the child by visiting her in a foster home. Ms. Q. was a 45-year-old unmarried sales manager who had spent her early adult life concentrating on her career and who was now looking to adopt a school-age child. Ms. Q. fell in love with Dee-Dee during her first visit to the child's foster home. Ms. Q. was captivated by Dee-Dee's large dark eyes and winning smile, as well as touched by the image of this thin, emotionally deprived little girl who had reached the age of 8 without a real mother in her life. Ms. Q. had been warned by the child protective services workers that Dee-Dee had displayed behavior problems in the past, but Ms. Q. attributed this behavior to the fact that this child had been with temporary foster parents who were not very interested in her. Ms. Q. was eager for the adoption process to get under way as quickly as possible.

The first step of the trial period involved visits by Ms. Q. in which she would take Dee-Dee out of the foster home for an afternoon and return her to the home at night. Ms. Q. was careful not to overwhelm the child by prematurely introducing a discussion of adoption, although she did respond truthfully to Dee-Dee's occasional questions on this subject. The day visits were followed by five very successful weekend visits in which Ms. Q. shared a number of rewarding experiences with the child that included quiet time at home where Dee-Dee would play with new toys or would play a board game with Ms. Q. It was during these weekend visits that Ms. Q. discussed more fully with Dee-Dee the subject of adoption and explicitly told her that the purpose of the visits was to prepare Dee-Dee to live with Ms. Q. permanently.

Dee-Dee responded happily to this information and expressed an eagerness to live with Ms. Q. as her daughter and to meet the rest of her adoptive mother's family. In the weeks that followed, Dee-Dee met Ms. Q.'s siblings, who were just as taken with this attractive little girl as Ms. Q. was herself. Dee-Dee began to have weekend visits during which she slept in her own room in the adoptive mother's house surrounded by lots of new toys. The child protective services worker assigned to Dee-Dee's case at that time worked with Dee-Dee in preparing a "life book" with pictures and descriptions of the birth parents and the child's siblings. The adoptive mother agreed to an informal arrangement in which she would get together with the adoptive mothers of the other four children so that they could have sibling visits periodically.

The final transfer of custody occurred, and Dee-Dee was placed with Ms. Q., with the first 2 months considered as a trial period. The first week of the placement passed splendidly. Dee-Dee was placed in a second-grade class in Ms. Q.'s local school district, and arrangements were made for an after-school program to provide coverage until Ms. Q. returned home from work. It was during this week that the adoptive mother reassured Dee-Dee that she would never leave her and that she loved her just as though she were her own daughter. Dee-Dee's affectionate responses to her during this honeymoon period delighted Ms. Q., confirming for her the correctness of her decision to reach out to a needy child with healing parental love.

By the time the second week of the placement arrived, the honeymoon was over. Dee-Dee began to display the controlling, demanding behavior that Ms. Q. had been warned of by the social workers. It came under the heading of "testing the limits," Ms. Q. had been told, and was a natural, expectable phenomenon associated with adoptive placement of a child who had been in foster care for a long time. Ms. Q. was ready. She responded with tolerance, understanding, and equanimity, while not relaxing her rules or behavioral expectations of Dee-Dee. Furthermore, on the advice of the social workers who had counseled Ms. Q. concerning the adoption, Ms. Q. instituted a behavioral "time out" procedure in which she managed to defuse several incidents by sending the child to her room for brief periods of time.

This technique produced a brief improvement in the child's behavior, leading Ms. Q. to conclude that she had turned around a potentially troublesome behavior pattern by following the advice of professionals. This result gave her a sense of mastery and encouragement that she could begin the task of parenting a very needy child without too much difficulty.

The succeeding weeks saw a complete deterioration of Dee-Dee's behavior to a state of incorrigibility. She attacked her adoptive mother in a variety of ways, including biting her, throwing things at her, locking her out of the house, and menacing her with a knife. By the time this distraught parent appeared at a therapist's office, she was approaching the breaking point, troubled with angry feelings toward the child and guilty over her failure to help Dee-Dee adjust to her home. Ms. Q. was also afraid of further physical attacks by Dee-Dee.

A few sessions with Dee-Dee alone and conjointly with the adoptive mother disclosed a hopeless situation, with Ms. Q.'s guilt being the only factor keeping the placement going. Dee-Dee's behavior proved completely refractory to a variety of behavioral and counseling interventions, and the adoptive mother was advised that guilt was not a satisfactory basis for perpetuating a relationship that had no chance of success. Dee-Dee was returned to foster care.

The failure of this adoption, and particularly this child's inability to adjust, can be traced to specific elements of her history. Prior to entering Ms. Q.'s home, Dee-Dee had been in three separate foster placements, with a brief return to the birth parents that separated the child's stay in the first and second foster homes. The timing and the duration of the first separation, which lasted 6 months when the child was 3 years old, produced a profound alteration in this child's pattern of attachments, weakening her already fragile and conflicted emotional connection to the birth parents to the point where she was no longer bonded to them. When she returned to foster care, her capacity to form attachments to caretakers was weakened and subsequently became further weakened by the transfer from one foster home to another. From nearly age 4 to age 8, this child did not fully accept any adult in a parental role. As far as the evolution of her emotional life was concerned, she was on her own.

By the time she entered Ms. Q.'s home, Dee-Dee had become very firmly entrenched in a position of pseudo-self-sufficiency and guarded hypervigilance. She had convinced herself that she was intrinsically unlikable and unlovable vis-à-vis any parental surrogate. Her capacity to form a relationship of trust and dependency with an adult, or to truly grow to love a mother or father surrogate, had been very seriously compromised by her history of repeated separations and disappointments in love objects.

It is inconceivable to most people that any child could possibly resist the security of a loving, caring, concerned parent in favor of the isolation and uncertainties of foster care. Indeed, no child with a normally developed ego would make that choice; humans thrive on attachment, acceptance, nurturance, approval, and affection. Only a child with significant defects in ego formation would opt to remain in a state of isolation and alienation. For such a child, the offer of intimacy carries an enormous threat: that of disappointment and abandonment that eventually produces a powerful network of defenses against the experience of love. For such a child, the state of pseudo-self-sufficient alienation is a safe one. It is safe because it is familiar, representing the status quo of the child's adjustment and pattern of adaptation to the uncertainties of interpersonal reality. At least in such a case, the child knows what he or she has and can derive self-comforting from remaining free of dangerous emotional involvement, directing pity toward the suffering, deprived self and directing contempt and hostility toward the rest of the interpersonal world.

This strategy offers protection against the crushing emptiness that follows rejection by yet another caretaker. There is safety in the familiar. Children in this position very often display aggressive, destructive behavior for the unconscious purpose of proving to themselves that the new caretaker really does not want them and is merely lying to them for some selfish purpose. When the proof is finally achieved, at the point where the child's disturbed behavior provokes a disruption of the adoptive placement, there is a feeling of relief, mastery, and triumph. This serves to reinforce the child's belief that guardedness and keeping others at a distance, except in situations where the child can exert total control, is the only viable means of self-protection. Thus, in spite of Ms. Q.'s genuine care and concern for Dee-Dee, and in spite of Ms. Q.'s growing love for the child, the adoption was doomed by a life history that robbed the child of the capacity to allow the love of another human being to touch her.

CASE 2: AN OLDER FOSTER CHILD ATTACHED TO HIS BIRTH FATHER

In contrast to Dee-Dee's complete alienation from her birth parents and subsequent inability to accept any adult in the parental role, there are children in the foster care system who are unable to bond with foster parents because of prior attachments. Ten-year-old Kenny is an example of this latter class of children. Kenny's mother was a drug abuser whose lifestyle was extremely unstable. His birth father, Mr. B., also drug involved, lived with the family until Kenny was 1 year old. Unlike many such fathers, who simply abandon their children upon terminating their relationship with the biological mother, Mr. B. actively sought to preserve his tie to his son.

Mr. B. was extremely emotionally needy and his experiences with members of his own family had been nothing but disappointments. Although he had had several minor brushes with the legal system, Mr. B. was not an antisocial personality. Rather, he was a dependent, anxious, mildly depressive person who worked hard at jobs when he was employed and who experienced transient lapses into nonviolent criminal behavior whenever he slipped back into drug abuse.

Kenny appeared to look up to his birth father, who played with the boy for endless hours during periods when the father was home and out of work. When the father visited his son after the father's separation from Kenny's birth mother, the father would take his son to the park, buy him toys and clothes, and shower loving attention upon him. Kenny was firmly established as the one bright spot in his father's life, which was otherwise marred by family alienation, periodic drug abuse, minor arrests, and general instability.

When Kenny's mother became too impaired by drug abuse to care for him, the local child protective services awarded custody to his father, who had stabilized to a significant degree in his adaptation to life. Kenny resided with his father from age 2 to age 7 years. Most of the time, Kenny was adequately cared for; however, there were periods when his father relapsed into drug abuse and physically neglected him. Even during these periods, however, this affectionate and enthusiastic child felt that his father loved him.

Kenny was placed into foster care at age 7 after his father was arrested on a drug possession charge. Kenny was placed with the W. family, consisting of a foster mother and father and their two birth children, who were close in age to Kenny. A sweet and adaptable child, Kenny adjusted well to his foster home. At the time of his placement into foster care, he was identified as perceptually impaired, possibly as a result of intrauterine exposure to drugs, and was placed in a special education program. In addition, at the time of his placement, Kenny displayed mild depressive symptoms that were attributable to the separation from his father.

Kenny's birth father visited his son faithfully when Kenny was placed into foster care. After a period of visitation in the social services office, the birth father was granted visitation at his home. Again, he took Kenny to the park and other interesting places, buying him clothes and toys. It began to look as though Kenny would be returned to his birth father eventually since the father remained stable, demonstrated unwavering concern for the child, and related appropriately to his son during visits. This progress came to an abrupt halt when the birth father was rearrested for drug-related offenses and was sentenced to a 1-year jail term.

At this point, the case goal changed from family reunification to foster home adoption since the W.s had become attached to Kenny and wanted to keep him permanently. The agency's position was that allowing this boy to remain indefinitely in the limbo of foster care would have a deleterious effect on his sense of identity and overall personality development. When asked about the issue of adoption by his therapist, Kenny, who had an imperfect understanding of this concept, replied that he wished to be adopted by Mr. and Ms. W.

There was no contact between Kenny and his father during the 1-year period of the birth father's incarceration. Kenny was not encouraged by his foster parents to write to his father, nor did the father's depressed spirits and sense of having failed the child allow him to reach out to contact his son either by telephone or letter.

Upon his release from prison, Kenny's birth father requested a resumption of visits. Although the child protective services opposed this on the basis of the revised case goal of adoption, the court granted the father's request. Kenny was delighted to see his father again and responded affirmatively when asked if he would like to come back home some day. Visitation with the father continued on a monthly basis for approximately a year and a half until the father was rearrested. At that point, the child protective services moved aggressively on its complaint for guardianship to permit adoption by the foster parents.

The birth father was ready to sign a surrender of his parental rights after signing a plea bargain that stipulated 4 years of jail time before parole eligibility. However, he changed his mind when Kenny, who had been brought to the county jail to see him for a bonding evaluation, stated that he loved his birth father and refused to be adopted by his foster parents, even though they had been very nice to him. When the birth father attempted to change Kenny's mind by telling him that it would be at least 4 years before his son could live with him again and that he would be grown up by that time, Kenny emphatically replied, "I'll wait!"

In this second situation, we see the failure of a child to form an exclusive attachment to foster parents, but for dramatically different reasons from those underlying the failure of Dee-Dee's adoption. Whereas in Dee-Dee's case the child's very capacity to form attachments was seriously compromised, with Kenny the enduring attachment to a dysfunctional parent overshadowed any other connection in the child's life. Kenny's psychological health depended to a significant extent upon the preservation of his inner mental image of the loved parent. Adoption by the foster family, as it was presented to him, meant making him a part of their family as though he were their own biological child. It would have ended all contact with the birth father at least until Kenny's adolescence, and it would have forced Kenny to take on the foster family's surname. These factors posed an enormous threat to Kenny's deep emotional connection to his father as his primary love object and to his identity as his father's son.

Kenny resisted being assimilated into a family that, despite years of foster care in which he received love and nurturance, was still alien in some respects. The profound tie formed in infancy exerted a powerful effect on this child. The parent's furnishing a child with a stable, positively valued internalized image as a love object is the most precious gift that the parent can bestow. A good parental object enables the child to maintain adequate self-esteem, sense of personal identity, and the capacity to form emotional connections of some depth with new figures later in life. Mr. B., despite his periodic entanglements with the law, had provided his son with such a psychological foundation.

Kenny fiercely defended his tie to this parental love object by resisting the proposed adoption. In the end, long-term foster care with the same family attended to the child's physical and emotional needs, while his deeper psychological needs, having to do with primary attachments and identifications, were spared the threat associated with becoming completely absorbed into another family through adoption. Kenny is an example of the type of older foster child, discussed in Bush and Goldman (1982), for whom adoption, as opposed to foster care status, represents a loss of the birth parent that overshadows the potential gain in security and stability.

CASE 3: A MENTALLY HANDICAPPED BIRTH MOTHER WITH A SEVERELY ASTHMATIC CHILD

This is a summary of *In the Matter of the Guardianship of S. C.* (1991). In this case, a mentally handicapped young woman, L. C., with marginal community adjustment gave birth to a child with medical problems, leading to the child's placement into foster care directly from the hospital. Some time later, the child, S. C., was diagnosed with very severe asthma that required a high degree of vigilance on the part of the caretaker, who needed to be alert to changes in the clinical picture and to be able to respond to these changes by administering the proper medication or, if necessary, transporting the child to a hospital emergency room for treatment. I became involved with the case as the court's independent expert, with the consent of both the deputy attorney general and the defense attorney. At a later point in the case, however, the defense engaged two additional experts, a psychologist and a pediatrician/allergist.

Under the legislative and judicial mandates in New Jersey to protect the child's best interest as far as practicable by providing welfare services to support and maintain the integrity of the biological family as a living unit, the New Jersey Division of Youth and Family Services expended great efforts in the direction of reunification. From July 1987 to January 1989, the Division worked with the birth mother, L. C., under a signed service agreement, outlining tasks and goals and coordinating a network of resources to assist the birth mother. L. C. was given medical training in managing her daughter's asthma and was placed with the Association for the Advancement of the Mentally Handicapped. She was also given parenting skills classes.

From the time of S. C.'s birth until the time of trial on September 1989, L. C. had lived at 13 different locations and had held five different jobs. She had been unemployed since November 1988. She had been furnished a rent-free apartment; assistance in securing employment; free medical care; paid food, electric, and heating bills; and a clothing and telephone allowance at the supervised residence run by the Association to which she was referred by the Division of Youth and Family Services. L. C. left this facility in order to move in with her boyfriend, a married man, whom she proposed as a potential coparent for S. C. if the child were returned to her.

The parental rights of the birth mother were terminated at trial on the basis of her limitations coupled with the child's extensive medical needs. The birth mother, who was represented by the Community Health Law Project, an advocacy group for the mentally disabled, appealed the termination by arguing that, among other grounds for reversal, the state had not met its burden of proving by clear and convincing evidence that L. C. should lose custody of her daughter. An interesting complication in the case was that, prior to the termination hearing, the foster mother died, leaving the minor S. C. in the care of the foster father as a single parent.

The case turned on three considerations: (1) the birth mother's characterological problems as they affected her capacity to provide adequate nurturance and structure for a young child; (2) the birth mother's cognitive and attentional capacities and degree of responsibility as they affected her ability to administer the appropriate medications to this child, be alert to changes in the child's clinical picture, and respond accordingly; and (3) the impact on the child of being removed from the home of her foster father, as such removal might affect both the child's psychological development and physical condition.

The appellate court noted that S. C. suffered from a degree of asthma that was life threatening and that she required constant and careful monitoring to ensure her survival. A medical expert for the state, who was Director of Pediatric Pulmonology at Newark Children's Hospital, labeled the child's asthmatic condition "extreme." A pediatrician and allergist who also testified at the trial, stated that the child was a severe asthmatic who could quickly go into respiratory failure, requiring a tube to be inserted for ventilation during an emergency room admission. This expert continued as follows:

> On such a child it is absolutely critical that the child be followed with the utmost care, get all the appropriate medications, and even that she—she still is a powder keg that has to be taken care of by someone who will recognize when the asthma is of such a state that more [medication] is required.

The court noted that S. C.'s medication regimen at that time consisted of a bronchial dilator, Somophyllin, four times daily; anti-nebulized medications, Ventolin and Intal, every 6 to 8 hours; an atopical steroid called Azmacort, every 6 hours; and bursts of Prednisone, depending on the child's clinical condition. The court also noted the necessity of precise administration of these medications, adding that undermedication is the major cause of asthma mortality. Furthermore, the court noted that the caretaker of this child must be alert to new trigger factors and warning signs because the physician relies heavily on information supplied by the caretaker. The first medical expert testified the following:

> There are a lot of therapeutic options in the management of asthma. And it needs a good team approach between the mother or the caretaker and the doctor. We have—she must learn to characterize the child to us. She must give us a profile of the child. The reason is because our—a lot of our decisions will depend on that.

It is noteworthy that the court did not devote a great deal of attention to L. C.'s personality and adjustment problems as factors justifying the termination; however, the court did note that all experts who testified in the case, with the exception of the director of the center for handicapped parents and their children where L. C.

was housed for a while, agreed that she was incapable of caring for S. C. independently. The primary issues treated in the opinion of the appellate court involved the birth parent's capacity to attend to her daughter's complex medical care requirements and the impact on the child's mental health and personality development of a removal from the foster father to whom she had become attached.

The birth mother had spent 4 years at Arthur Brisbane Child Treatment Center as a child, where she was treated for psychiatric problems. In regard to the subject's personality functioning, I testified:

> Based on my administration of these techniques, it is my opinion that [L. C.] suffers from a degree of personality immaturity that would preclude her being able to provide adequate parenting to a young child in terms of consistent attunement, consistent responsibility, consistent attentiveness to a young child's needs. In fact, [L. C.] tends to see herself as being in the role of a dependent child in relation to other people and that this seems to be the way in which she maintains a positively valued self-image, by clinging to this safe position of being a dependent child in relation to the adults who represent parent figures.

Another psychologist, who was Chief Senior Clinician at a hospital-based family clinic, also examined the defendant. The psychologist found that L. C. suffered from generalized anxiety disorder and possibly from some form of paranoid disorder. The psychologist also noted that L. C. presented some borderline personality features, including an inability to develop relationships, inability to plan, and an unstable living situation.

The area on which the appellate opinion focused most strongly was that of L. C.'s incapacity to administer the proper amounts of medication to the child or to pick up on changes in the child's clinical picture that would signal an impending medical crisis of life-threatening proportions. My psychological testing of this client disclosed borderline retarded intellectual functioning. A learning disability evaluation from the Brisbane facility indicated that as a child L. C. had severe learning problems in the areas of auditory association, visual memory, and auditory memory. Concerning these results, I testified the following at the trial:

> These problems were never satisfactorily addressed as far as I have been able to determine from my review of the records. That is to say that

> [L. C.] never had any kind of specific therapy or other treatment with a learning consultant to remediate these particular specific learning disabilities.

The Chief Senior Clinician at the hospital-based program who examined L. C. also felt that L. C. was too cognitively limited to parent this child adequately. Even L. C.'s expert, a psychologist in private practice, opined that her intelligence test results showed a deficit that would hinder L. C. from caring properly for S. C. without supervision. The defense expert testified the following:

> If [L. C.] has [S. C.], the minimal supervision that I would suggest would be 2 hours a day of direct one-to-one supervision from a—some type of staff individual that's involved and, in addition, someone that's on call 24 hours a day that either—that lives in either the apartment next door or within 5 minutes at the most away due to S. C.'s medical condition.

Beyond the general issue of L. C.'s intellectual limitation, the experts in the case offered specific testimony as to how this impairment would prevent L. C. from being able to manage S. C.'s medication needs. Regarding L. C.'s response to training in monitoring her daughter's breathing, a registered nurse testified for the state as follows:

> When we got to the aero chamber and [L. C.] didn't know how to count the breaths, I was shocked. Because with asthma—breathing—that's the name of the game. Breathing—how the child is breathing. Is the child wheezing? Is it labored breathing? Is it easy breathing? That's the basis of the whole thing. That's the basis of the child's survival . . . being able to breathe easily and knowing how to assess the breath sounds and all of this.
>
> * * *
>
> So that when that question came up, How mechanically do I count the breaths? in my mind, I thought, well, How—how deep is the lack of knowledge that I'm working with?

I opined that L. C.'s borderline intellectual functioning, coupled with her pattern of irresponsibility, would prove life threatening for S. C. if the child's medication management were entrusted to the birth mother. My testimony on that issue was extensively quoted in the appellate court's opinion:

> In my opinion, [L. C.] would probably be able to perceive visual cues from the environment with a substantial degree of accuracy. But in terms of interpreting the significance of those cues as they dictate various courses of action . . . she lacks a substantial capacity to do this.
>
> * * *
>
> It is my understanding of the tasks involved in [S. C.'s] medical care that this child is extremely fragile and requires a high degree of vigilance on the part of the caretaker to recognize the various symptoms of her disorder that could signal a life-threatening asthmatic attack. This child's situation, I understand, varies in terms of the care that is required, the specific procedures that are required to address different kinds of emergencies; and in order to manage such a child, the caretaker would have to be sensitive to the variety of symptoms that appear and would have to have an adequate understanding of the implications of each particular constellation of symptoms in terms of the particular intervention that would be required.
>
> * * *
>
> In my opinion, [L. C.] would not be able to accurately report her daughter's condition to a physician who has been treating her unless that physician were extremely knowledgeable about [S. C.'s] particular circumstances and was able to ask very specific questions designed to elicit particular information that was related to the presence or absence of any particular physical condition and which would dictate some particular form of intervention.
>
> * * *
>
> The fact that [L. C.] has a deficiency in retaining learned information would suggest that she would have a great deal of difficulty in implementing any kind of new medical procedures that she might be shown for managing [S. C.'s] care.
>
> * * *
>
> The inability to retain material and to rely specifically on—on rote memory which tends to be deficient would cause somebody not to be able to adjust to slight variations in procedures, and I understand that such variations are required in administering the—the medication that [S. C.] is on according to various circumstances that present themselves with her physical symptoms.

The final issue that the court treated at length in its opinion was that of S. C.'s attachment to the foster father. Both I, as the court's independent expert, and the defense expert found that S. C. had formed a strong bond with her foster family. Both experts agreed that the removal of this child from her foster home would be detrimental to the child. Both experts agreed that if removed from the foster family, S. C. would suffer a short-term reaction consisting of depression, crying, temper tantrums, loss of appetite, and regression. Both agreed that if the problems were not handled quickly and sensitively that they would become chronic. There was significant disagreement, however, over the extent and duration of the harm associated with a removal. I testified that S. C.'s personality development would be adversely affected and that a removal from the foster family to whom she had become attached would injure her capacity for basic trust, optimism, and self-esteem and would prevent her from having the ability to form stable relationships. The defense expert did not predict long-term harm of this type. Both experts agreed that the birth mother had trouble comprehending the trauma that S. C. would suffer if removed from the foster home and that this fact would make it more difficult for L. C. to cope with S. C.'s emotional crisis. It was also undisputed that these emotional consequences would place S. C. at increased risk for exacerbation of her asthmatic condition. Regarding the issue of psychological harm associated with the loss of the child's primary attachment figure, the court wrote the following:

> S. C. has been in foster care since birth and has been with her current foster family since she was 4 months old. Both Dr. Dyer and Dr. Bruey [expert psychologist for the defense] testified that S. C. has a strong and powerful bond with her foster family. S. C. has formed strong ties of emotion, love, and dependence with her foster family. Foster care has continued for such an extended period of time that a parent–child relationship has been created, albeit not one based upon blood but upon love, affection and need. Thus, the trial court properly concluded that either the sudden or gradual disruption of that relationship would damage S. C. Nothing in New Jersey's statutory scheme requires the attempted creation of a new psychological relationship with the natural mother at the cost of a child's present well-being in an established home in which the child is happy and flourishing.

In regard to the complication in this case created by the death of the foster mother, the defense felt that this circumstance cast the litigation in a new light and that the court should view the issues less as a typical termination matter and more as a divorce-related child custody case. As noted in Chapter 11, this equation of termination of parental rights and divorce/custody cases is a common tactic among attorneys representing birth parents. It is rarely successful, as was the case in S. C. The appellate court wrote the following:

> L. C. suggests that because the foster mother is now dead that she and S. C.'s foster father stand in relation to S. C. in the same posture as divorced parents stand in relation to their children. L. C. views herself as the noncustodial parent and asserts that the court would not "think of terminating the visitation rights of a divorced, noncustodial parent except upon finding behavior far more distressing than can be attributed to L. C." L. C. contends that parental rights are divisible into rights of custody and visitation and an inability to exercise one right does not preclude exercise of the others. We disagree. What L. C. fails to recognize is that this is not a divorce case where visitation is almost invariably granted to the noncustodial spouse. This is a case for termination of parental rights.

The court also addressed the question of who was responsible for payment of the defense experts. The court cited *Ake v. Oklahoma* (1985) in which it was ruled that an indigent defendant does not have a constitutional right to choose a psychiatrist or to receive funds to hire one independently. The court noted that I was initially retained as the court's independent expert with the consent of both parties, to be paid by the New Jersey Division of Youth and Family Services. The court also noted that the Community Health Law Project, representing the defendant, was especially funded to litigate cases such as this and that it therefore bore the financial burden and responsibility to pay counsel and necessary expert fees.

It should be noted that the present situation in family courts in New Jersey is different. Subsequent to the S. C. ruling, there was a court decision that ordered the state to pay for experts hired by the defense, so long as these experts were chosen from an approved list of individuals who were under contract to provide examinations for the state and agreed to accept the specified contract rate when working for the defense. Although defendants are thus allowed access to their own experts through this agreement, such access is not unlimited. If the defense attorney is not satisfied with the results of the expert evaluation, any additional experts that the defense might choose to engage will be at the defendant's own expense. The court does not expect the state to fund defense attorneys' expert shopping and sees no violation of the defendant's due process inherent in this limitation.

CASE 4: PSYCHOLOGICAL AND BONDING ASSESSMENTS OF A CHRONIC PSYCHIATRIC PATIENT AND HER CHILDREN

Brianna was first referred to the New Jersey Division of Youth and Family Services by the birth father of her child after Brianna was hospitalized for psychiatric treatment. Brianna's child, Felicia, was placed into foster care as a toddler and remained in the foster care system until adolescence. Several years later, Brianna delivered another child, who was born with cocaine in his system. The child's intrauterine drug exposure plus the birth mother's chronic psychiatric disorder gave the New Jersey Division sufficient leverage to place the baby into foster care directly from the hospital after birth. Brianna subsequently had a relapse and was referred to the psychiatric outpatient program at a local hospital upon her discharge from the state hospital. A few months later, however, Brianna suffered another relapse and was admitted to the county psychiatric hospital, where she stabilized on medication. She eventually managed to establish herself in her own apartment through a housing program for the disabled and remained crisis free for nearly a year.

The client's infant son remained in foster care, as his mother was clearly unable to provide for his needs. In spite of her recent history of psychiatric crises, Brianna successfully petitioned the court for a return of custody of her teenage daughter, Felicia, who had been in the system since she was a toddler. Because of her behavior problems, this child went from foster home to foster home and ultimately to a group home before being returned to Brianna. Support services included parenting skills training for Brianna and a youth services worker assigned to Felicia.

A psychological examination of Felicia shortly after her return to the birth mother and a collateral interview with Brianna indicated that Brianna was passive, mildly limited cognitively, and inadequate to the task of managing the behavior of her defiant, negativistic teenage daughter. Felicia was sullen, emotionally flat, and hostile. She had enormous resentment toward her mother for allowing her to spend her entire childhood in foster care, as well as toward the foster care system for putting her through multiple experiences of humiliation, frustration, rejection, and trauma. Felicia was functioning within the mildly retarded range intellectually and her personality organization was that of a self-absorbed, demanding, infantile adolescent with singularly poor impulse control.

Individual therapy was recommended for Felicia, as well as continued parenting skills training and in-home behavior management training for Brianna. The evaluator also expressed pessimism as to the viability of this placement. A few months after the evaluation, Brianna asked for her daughter's removal because the former was entirely unable to cope with Felicia's aggressive and defiant behavior.

A year later, Brianna was referred for a formal psychological evaluation to assess her prognosis for successfully parenting her 2-year-old son, Jonathan. Brianna was mildly confused and rambling in her communications with the examiner. She was grossly in contact with reality and did not display any indication of mood disorder. During the preliminary interview, Brianna stated that she had lived with her birth mother until age 6 years and then with an aunt until she was 9. After that, she lived in a foster home. She stated that she was placed into foster care because her aunt's husband sexually abused her. She stated that there was never any criminal prosecution of her uncle and that she was never provided with any therapy or counseling to address this. When asked how many times she had been hospitalized, Brianna replied that she did not know. Her memories of her recent psychiatric treatments were vague, and she could not recall at which hospital she had been treated the last time. She complained that her brother put her into the hospital because he felt that she should have been taking her medication, although there was actually nothing wrong with her.

Psychological testing found that Brianna was functioning within the borderline range intellectually, but with indications of significantly higher potential that was apparently masked by her psychiatric problems. The subject's Millon Clinical Multiaxial Inventory–II results depict her as excessively self-centered and paranoid to the point of being actively delusional. An interesting feature of Briannas Millon test record was that the validity indicators (technically, modifier indices) were elevated in the direction of a socially desirable response set. In other words, Brianna's approach to this self-report personality inventory was that of impressing the examiner positively, yet she registered scores in the delusional range. This is an indication of the extreme ego-syntonicity of the subject's psychopathology, which was experienced as a natural part of the self that she had no reason to attempt to conceal in spite of her overall attempt at impression management. The examiner's recommendation was that Brianna not be considered as a viable candidate for custody of any of her children.

As noted in Chapter 2, a psychiatric diagnosis alone is not sufficient to justify termination of an individual's parental rights. There must be a showing of a specific nexus between the individual's impairments and specific aspects of parenting skills. The psychological report stated that Brianna's problems interfered with her judgment and her reality contact to such an extent that she would be unable to provide the degree of safety, vigilance, emotional security, structure, and stimulation that a young child requires and that her prognosis for change through therapy was very poor. It was the evaluator's opinion that Brianna was barely able to manage a marginal existence outside of the hospital for herself, let alone attend to the needs of a child.

Brianna was also observed with her son, Jonathan for a bonding assessment. During the preliminary interview, Brianna related that she was securing an apartment. She stated that she was about to begin individual psychotherapy at a hospital outpatient clinic and that she would check with a psychiatrist at that facility concerning medication management. She indicated that she was not on any sort of medication but that she felt good because she was not under any pressure. She stated that she was not involved in any educational activity and was not employed. Nevertheless, Brianna reported that she had a full schedule between going to various clinics and court. She admitted to having been addicted to cocaine when she gave birth to Jonathan, who tested positive for that drug at birth.

Brianna was observed with Jonathan for 30 minutes. When she attempted to bring the child in from the waiting room, he would not go unless accompanied by his foster mother, whom he followed back out when she left the consultation room. Jonathan buried his head in his foster mother's lap when she sat down in the waiting room. Eventually, Brianna was able to persuade Jonathan to accompany her into the consultation room, with the foster mother's encouragement.

Brianna attempted to engage Jonathan in play with some number blocks, quizzing him on number recognition. The child remained silent and turned his head away from his birth mother when she spoke to him. Brianna talked to Jonathan continuously and showed him family dolls, trying to get him to respond to her labeling them as various family members. She attempted to engage him by making animal noises while holding up toy farm animals. At that point, the child rose and wandered behind the examiner. The child returned when Brianna summoned him back to the low play table. Brianna rewarded Jonathan's play activities with verbal praise, to which the child was unresponsive. Jonathan whispered "three" when his mother held up a block with that number on it. He responded "moo" when his mother told him that the toy cow that he was playing with made that sound.

Jonathan began to throw things on the floor. When Brianna handed him a toy rooster he dropped it on the floor. He wandered over to the examiner's desk but returned to the play table when his mother called him back. As Jonathan touched some family dolls, Brianna told him that he had a sister named Felicia. Jonathan returned to the examiner's desk and attempted to open a drawer. Brianna called him back, but the child continued his efforts to open the drawer and ignored her. Brianna came over to Jonathan and picked him up, whereupon he started to cry. Brianna cautioned her son abruptly, "Don't you start with me! Why are you crying?" She placed him on the floor near the low play table as he continued to cry. Brianna called her son over, and he approached her. As she wiped his tears, Jonathan turned toward the examiner with an extremely distressed look. He sobbed and sucked on a finger. Brianna attempted to comfort her son by talking to him. She held on to the child so that he could not move away. Jonathan continued to cry and did not respond to Brianna's attempts to engage him in conversation. He attempted to pull away from his birth mother without success. When she released him, he stood against the wall, sobbing and looking at the examiner. He did not respond at all to his birth mother's further attempts to engage him; and at that point, the examiner ended the session.

Jonathan stopped crying when the examiner opened the door to the waiting room. He then flopped down into a kneeling position and resumed sobbing. Brianna led him out of the room. Jonathan buried his head in his foster mother's side and stopped crying. The foster mother put her arm around him and wiped his face. Jonathan looked up at his birth mother and immediately buried his face in the foster mother's side once more.

his birth mother, he would suffer a traumatic loss that would produce severe and enduring harm. The most probable long-term effects would include impairment of basic trust, impairment of self-esteem, impaired capacity for establishing intimate emotional ties to others in the future, and diminished optimism and self-confidence. This child's inner template for intimate relationships would be marked by issues of abandonment, mistrust, and rage over the loss of his central parental love objects, which would render him vulnerable to conditions such as depression and severe personality disorder as an adolescent and adult.

Rather than continue to work with Brianna toward the return of Jonathan, the state filed a guardianship petition for him. Some years later, Brianna was arrested for inflicting very severe injuries on her new baby, whose existence was not known to the child protective services. Without having access to the full details of that event, one is tempted to speculate that Brianna's rageful projection onto Jonathan during the bonding assessment, in the form of her perception that this frightened child was "starting" with her by crying, characterized her interactions with her new baby as well. There may have been a fuller, psychotic degree of projection onto the baby, that was acted upon in a violent manner in the absence of another adult supervising that interaction.

CASE 5: BONDING ASSESSMENTS AND EXTREME DISTRESS ASSOCIATED WITH VISITATION

This case was referred to New Jersey's Division of Youth and Family Services when the birth mother disappeared, leaving the children home alone. The children appeared at school with soiled clothing and a strong body odor. The caseworker found that the children's clothing was filthy and that there was no food in the home. The mother's whereabouts were unknown and the father was under arrest for narcotics distribution. The children were placed into foster care at that time.

Although there had been a previous charge of negligence, relatives of the birth mother described her as a responsible and dedicated mother who had been the victim of her husband's violent behavior. Prior to the husband's arrest, the birth father had inflicted numerous injuries to the birth mother and had made terroristic threats.

The behavioral picture was entirely different when Jon observed with his foster parents. The foster mother related than was not a very friendly child and that he was reticent about everyone. This tendency was reflected to some ext child's Vineland Adaptive Behavior Scale results, which w wise normal. During the observation, which included b parents, Jonathan positioned himself physically close to mother. He appeared to be happy, relaxed, and secure duri sion, and in spite of the behavior reported by the foster mo than was friendly toward the examiner, smiling at him sev Upon being told by his foster father that he could not tou clock on a table near the examiner, Jonathan ran to his fos and buried his head in her lap, hugging her. Jonathan accep cal affection from his foster mother and interacted well foster parents. The child refused to talk at all, however, the examiner made a point of requesting that the foster mc get him to speak. The foster mother replied that Jonath talked outside the home, but that when he is home wit talks nonstop.

The report on these bonding assessments stated that d athan's biweekly visitations with his birth mother, he did to have a positive emotional investment in her. The bi clearly did not occupy a position of centrality in this child' than displayed distress and anxiety when observed wit mother, who was unable to comfort him. While generally appropriate parental behavior during the session, the bi was at times overly confrontational and critical of the example, when she responded to his crying by telling "start" with her.

Jonathan was profoundly attached to his foster pa were competent, caring adults interested in his welfare. takers were assessed as being Jonathan's central parental and identification figures. They were his primary sou turance, protection, emotional security, and affection. B her position in the center of Jonathan's emotional world mother had the power to calm and soothe him when he tress.

Far from being a superficial matter, these parental represent the building blocks of future personality deve Jonathan were to be removed from his foster parents and

When interviewed about his wife's disappearance and the situation of the children, the birth father stated that his wife had been kidnapped. The caseworker observed that the birth father, who had left all of his relatives in his native country, had an intimidating personality and talked very loudly. The three older girls in the family attended a total of four different schools within the span of 2 years. All three girls had academic problems and were bedwetters. Another child, Claudio, who was 2 months of age when he was placed into foster care, did not have any history of intrauterine drug exposure and was free of health problems.

After a time, the birth mother resurfaced. The reasons for her disappearance remained obscure. The Division of Youth and Family Services directed the birth parents to engage in counseling and to undergo a drug evaluation. After a period of intense hostility between the parents, they reunited and stated to the caseworker that they wished to seek custody of all the children and to parent them jointly.

The children were in a few different foster homes at this time. The older children experienced difficulty in adjusting to placement and displayed sadness at the end of visits with their birth parents. The oldest girl was frequently observed by the foster mother talking to herself. Claudio, now age 14 months, resisted being physically close to either parent during visits and would not allow his birth father to come anywhere near him. In her report, the caseworker observed that Claudio was bonded to his foster parents and that he remained upset after visits with his birth parents, refusing to eat and demanding to sleep with the foster parents. The case goal remained family reunification, providing that the parents engaged in the mandated drug screening and counseling.

The birth parents subsequently became unemployed. The birth father sustained an injury in an automobile accident and filed suit. He expressed the hope that the proceeds of this lawsuit would enable the couple to obtain a permanent home. Although they had been court mandated to attend counseling, neither of the birth parents did so, stating that they did not feel that they needed this service. They had not obtained a larger apartment suitable for housing all of their children but did comply with the requirement of monthly visitation with the children at the Division of Youth and Family Services office. The Division felt that these birth parents had not made much of an effort toward reunification, and the case was referred to the adoption unit of the agency. At that point, the children had been in placement for over a year.

Claudio was seen for a bonding assessment with his foster parents. The child was age 19 months at the time of this assessment. The foster mother was a nurturing individual who was caring for Claudio and one other infant in her home. The foster father was employed as a semiskilled repair worker.

These foster parents did not have any birth children and reported that they fell in love with Claudio and decided to try to adopt him as soon as he was placed with them. Claudio had been with these foster parents since age 4 months. He had adjusted very well to this foster home, and he did not have any medical or developmental problems.

The foster parents related that Claudio reacted with sleep problems after the monthly visits with his birth parents. He also became clingy and demanded to be held upon returning from these visits. When the caseworker came to pick him up to transport him to the visits, Claudio would cry and cling to the foster mother.

Developmental assessment with the Vineland indicated that this child was functioning within the normal range in all measured areas, except for motor skills, where he was significantly above average. He was happy, relaxed, and secure when observed with the foster parents, smiling frequently at them. The foster parents were both obviously in love with this appealing, active 19-month-old boy. The overall quality of the observed interaction was excellent, and the foster parents appeared to be sensitive, competent caretakers who were meeting this child's emotional and developmental needs very well.

The report stated that Claudio had formed a profound attachment to these caretakers, with whom he had been in uninterrupted placement since age 4 months. Clearly, these foster parents were Claudio's central parental love objects. The report went on to state that a return of custody to unstable, inadequate caretakers such as the birth parents would be catastrophic for Claudio. In support of this prediction of harm, the report indicated that for a child as young as 19 months, the effects of the loss of the child's central parental love objects, even if that child were then transferred to an optimal caretaker, would necessarily impair basic trust, self-esteem, and the ability to form intimate emotional ties to others in the future.

My reading of recent clinical and research literature would result in a somewhat different wording of this proposition from that contained in the bonding assessment report in this case. It is possible that for many children at age 19 months a permanent transfer to an optimal caretaker would result in a merging of the memory traces of the present and former caretakers with little impairment of ego structure. However, when a child's relationship with the foster caretakers has been excellent, and for children who are precocious enough to have developed some degree of differentiated stable object representation of the former caretakers, there would be significant long-term damage to personality development resulting from such a loss. Clearly, this type of harm would take place in the case of a child who is well into rapprochement, perhaps beginning shortly after 2 years of age, with some variation among children, depending on cognitive and emotional factors. Equally as clear, the harm would be substantial in the case of a child who was transferred to caretakers who were inadequate.

The family court judge assigned to this case heard arguments from the Division of Youth and Family Services and from attorneys representing the birth parents. The Division had decided to initiate guardianship proceedings on behalf of Claudio. In spite of the birth parents' lack of cooperation with the case plan, the judge ordered that the oldest children be returned to them, with continued agency supervision. All of those children had shown distress over being in foster care, and all three children had expressed a desire to be reunited with their parents. The judge requested an additional report regarding the probable impact on Claudio if the parents' request for overnight weekend visits with this child were granted.

The supplemental report stated that in view of the fact that this child reacted with sleep problems, clinging, and crying when brought for day visits with his birth parents once per month, it was the opinion of the examining psychologist that overnight weekend visits would have an even more destructive effect on this child. It was clear that Claudio had bonded with his foster parents, which was to be expected as a natural result of placing so young an infant with competent and attuned caretakers for an extended period of time. Disruption of this child's sense of emotional security by forcing him to undergo periodic separations of 1 or 2 days from his foster parents would, in all psychological probability, cause this child to experience unbearable separation anxiety and, if continued over a significant period of time, would also impair his capacity for basic trust. It was unlikely that these contacts would result in the development of a bond with the natural parents in this particular case. The most probable effect would be to inflict needless trauma upon this child, for whom the foster parents were his "psychological parents."

The overnight visitation was not granted; however, the court increased the frequency of the daytime visits to weekly. Shortly after the above supplemental report concerning visitation was issued, the foster parents began writing to the judge and to the state's examining psychologist, describing Claudio's reactions to the visits with his birth parents. Although these letters clearly lack the objectivity of a professional observer, such as the Robertsons' (1989) descriptions of 2-year-olds in foster care for much briefer periods of time, these communications from the foster parents are strikingly consistent with the kinds of phenomena observed in the professional literature (see Chapter 9). The foster parents wrote to the judge that on the days when Claudio was transported to the visits with his birth parents, he realized where he was going and protested desperately. Upon returning to the foster home, Claudio felt so insecure that he clung to the foster parents. For several days after each of these visits, Claudio experienced nightmares and awakened in tears. This pattern increased with the greater frequency of the visits.

The foster parents wrote to the examining psychologist and described further behavioral reactions that Claudio was displaying in response to the increased visitation with his birth parents. The foster parents related that when social workers came to transport Claudio for a visit with his birth parents, the child ran toward the foster parents, embraced them, and would not let go. When one of the caseworkers tried to pick him up to take him to these visits, Claudio cried desperately. The foster parents noted that normally Claudio was a very friendly child who took to others immediately. They also stated that for several days after such visits the child was anxious and insecure outside of their presence. The sound of the doorbell would cause him to panic and hide, and he had regressed in his toilet training to the point where he again needed diapers.

A month later, the examining psychologist received another letter from the foster parents who complained of an escalation in Claudio's anxious and regressive behaviors. The foster parents stated that, in addition to the regression in toilet training, Claudio had also lost much of his vocabulary. They related that he did not seem interested in learning any new words or in practicing any of the ones he already knew. They also commented that, whereas he had previously been a very happy and loving child, he was now unhappy and aggressive all the time.

In a subsequent letter documenting Claudio's changes in behavior as they correlated with the frequency of his contacts with his birth parents, the foster parents wrote that for the 3 consecutive weeks when there were no visits with Claudio's birth parents the child became happy, relaxed, and playful again. He gave up the pacifier and used the potty instead of needing to be in diapers. However, when the visits resumed, he returned from the first visit in a very aggressive and perturbed state. He asked the foster mother for his pacifier and again needed diapers. The foster parents also expressed the opinion that Claudio's insecurity was caused in part by his seeing that the foster parents, to whom he looked for protection, were powerless to protect him.

The examining psychologist subsequently observed Claudio with his birth parents. Although the child was stable in the waiting room with his three older sisters and the caseworker, he burst into tears when brought into the consultation room with his birth parents and the examiner. After an unsuccessful attempt at calming him down, the birth mother asked the examiner for permission to allow Claudio's sisters to come in. The child calmed somewhat, but attempted to leave the room a few minutes later. His birth mother prevented him from doing this by physically restraining him. The birth mother finally succeeded at engaging him in playing with blocks with his sisters while his birth father sat on the other side of the room watching Claudio. The examiner then instructed the parents to send the older children out of the room one by one . After the second child departed, Claudio dumped some blocks out of a bucket and tried to throw one at his birth mother, who deflected the missile with her hand and took the other blocks away from him. A few moments later, Claudio threw two more blocks at his birth mother and then repeated this action with two larger blocks.

Claudio took the arm of one of his sisters and led her out into the waiting room. He then attempted to leave the office entirely, but was restrained by another sister. Both parents went out to the waiting room to retrieve him, and the birth father carried him back. Claudio then stood across the room from his birth father, scowling at him. The birth father called loudly, "Come here, Claudio!" The child took a single step toward his birth father and then kicked over a block wall that one of his sisters had made. The birth mother was able to distract Claudio for a few moments with a toy, but the child then backed away from her and scowled at her. The birth father took Claudio out to the bathroom even though Claudio had not asked to go.

Upon returning to the waiting room, Claudio played at a table in the corner away from his mother. A sister was able to coax him into the consultation room; however, once inside, he kicked over her blocks and ran out. He then pulled on his caseworker's arm to bring him into the room with him. After Claudio once again ran out of the consultation room, his birth mother picked him up. Claudio reached for his caseworker, straining away from the birth mother, who continued to hold him. Claudio, now back in the consultation room on the floor, kicked some more blocks on the floor and ran out again. The observation was terminated by the examiner at that point.

The report concluded that Claudio viewed the visitation with his birth parents as a threat to the stability of his placement with his foster parents. This sense of threat was clearly indicated by the unusual aggressive behavior that this child displayed toward the birth parents. Further, given the extremely poor quality of the relationship between this child and his birth parents, it was the evaluator's opinion that no program of therapy, supervised visitation, or other intervention could result in a significant positive change in that relationship. The evaluator recommended Claudio's visitations with his birth parents end immediately and that the Division of Youth and Family Services pursue a case goal of foster home adoption.

In testifying about this case, the issue of the adequacy of the birth parents needed to be addressed. This was problematic, in light of the fact that the evaluator had not assessed these individuals directly, apart from observing their behavior with Claudio. According to the section of the APA's ethical code that deals with forensic activities, a forensic psychologist is not permitted to offer opinions regarding parties with whom the psychologist has not performed an examination adequate to support the opinions (Standard 7.02b). In the instant situation the evaluator had met with the birth parents; however, the type of assessment that would have permitted conclusions about their individual psychological functioning had not been performed. Thus, any opinion in regard to any issue apart from the birth parents' observed adequacy and appropriateness in interacting with Claudio would not have been supported by the data.

Canter et al. (1994) state that the APA ethical code does allow one to address certain clinical issues obliquely in this type of situation. The witness may respond to hypotheticals concerning individuals similar to the litigants without offering testimony concerning the particular individuals who have not been individually examined. However, it then becomes incumbent upon counsel to demonstrate that the parties do in fact present these traits; the witness obviously cannot offer that type of conclusion.

The manner in which this situation was handled in the state's expert testimony in the matter of Claudio's parents was via a series of such hypotheticals that addressed the documented history, the court-mandated interventions, and the probable effects on the child of being raised with caretakers who had chronic problems such as those documented in the record. For example, could parents who were involved in drugs and who had a history of unstable living conditions, neglect of their children, and domestic conflicts, including the father's terroristic threats, be reasonably expected to raise a child without substantial risk of harm? If such parents were mandated by the court to undergo counseling and refused to engage in such services because they felt no need for them, could they be expected to make any significant change in their situation? Would Claudio's severe behavioral reaction and long-term personality damage, predicted by the examining psychologist if Claudio were removed from his foster parents, be compounded by his being transferred to birth parents who had presented the above problems, been mandated to undergo counseling, and refused?

Because of the birth parents' egregiously poor record, which was amply documented by casework and law enforcement personnel, counsel for the state was able to introduce their deficiencies as parents convincingly via the hypotheticals without having them examined individually. Of course, from the perspective of achieving a comprehensive clinical picture of the family, it would have been much better if the birth parents had been examined individually, if they had been willing to participate. In fact, one wonders if the court would have been as quick to return the older children to these birth parents if the parents had been examined individually by using the interview techniques and psychological tests discussed in Chapter 5. In any event, the termination case involving Claudio was clearly a "bonding case" rather than a "fitness case," and issues of parental competency were secondary to the psychological damage that would have resulted had Claudio been subjected to the loss of his central parental love objects.

CHAPTER 13

Illustrative Cases II

Analysis of the Baby Jessica Case

The news over the past decade has featured sensational accounts of disrupted adoptions relating to birth parents' rescinding their surrender of rights, in some cases because a birth father simply has been unaware of his child's existence. One notable case of this type is the case of Anna Schmidt, aka Jessica DeBoer, referred to in the media as "Baby Jessica." In this case, the birth mother named another individual as the birth father and that individual's rights to the child were erroneously terminated by the court in order to permit an adoption to go forward. It is useful to apply some of the clinical theory discussed in Chapter 8 and the legal concepts discussed in Chapter 2 to the specifics of this case, which aroused tremendous public sympathy for the adoptive parents during the height of the publicity over its litigation. The Baby Jessica case illustrates many of the clinical and legal issues discussed earlier in this work and, despite the unusual circumstances involved, has a good deal of applicability to more conventional termination of parental rights cases.

FACTUAL BACKGROUND OF THE CASE

Cara Clausen, the birth mother, was a 28-year-old Iowa resident who had broken up with her boyfriend, Daniel Schmidt, and subsequently began to date one Scott Seefeldt. She became pregnant in 1990; and when she gave birth to Baby Jessica on February 8, 1991, she put Seefeldt's name on the birth certificate. Two days later, she waived her parental rights and put the baby up for adoption. A childless couple, Jan and Roberta DeBoer of Ann Arbor, Michigan, had heard through relatives in Cedar Rapids, Iowa, that a baby might be available through private adoption channels. Private adoption is legal in Iowa. The DeBoers retained an attorney named John Monroe to represent them.

Monroe met with Cara Clausen at the hospital and gave Clausen papers to sign, thus waiving her parental rights to the baby to free the child for adoption by his clients. According to Monroe and the DeBoers, Clausen freely signed away her parental rights to Baby Jessica after the mandatory 72-hour waiting period. With Cara Clausen's signature on a surrender document, as well as that of Scott Seefeldt, the individual whom Monroe thought was the birth father, the DeBoers's attorney felt that he had done a good job on behalf of his clients and also on the infant's behalf. By March 1, the DeBoers had filed the required adoption petition and had received the court's permission to remove the infant from Iowa to their residence in Michigan. Even after this, Clausen sent the DeBoers a letter indicating that she wanted the adoption to proceed.

Within the next few days, however, Cara Clausen informed Daniel Schmidt that the baby she had signed over for adoption was actually his. Clausen attended a meeting of a support group called Concerned United Birth Parents and met an individual in that group who persuaded her to change her mind about the surrender of her daughter for adoption. A member of the group referred Clausen to a friend of hers, Jacqueline Miller, who was an attorney and who filed a motion in the Iowa District Court requesting restoration of Clausen's parental rights. The petition stated that Clausen had been fraudulently induced to sign her rights away and that the termination had been predicated upon false information, namely, that Scott Seefeldt was the birth father, whereas the actual birth father was Daniel Schmidt. Clausen also alleged that she had not received adequate counseling in the hospital, that Monroe had visited her and induced her to sign the surrender of rights before the mandatory 72-hour waiting period had elapsed, and that she was still under the influence of drugs that she had been administered during the delivery process. On March 12, Jacqueline Miller, Cara Clausen's attorney, filed a motion on Daniel Schmidt's behalf declaring him to be the birth father and requesting that the court vacate the termination order.

In an interview with the publication *Midwest Today* (Lawrence, 1993), Monroe denied all of these allegations. Regarding the encounter with Clausen he stated: "The only reason it went awry is because she had lied to me about who the father was. She would have never gotten anything turned around, gotten the termination reversed or anything if we had terminated the right birth father. Because she had notice of the termination hearing and she didn't resist." Monroe also asserted that Clausen did receive counseling at the hospital, both from a physician and from a hospital social worker.

On March 21, a hearing was held in Cedar Rapids. The family court threw out the case for lack of jurisdiction. Clausen and Schmidt appealed the decision and asked that Schmidt be given a blood test to establish his paternity. This order for blood testing was granted by the court on April 29, and the tests were conducted on July 8, 1991. The results came back on July 22, confirming that Schmidt was indeed the birth father.

In the meantime, the DeBoers decided to fight Schmidt and Clausen on the custody issue even though it was clear that the wrong individual had been named as the birth father in the termination order. The DeBoers subsequently explained that they had been informed by the Iowa Department of Human Services and by adoption officials in Michigan that if they relinquished their guardianship of Jessica, she would be placed in temporary foster care until the situation was resolved. They were reluctant to place the child with a strange family where she might be kept for months while the litigation proceeded. Furthermore, they discovered that Schmidt had legally abandoned a 14-year-old son named Travis and that he had also fathered a daughter, then age 12, out of wedlock whom he had refused to meet. The DeBoers decided to contest the Iowa court's order on the grounds that Schmidt was an unfit birth father. They petitioned the court to terminate Schmidt's rights and to grant a jury trial and a hearing based on the child's best interests.

Cara Clausen and Daniel Schmidt were married in April. They pursued custody jointly from that point, with the intention of coparenting their baby as husband and wife.

On December 27, 1991, the Iowa District Court ruled that the DeBoers had not demonstrated that Schmidt had abandoned the child. The court ordered that custody of the baby be awarded to

Daniel Schmidt and that child welfare officials investigate Schmidt's fitness as a parent. After an unsuccessful appeal of the district court's decision, the DeBoers filed a motion for a new hearing, which was also denied on November 20, 1992, by the Iowa Supreme Court. The decision noted that, although Schmidt had a poor record as a parent and it was "alluring" to consider Jessica's best interests, Schmidt's rights as a birth father were determinative.

The DeBoers litigated the matter in the Circuit Court for Washtenaw County, Michigan, and were successful in obtaining a temporary order blocking the transfer. They had been cited by the Iowa court on December 3 for contempt and ordered to turn over the baby immediately. At this point, Baby Jessica was 20 months old. On January 5, 1993, the circuit court ruled that Jessica DeBoer was a resident of Michigan and that, since the Iowa courts had failed to consider her best interests, the Michigan court would do so.

On January 29, hearings began in Michigan on Jessica's best interests. The Schmidts engaged an attorney by the name of Marian Faupel to represent them in Michigan. Faupel introduced records indicating that as a young adult Jan DeBoer had been arrested for breaking and entering and for driving under the influence of alcohol. The DeBoers put the mothers of Daniel Schmidt's two other children on the stand to testify that he had neglected them.

The court-appointed psychologist, Dr. Beth Clark, stated that neither of the birth parents realized the severity of the problems that Jessica would face if she were to be removed from the DeBoers and given to them. Dr. Clark also testified that Daniel Schmidt had a potential for substance abuse and that he had various character flaws, including an explosive temper and a lack of self-control. She further testified that he tended to confuse his own emotional needs with those of his children. A child psychoanalyst from the University of Michigan, Dr. Jack Novick, testified that Jessica would be traumatized if she were to be removed from the DeBoers. Dr. Novick described the process of identity formation in a 2-year-old child, stressing the primacy of the mother in the child's emotional life. He further stated that if a 2-year-old were to be removed from her psychological parents, the separation from her primary attachment figure would be like losing a piece of herself. He predicted severe adverse psychological consequences, including the child's blaming herself for the loss and an impairment of the child's capacity to form attachments in the future.

In February 1993, the trial judge cited a number of guidelines from the Michigan Child Custody Act and ruled that the DeBoers were superior as parents in every applicable area. He also stated that if Jessica were "plucked from her parents" she might never recover. At around the same time that the Michigan trial court decision was rendered, the Iowa Juvenile Court announced a summary judgment restoring Cara Schmidt's parental rights to Baby Jessica. The Schmidts appealed the Michigan trial court's decision, arguing that the Iowa court's ruling should be honored by Michigan. In July 1993, the Michigan Supreme Court ruled six to one that Michigan had no jurisdiction in the case and that Jessica would have to be returned to the Schmidts within a month. That would place Jessica at 2½ years of age at the time of the mandated transfer of custody.

ANALYSIS

At the time that the hearings began in Michigan in January 1993, the Baby Jessica case began to resemble a typical divorce/child custody case rather than a termination of parental rights case. The DeBoers appeared to be arguing that they should be allowed to keep Baby Jessica because they were able to provide a better environment for her and because Daniel Schmidt presented certain undesirable personality characteristics that made him a less desirable father figure for the child than Jan DeBoer. To counter this, as mentioned in the previous section, Schmidt's attorney Faupel introduced negative character evidence concerning Jan DeBoer, namely, the arrest, in Ann Arbor, Michigan, for breaking and entering and for driving under the influence of alcohol. The DeBoers called the mothers of Schmidt's two older children, who testified that Schmidt had neglected the children. Schmidt countered with testimony from his 14-year-old son, who stated that Schmidt had treated him better than had his adoptive father.

Had this case been heard after *Daubert*, much of the testimony of the court-appointed psychologist, Dr. Clark, might have been successfully challenged by the defense on the grounds of *helpfulness*, which, as noted in Chapter 10, is the quality that characterizes evidence that "logically advances a material aspect of the proposing party's case." In other words, the evidence must be directly related to the ultimate legal issue before the court. Furthermore, the evidence must not be more prejudicial than probative. It appears that the testi-

mony offered by Dr. Clark did not address any criterion relating to the termination of Daniel Schmidt's parental rights to Baby Jessica.

As demonstrated by the numerous cases cited in Chapter 2 concerning the relationship of diagnosis to termination of parental rights, courts have held overwhelmingly that a psychiatric diagnosis alone is insufficient to demonstrate parental unfitness. The testimony must provide a nexus between the diagnosis and some specific defect in the individual's parenting capacity. In the instant matter, however, there was no specific showing that Daniel Schmidt's purported lack of impulse control, hot temper, or even potential for substance abuse created a risk that the child would be abused or neglected while in his care. Clearly, a knowledge that one of the litigants presented those characteristics would be helpful to the court in a typical divorce-related child custody action. In the instant case, however, it was arguable that the testimony to the effect that Schmidt had these traits simply biased the judge against him while doing nothing to assist the court in ruling on the ultimate legal issue, which was the termination of Schmidt's parental rights.

On the other hand, the testimony of Dr. Novick, concerning the probable effects on the child associated with a removal from the adoptive parents, was arguably helpful to the court under a termination scenario. That testimony related to factors included in Michigan's termination of parental rights statute involving the age of the child and length of time that the child had been in placement. I might not have been considered too great a conceptual leap to ass that those factors serve to protect a vulnerable younger child has formed an attachment to foster or adoptive caretakers and might be traumatized by a removal from those parental figure the testimony could be ruled admissible for the purpose of e ing the degree of harm to the child that failure to termi would cause. It would have assisted the judge as a facto sidered in making the Solomonic decision in balancing the birth parents, who had in fact already won in th against the impact on the child of removal from th

In contrast to the "placement with the better best interests" approach typical of a divorce/chil the Michigan court employed, courts in othe have focused exclusively upon the statutory c regarding such factors as social class, alleg tions of neglect of other children, the cul

n
is
th
the
for-
ratin

raised in a university town, and the rest as irrelevant. The trial court in the New Jersey case of Baby M., for example (*In the Matter of Baby M.*, 1988) stated: "It is clear that a 'best interests' determination is never sufficient to terminate parental rights; the statutory criteria must be proved." Indeed, the Iowa Supreme Court in its September 1992 eight-to-one ruling in this case in favor of the birth parents stated that courts "are not free to take children from parents simply by deciding another home offers more advantages."

Thus, in light of the standards for termination of parental rights discussed in Chapter 2, it is remarkable that the Michigan court focused on the type of character testimony that was allowed in. Had the trial court followed the Michigan statute for termination of parental rights rather than the child custody statute, the outcome would have been dramatically different. According to the Michigan statute for termination of parental rights, the following factors must be considered as part of the termination process: (1) failure to visit or communicate; (2) failure to provide a home when able to do so; (3) abandonment of infant and no identification of birth parent for a specified time; (4) extreme or repeated abuse or neglect; (5) long-term incarceration—early parole unlikely; (6) failure to improve in response to agency assistance; (7) development of case plan; providing of services pursuant to plan; (8) consideration of length of time that the child is in placement; (9) consideration of child's age.

(If the case had been heard in Iowa, the following criteria would have applied: [1] extreme disinterest/abandonment; [2] failure to visit or communicate; [3] extreme, or repeated abuse or neglect; [4] failure to improve in response to agency assistance; [5] development of case plan; [6] providing of services pursuant to plan; [7] consideration of specific length of time that the child is in placement.)

In response to the first consideration under Michigan law, Daniel Schmidt had been trying to regain custody of his daughter since she was less than a month old. As to the second consideration, there was every indication that the Schmidts could provide a suitable home for he child. It is interesting to note in this regard that, while this may ot have been a paramount issue in the hearing, the press made a big sue of the alleged social class disparity between the Schmidts and DeBoers, portraying the Schmidts as unsophisticated people and DeBoers as sophisticates from a university town. Indeed, a made-elevision movie about the case portrayed the Schmidts as deco-g their house with hubcaps (which the Schmidts denied ever hav-

ing incorporated as an item of decor) and the DeBoers as sipping fine wine at an upscale restaurant while agonizing over the custody of the baby. In fact, the Schmidts' family income was actually slightly higher than that of the DeBoers, and Cara Clausen Schmidt's father owned a business. Even if Daniel Schmidt conformed in every detail to the worst stereotypic portrayal of him in the media, that fact would not have any bearing as to the termination of his parental rights to an infant whom he had been trying to reclaim since she was a month old.

Regarding the third consideration under Michigan law, listed above, regarding termination of parental rights, Daniel Schmidt could hardly have been accused of abandoning the infant, as he had no knowledge of her existence until after the birth mother had signed away her rights to her. Schmidt came forward as the birth father as soon as he was apprised of the situation, which was within days of the child's birth. As to the fourth consideration, there was no issue of abuse or neglect whatsoever, because the child had never been in the birth father's custody. Furthermore, there had never been an adjudication of abuse or neglect against Schmidt regarding his other two children, one of whom in fact testified that Schmidt had treated him well. As to the fifth, sixth, and seventh considerations, there had been no social service intervention and no case plan, and thus nothing that Schmidt could have failed to respond to. Moreover, Schmidt gave every indication that he was willing to provide a stable and secure home and family for the child. He was employed, had married the birth mother, and had come forward immediately upon learning of his paternity of the child.

It is in regard to the last consideration, namely, the age of the child and the length of time that the child has been in placement, that there are legitimate issues. At the time that Daniel Schmidt first petitioned the court for the return of Baby Jessica, the child was one month old. Had the child been given over to Schmidt at that time as a biological father whose parental rights had not been terminated and who had not failed the child in any way, no one would have had any question about any psychological ill effects associated with the transfer, separate and apart from the DeBoers' concerns about Daniel Schmidt's personal characteristics, and also assuming that Jessica would have passed directly from the DeBoers' hands to Schmidt.

Regarding the last consideration, when asked why they decided to resist the efforts of the birth parents to gain custody of Baby

Jessica, the DeBoers indicated that they were concerned about the possibility of psychological harm resulting from the transfer process itself. The DeBoers had been informed by social service personnel in both Iowa and Michigan that if the DeBoers were to give up the temporary guardianship that they had been awarded pending adoption and release the child to the birth parents, Jessica would be housed in a temporary foster home until the matter was resolved. The DeBoers feared that this disruption, in which their preadoptive daughter would be given to at least one and possibly more than one temporary caretaker prior to being returned to Cara Clausen and Daniel Schmidt would scar her psychologically.

Although this argument has a certain intuitive appeal, the research indicates that children who are moved before age 6 months do not appear to suffer any long-term harm (Bowlby, 1953). This is the consensus; however, the research community is not completely unanimous on the point. Goldstein et al. (1979) predict varying degrees and types of psychological harm associated with removal of a child from his or her psychological parents at different developmental periods. They predict discomfort, distress, and delays in orientation resulting from disruptions of continuity of care in infants from birth to age 18 months. This does not appear to be a prediction of long-term psychological harm, however.

Citing a number of developmental studies of adopted children, Milchman (1996) states: "Children adopted a while after birth experience delayed bonding, as well as bonding loss if they were attached to someone prior to the adoption. Children adopted after 5 months of age show increased risk of manic and depressive symptoms through adulthood . . . which is not due to genetics, adoptive home problems, or early neglect" (p. 8). Certainly, if the infant were to be subjected to abuse, neglect, or even substandard care in one or more foster homes, there would be significant cause for concern in regard to long-term psychological effects of these experiences.

Aside from these considerations, however, it is safe to state that if the DeBoers had simply returned the child to the birth mother as soon as it became clear that their legal position was shaky because the wrong birth father had been terminated, Baby Jessica at age 3 or 4 months, or even somewhat older, would have emerged from the transfer process unscathed.

The situation became more clouded as the litigation intensified. On December 27, 1991, the DeBoers were ordered by the Iowa district court to transfer Jessica to the birth parents. At that time, Jessica was 10½ months old. Developmentally, she had in all likelihood achieved a specific recognition of Jan and Roberta DeBoer as "Daddy" and "Mommy" figures and had completed a period of stranger anxiety in which the approach of anyone who is "not Mother" provokes emotional upset. Jessica would have started to imitate her adoptive parents' actions and would have begun to achieve supported walking and vocalization. She would have become accustomed to the adoptive parents' routines, baby games, affectionate behaviors, and other intimate features of older infants' relationships with their parents. Jessica would have begun to display significant separation reactions when separated from the adoptive parents for even brief periods of time (Mahler et al., 1975). Still, as far as can be determined from the clinical literature, in particular the intensive studies of children in foster care performed by the Robertsons and the studies of prison nursery children by Spitz, the most likely outcome associated with removal of Jessica at age 10½ months would have been short-term distress or even reversible clinical depression, but not significant long-term harm.

The Iowa Supreme Court found for the Schmidts in September 1992, at which time Baby Jessica was 20 months old. This was perhaps the last juncture at which the child could have been removed from the adoptive parents without the threat of serious psychological damage. Developmentally, Jessica would be expected at age 20 months to have mastered walking and even running, to a degree. She would have developed rudimentary verbal communication skills and would have been speaking in short sentences. She had probably achieved a great deal of progress in toilet training and feeding skills. Intrapsychically, she would be expected at that age to have just completed a developmental phase in which the child's focus shifts dramatically away from the parents and outward to the wider world. The achievement of mobility brings a joy of discovery, and children from 1 year to 18 months (with considerable variation in this timetable among individual children) are observed to have "a love affair with the world," running free and exploring with only occasional trips back to Mommy as a secure base who can provide brief emotional refueling (Mahler et al., 1975).

A child of approximately 20 months of age is still very immature cognitively and has not achieved a high degree of what is termed "object constancy" and "object differentiation." This refers to the capacity to maintain a positively valued, cohesive inner image of the parental love object that is stable across time and well differentiated from mental representations of other individuals, even when the parent is physically unavailable. As noted by the Robertsons (1989) in their study of foster children (reviewed in Chapter 9), the younger subjects, who were below 2 years of age, accepted their foster parents without great conflicts stemming from loyalty to the absent birth parent, whose image faded after a period of time. The Robertsons speculate that if these foster children had been allowed to remain with them permanently, then eventually the memory traces of the birth parents would have merged with those of the new foster parents and the transfer would be achieved without major damage to the child's developing psychic structure.

At around 18 months or so, the child's infatuation with exploring the environment gives way to a sense of vulnerability and renewed dependence on the mother. This period of normal developmental crisis is termed the "rapprochement" subphase of development in ego psychological theory because of the child's turning toward the mother once more and ultimately establishing a relatively conflict-free relationship with her as the resolution of this period of testing and trying. The toddler tests limits behaviorally, becomes demanding, coercive, and oppositional, and manifests a desperate dependency on the mother. This subphase is experienced by many mothers as a totally unexpected burden because the child had seemed to be so free and independent during the preceding subphase. During rapprochement it is not unusual for the child to protest the mother's unavailability, even if she is only in the bathroom with the door closed. This neediness reflects an aspect of the normal psychological transformations of rapprochement whereby the child's capacity to function independently and to experience comforting and support from the mental image of the mother is weakened. This is due, in part, to the child's increasing cognitive awareness of real-world threats and of the mother's absence as the child's perception and mentation mature.

For a child to suffer the irretrievable loss of the mother during this critical subphase of rapprochement is to inflict a very heavy blow on the immature personality that will distort its development (Blanck & Blanck, 1975; Mahler et al., 1975). I agree with the testimony of Dr. Novick in the Michigan trial as to the probable effects of inflicting such a loss on Baby Jessica (see Chapter 8, Mahler et al.'s [1975] theoretical formulations). At the time of the mandated transfer of Baby Jessica to the birth parents, the child would have been well established in the rapprochement subphase, assuming that she was free of cognitive or other limitations that would have affected the dynamics discussed above. Thus, Jessica would have suffered the loss of a specific emotional tie with Roberta DeBoer, and secondarily with Jan DeBoer, during the developmental period when adequate resolution of normal conflict and instability is vital for healthy personality formation. A traumatic loss such as this tends to prevent the child from moving psychologically past this stage. It is also clear that the normal developmental drama cannot simply be picked up with a different "mother," since it is the specificity of the child's desperately dependent and ambivalent tie to the mother during this subphase that drives the process. A child who would be able to attach to a new mother figure immediately and pick up as though she were with the original parental love object would clearly have an attachment disorder of the indiscriminate type, which there is no evidence that Jessica had (Zeanah et al., 1993).

Apart from the object loss itself, there are two significant factors that would be expected to compound Jessica's trauma. The first is that the birth parents, consistent with what Dr. Clark testified to at trial, did not seem to have any realistic appreciation of the magnitude of the impact that this loss had on Jessica. In their television interview with *Dateline*, the Schmidts appeared to blame Jessica's upset on the day of the transfer on the presence of the media and of DeBoer supporters. They stated that after they left the scene of commotion that attended the handing over of the child, with weeping adoptive parents and angry supporters causing Jessica to cry, the child adjusted well for the rest of the drive. This is oddly reminiscent of Robertson's myth of the happy children's ward, wherein children's low-key state and despair following the initial phase of protest at being separated from parents was interpreted by the ward staff as the children's having "settled in." If the Schmidts deny the validity of the psychological testimony that they heard on this issue in the Michigan trial, this would seriously limit their understanding of their daughter's emotional states and needs, making it more difficult for them to achieve any possible mitigation of her suffering. One would hope that the Schmidts were sufficiently persuaded by the psychological testimony that they at least did not burden Jessica with the rigid expectation that she should behave toward them as though they had been her caretakers from birth and should refrain from any expression of distress, longing for the adoptive parents, or resisting the birth parents' authority over her.

The second troublesome factor is the Schmidts' changing of the child's name from Jessica to Anna. For a child in the midst of the disruption and disorientation of a removal from her central parental love objects, from whom she is not fully differentiated psychologically, having to respond to a name other than her own would create a further impediment to her coping with this crisis. This is a rare circumstance about which there is no empirical literature. Clinically, there is a risk that the child's "Anna" self could come to be associated with the new environment and her "Jessica" self with the traumatic removal and the previous parents who, in the child's egocentric view, had given her away perhaps because there was something intrinsically unlikable, defective, or unlovable about her. The overall effect would be to limit her capacity to form a cohesive, positively valued sense of self.

The only evidence currently available as to Jessica's reaction to the loss of her adoptive parents at age 2½ exists in the form of a videotaped interview with the Schmidts conducted by Diane Sawyer of *Dateline* (1994). Much of this tape shows Jessica as a happy, energetic 3-year-old, running around the house and playing with her baby sister, Chloe. However, the fact that Jessica was able to display such positive affect 6 months after the transfer is not inconsistent with the predictions of intrapsychic developmental harm offered above. It is only when the interview turns to the subject of "Peach Street," where the DeBoer home was located, that the viewer sees evidence of the trauma. It should be noted here that all of the interviewer's questions were approved in advance by the court-appointed therapist who was supervising Anna and that, just before the sequence about to be described, there is a break in the continuity of the tape, suggesting that something was edited out. Whether this involves some verbalization or emotional reaction of the child cannot be determined.

As the interviewer speaks to Anna about Peach Street, Daniel Schmidt cradles the child in his arms, reassuring her. Whereas the child portrayed in the initial clips from this interview is happy and apparently carefree, the child facing this line of questioning is obviously low-key and distressed. Anna turns her head away from the interviewer and remains silent after responding briefly to questions about who lived with her at the Peach Street house. The change is profound and dramatic.

Another phenomenon described by the Robertsons is touched upon in the *Dateline* story. Cara Schmidt relates to the interviewer that Anna on one occasion broke into tears upon being read a book that had been one of her favorites in her former home with the DeBoers. The birth mother states that she used this opportunity to discuss the adoptive family with Anna and that when she did this, "The flood gates opened up." This is an example of the type of sudden reawakening of the original traumatic experience by a stimulus associated with it that the Robertsons documented in children who had been separated from their parents during hospital stays or by placement into temporary foster care. The fundamental difference between those children's experience and that of Anna, however, is that while all of the children studied by the Robertsons were separated for relatively brief periods and all were told from the outset that they would be reunited with their parents, Anna was told that she was now with "Mommy" and "Daddy" and there was no indication to her that she would ever be returning to her adoptive parents.

References

Abel, G., Becker, J. V., Mittleman, M., Cunningham-Rathner, J., Rouleau, J., & Murphy, W. (1987). Self-reported sex crimes of non-incarcerated paraphiliacs. *Journal of Interpersonal Violence, 2,* 3–25.

Abidin, R. A. (1986). *Parenting Stress Index* (2nd ed.). Charlottesville, VA: Pediatric Psychology Press.

A. C. v. C. B., 113 N.M. 449, 829 P.2d 660 (1992).

Ackerman, M. J., & Kane, A. W. (1990). *How to examine psychological experts in divorce and other civil actions.* Eau Claire, WI: Professional Education Systems.

Ackerman, M. J., & Kane, A. W. (1996). *Psychological experts in divorce, personal injury, and other civil actions* (2nd ed., 1996 cumulative supplement). New York: Wiley.

Ackerman, M. J., & Kane, A. W. (1997). *Psychological experts in divorce, personal injury, and other civil actions* (2nd ed., 1997 cumulative supplement). New York: Wiley.

Adam, K. S. (1994). Suicidal behavior and attachment: A developmental model. In M. B. Sperling & W. H. Berman (Eds.), *Attachment in adults* (pp. 275–298). New York: Guilford Press.

Adam, K. S., & Adam, G. (1978). *Attachment theory and attempted suicide.* Paper presented at the 15th Annual Congress of the Royal Australian and New Zealand College of Psychiatrists, Singapore.

Adam, K. S., Bouckoms, A., & Streiner, D. (1982). Parental loss and family stability in attempted suicide. *Archives of General Psychiatry, 39,* 1081–1085.

Adopted youths are normal in self-esteem, study finds. (1994, June 23). *The New York Times,* p. A14.

Ainsworth, M. D. S., Blehar, M. C., Waters, E., & Wall, S. (1978). *Patterns of attachment: A psychological study of the Strange Situation.* Hillsdale, NJ: Erlbaum.

Ake v. Oklahoma, 470 U.S. 68, 83, 105 S. Ct. 1087, 84 L. Ed. 2d 53, 66 (1985).

American Humane Association. (1989). *Highlights of official child neglect and abuse reporting.* Denver, CO: Author.

American Psychiatric Association. (1994). *Diagnostic and statistical manual of mental disorders* (4th ed.). Washington, DC: Author.

American Psychological Association. (1992). *Ethical principles of psychologists and code of conduct.* Washington, DC: Author.

American Psychological Association. (1994). Guidelines for child custody evaluations in divorce proceedings. *American Psychologist, 49,* 677–680.

American Psychological Association. (1998). *Guidelines for psychological evaluations in child protection matters.* Washington, DC: Author.

American Psychology–Law Society. (1991). Specialty guidelines for forensic psychologists. *Law and Human Behavior, 15,* 655–665.

Anastasi, A., & Urbina, S. (1997). *Psychological testing* (7th ed.). Upper Saddle River, NJ: Prentice Hall.

Anthony, E. J. (1987). Risk, vulnerability, and resilience: An overview. In E. J. Anthony & B. J. Cohler (Eds.), *The invulnerable child* (pp. 3–48). New York: Guilford Press.

Arena v. Saphier, 201 N.J. Super. 79 App. Div. (1985).

Awad, G. A., Saunders, E., & Levene, J. (1984). A clinical study of male adolescent sex offenders. *International Journal of Offender Therapy and Comparative Criminology, 28,* 105–116.

Barth, R., & Berry, M. (1987). Outcomes of child welfare services under permanency planning. *Social Service Review, 61,* 71–90.

Beck, A. T. (1972). *Depression: Causes and treatment.* Philadelphia: University of Pennsylvania Press.

Beck, A. T., Rush, A. J., Shaw, B. F., & Emery, G. (1979). *Cognitive therapy of depression.* New York: Guilford Press.

Bender, L. (1938). *Manual for the Bender Gestalt Test.* New York: American Orthopsychiatric Association.

Black v. Gray, 540 A.2d 431 (Del. 1988).

Blanck, G., & Blanck, R. (1974). *Ego psychology: Theory and practice.* New York: Columbia University Press.

Blanck, G., & Blanck, R. (1986). *Beyond ego psychology: Developmental object relations theory.* New York: Columbia University Press.

Block, J. H., & Block, J. (1980). The role of ego-control and ego-resiliency in the organization of behavior. In W. A. Collins (Ed.), *Minnesota Symposium on Child Psychology* (Vol. 13, pp. 39–70). Hillsdale, NJ: Erlbaum.

Blos, P. (1962). *On adolescence: A psychoanalytic interpretation.* New York: Free Press.

Boll, T. J. (1978). Diagnosing brain impairment. In B. B. Wolman (Ed.), *Clinical diagnosis of mental disorders: A handbook.* New York: Plenum Press.

Bottoms v. Bottoms, 444 S.ER.2d 276 (Va. Ct. App. 1994).

Bowlby, J. (1944). Forty-four juvenile thieves: Their characteristics and home life. *International Journal of Psycho-Analysis, 25,* 19–52, 107–127.

Bowlby, J. (1953). *Child care and the growth of love.* Baltimore, MD: Penguin Books.

Bowlby, J. (1977). The making and breaking of affectional bonds: I. Etiology and psychopathology in light of attachment theory. *British Journal of Psychiatry, 130,* 201–210.

Bowlby, J. (1988). *A secure base: Parent–child attachment and healthy human development.* New York: Basic Books.

Bricklin, B. (1990). *Manual for the PASS.* Furlong, PA: Village Publishing.

Briere, J. (1992). *Child abuse trauma: Theory and treatment of the lasting effects.* Newbury Park, CA: Sage.

Briere, J., & Lanktree, C. (1992). *Further data on the Trauma Symptom Checklist for Children: Reliability, validity, and sensitivity to treatment.* Paper presented at the Conference on Responding to Child Maltreatment, San Diego, CA.

Brodzinsky, D. M., Smith, D. W., & Brodzinsky, A. B. (1998). *Children's adjustment to adoption: Developmental and clinical issues.* Thousand Oaks, CA: Sage.

Bush, M., & Goldman, H. (1982). The psychological parenting and permanency principles in child welfare: A reappraisal and critique. *American Journal of Orthopsychiatry, 52,* 223–235.

Butcher, J. N., Dahlstrom, W. G., Graham, J. R., Tellegen, A., & Kaemmer, B. (1989). *Manual for the Minnesota Multiphasic Personality Inventory–2.* Minneapolis: University of Minnesota Press.

Caban v. Mohammed, 441 U.S. 380 (1979).

Canter, M. B., Bennett, B. E., Jones, S. E., & Nagy, T. F. (1994). *Ethics for psychologists: A commentary on the APA ethics code.* Washington, DC: American Psychological Association.

Carnegie Corporation of New York. (1994). *Starting points: Meeting the needs of our youngest children.* New York: Author.

Carrol v. Otis Elevator, 896 F.2d 210.

Child Welfare League of America. (1993). *Charting the new course: Children's legislative agenda.* Washington, DC: Author.

Child Welfare League of America. (1997). *Child abuse and neglect: A look at the states from 1986 to 1995.* Washington, DC: Author.

Cicchetti, D. V. (1994). Guidelines, criteria, and rules of thumb for evaluating normed and standardized assessment instruments in psychology. *Psychological Assessment, 6,* 284–290.

Clausen, J. (1968). Perspectives in childhood socialization. In J. Clausen (Ed.), *Socialization and society.* Boston: Little, Brown.

Clifford, R. C. (1997). *Qualifying and attacking expert witnesses.* Costa Mesa, CA: James Publishing.

Colorado ex rel. S. J. C. (Colo. Sup. Ct. 1989).

Committee on Ethical Guidelines. (1991). Specialty guidelines for forensic psychologists. *Law and Human Behavior, 15,* 655–665.

Commonwealth of Massachusetts v. Louise Woodward (Mass. Sup. Ct. 1997).

Conte, J. R. (1991). The nature of sexual offenses against children. In C. R. Hollin & K. Howells (Eds.), *Clinical approaches to sex offenders and their victims.* Chichester, UK: Wiley.

Crawford, S. (1987). Lesbian families: Psychosocial stress and the family-building process. In Boston Lesbian Psychologies Collective (Eds.), *Lesbian psychologies: Explorations and challenges* (pp. 195–214). Urbana, IL: University of Illinois Press.

Dateline. (1994, March 10). *Baby Anna.* Televised report by Diane Sawyer.

Daubert v. Merrell-Dow Pharmaceuticals, Inc., 509 U.S. 579 (1993).

Davis, P. C. (1987). "There's a book out": An analysis of judicial absorption of legislative fact. *Harvard Law Review, 100,* 1539–1556.

Davis, R. D., Wenger, A., & Guzman, A. (1997). Validation of the MCMI-III. In T. Millon (Ed.), *The Millon inventories: Clinical and personality assessment* (pp. 327–359). New York: Guilford Press.

Dawes, R. M. (1994). *House of cards: Psychology and psychotherapy built on myth.* New York: Free Press.

DeMause, L. (1980). Our forebears made childhood a nightmare. In G. J. Williams & J. Money (Eds.), *Traumatic abuse and neglect of children at home.* Baltimore: Johns Hopkins University Press.

Dietrich, D. R. (1989). Early childhood parent death, psychic trauma, and object relations. In D. R. Dietrich & P. C. Shabad (Eds.), *The problem of loss and mourning* (pp. 277–335). Madison, CT: International Universities Press.

Duckworth, J. C., & Levitt, E. E. (1994). Review of the Minnesota Multiphasic Personality Inventory–2. In D. J. Keyser & R. C. Sweetland (Eds.), *Test critiques* (Vol. 10). Austin, TX: Pro-Ed.

Duquette, D. N. (1981a). The legal aspects of child abuse and neglect. In K. C. Faller (Ed.), *Social work with abused and neglected children: A manual of interdisciplinary practice.* New York: Free Press.

Duquette, D. N. (1981b). Legal roles. In K. C. Faller (Ed.), *Social work with abused and neglected children: A manual of interdisciplinary practice.* New York: Free Press.

Dyer, F. J. (1993). Scientific credibility of the expert in guardianship proceedings. *New Jersey Psychologist, 43,* 29–32.

Dyer, F. J. (1996). Scientific validity of the psychological expert witness: The end of the expert's black box. *New Jersey Psychologist, 46,* 20–22.

Dyer, F. J. (1997). Application of the Millon inventories in forensic psychology. In T. Millon (Ed.), *The Millon inventories: Clinical and personality assessment* (pp. 121–139). New York: Guilford Press.

E. I. du Pont de Nemours and Co. v. Robinson, 923 S.W.2d at 559 (Tex. 1995).

Elliott, C. D. (1990). The nature and structure of children's abilities: Evidence from the Differential Ability Scales. *Journal of Psychoeducational Assessment, 8,* 376–390.

Ellis, A. (1977). *Reason and emotion in psychotherapy.* Secaucus, NJ: Citadel Press.

Elonen, A. S., & Schwartz, E. M. (1969). A longitudinal study of emotional, social, and academic functioning of adopted children. *Child Welfare, 48,* 72–78.

Esquilin, S. C. (1995). Sexually aggressive behavior in children: Assessing significance and planning treatment. *New Jersey Psychologist, 45,* 13–15.

Everly, G. S. (1993). Psychotraumatology: A two-factor formulation of post-traumatic stress. *Integrative Physiological and Behavioral Science, 28,* 270–278.

Exner, J. E., Jr. (1993). *The Rorschach: A comprehensive system: Vol. 1. Basic foundations* (3rd ed.). New York: Wiley.

Faller, K. C. (1996). *Evaluating children suspected of having been sexually abused.* Thousand Oaks, CA: Sage.

Faller, K. C., Bowden, M. L., Jones, C. O., & Hildebrandt, H. M. (1981). Types of child abuse and neglect. In K. C. Faller (Ed.), *Social work with abused and neglected children.* New York: Free Press.

Faller, K. C., & Stone, J. B. (1981). The child welfare system. In K. C. Faller (Ed.), *Social work with abused and neglected children.* New York: Free Press.

Fanshel, D., Finch, S. J., & Grundy, J. F. (1990). *Foster children in a life course perspective.* New York: Columbia University Press.

Fein, E. (1991). Issues in foster family care: Where do we stand? *American Journal of Orthopsychiatry, 61,* 578–583.

Finkelhor, D., & Browne, A. (1985). The traumatic impact of child sexual abuse: A conceptualization. *American Journal of Orthopsychiatry, 55,* 530–541.

Fitzgibbon v. Fitzgibbon, 197 N.J. Super. 63 Ch. Div. (1984).

Fonagy, P., Target, M., Steele, M., Steele, H., Leigh, T., Levinson, A., & Kennedy, R. (1997). Morality, disruptive behavior, borderline personality disorder, crime, and their relationships to security of attachment. In L. Atkinson & K. J. Zucker (Eds.), *Attachment and psychopathology* (pp. 223–274). New York: Guilford Press.

Friedrich, W. (1990). *Psychotherapy of sexually abused children and their parents.* New York: Norton.

Frye v. United States, 54 App. D.C. 46, 293 F. 1013 (1923).

G. E. v. Joiner, 96-188 (D. Dec. 15, 1997).

Goldberg, C. (1997, November 12). Pediatric experts express doubt on au pair's defense. *The New York Times,* p. A14.

Goldstein, J., Freud, A., & Solnit, A. J. (1979). *Beyond the best interests of the child.* New York: Free Press.

Goodman-Delahunty, J. (1997). Forensic psychological expertise in the wake of *Daubert. Law and Human Behavior, 21,* 121–140.

Graham, J. R. (1987). *The MMPI: A practical guide* (2nd ed.). New York: Oxford University Press.

Grisso, T. (1986). *Evaluating competencies: Forensic assessments and instruments.* New York: Plenum Press.

H. A. C. v. D. C. C., heard in Colorado in 1979.

Hardin, M., & Lancour, R. (1996). *Early termination of parental rights: Developing appropriate statutory grounds.* Washington, DC: American Bar Association.

Harris, D. B. (1963). *Children's drawings as measures of intellectual maturity.* San Diego, Harcourt Brace Jovanovich.

Hartmann, H. (1964). *Essays in ego psychology.* New York: International Universities Press.

Heilbrun, K. (1992). The role of psychological testing in forensic assessment. *Law and Human Behavior, 16*, 257–272.

Holden, E. W., & Walker, C. E. (1985). Review of Michigan Screening Profile of Parenting. In D. J. Keyser & R. C. Sweetland (Eds.), *Test critiques* (Vol. 4). Kansas City, MO: Test Corporation of America.

Holtzman v. Knott, *In re* H.S.H.-K., 533 N.W.2d 419 Wis. (1995).

Howze, K. A. (1996). *Making differences work: Cultural context in abuse and neglect practice for judges and attorneys.* Washington, DC: American Bar Association.

Hutt, M. (1969). *The Hutt adaptation of the Bender Gestalt Test.* New York: Grune & Stratton.

In the Matter of Baby M., 109 N.J. 396, 537 A.2d 1227 (1988).

In the Matter of Guardianship of J. T. (N.J. App. Ct. 1993).

In the Matter of the Guardianship of K. H. O., A.4669-96T3 (N.J. Super. App. Div., D. Feb. 20, 1998).

In the Matter of Guardianship of K. L. F., a Minor, A-104/105 September Term, 1991 (N.J. Sup. Ct., D. June 30, 1992).

In the Matter of the Guardianship of S. C., A-1273-89T3F (N.J. App. Ct., D. Mar. 12, 1991).

In the Matter of K. L. F., 129 N.J. 32 (1992).

In re Adoption of T. M., 389 Pa. Super. 303, 566 A.2d 1256 (1989).

In re Adoption of Tammy, 416 Mass. 205 (1993).

In re Andrea, 221 Cal. App. 3d 547, 270 Cal. Rptr. 534 (1990).

In re Angel B. (Me. 1995).

In re C. C. (Neb. Sup. Ct. 1987).

In re C. P. B. and K. A. B., 641 S.W.2d 456 (Mo. Ct. App. 1982).

In re C. S. (N.D. Sup. Ct. 1988).

In re The Custody of a Minor (Mass. Sup. Jud. Ct. 1979).

In re Donald L. L. (N.Y.S. App. Div. 1992).

In re E. M. (Pa. 1993).

In re Elizabeth R., 35 Cal. App. 4th 1774, 42 Cal. Rptr. 2d 200 (1995).

In re Guynn (N.C. Ct. App. 1993).

In re J. M. (Okla. Sup. Ct. 1982).

In re J. S., 227 Neb. 251, 417 N.W.2d 147 (1987).

In re Jeffrey R. L. (W. Va. 1993).

In re Jonathan Michael D., 194 W. Va. 20, 459 S.E.2d 131 (1995).

In re Joshua O. (N.Y. App. Div. 1996).

In re Kelly (Conn. App. Ct. 1992).

In re M. M. D., 94-FS-629 (D.C. Ct. App. June 30, 1995).

In re Petition of K. M. and D. M. to Adopt Olivia M., 653 N.E.2d 888 (Ill. App. Ct. 1995).

In re Romance M., 622 A.2d 1047 (Conn. App. Ct. 1993).

In re Scott (N.C. Ct. App. 1989).

In re Waggoner (Idaho, Canyon Co. Dist. Ct., Nov. 27, 1979).

In re Welfare of A. J. R. (Wash. Ct. App. 1995).

Jacobson, E. (1964). *The self and the object world.* New York: International Universities Press.

Jacobson, E. (1971). *Studies in depression.* New York: International Universities Press.

James, B. (1994). *Handbook for treatment of attachment–trauma problems in children.* New York: Lexington Books.

Johns, J. L., & Van Leirsburg, P. (1994). Review of the Slosson Intelligence Test—Revised. *Test critiques* (Vol. 10, pp. 672–679). Kansas City, MO: Test Corporation of America.

Johnson, J. H., Floyd, B. J., & Isleib, R. (1983). *Parental stress, empathy, and dimensions of adult temperaments as predictors of child abuse and neglect.* J. Hillis Miller Mental Health Center, University of Florida.

Johnson, M. B. (1996). Examining risks to children in the context of parental rights termination proceedings. *New York University Review of Law and Social Change, 22,* 397–424.

Jones, M. A. (1983). *A second chance for families—five years later: Follow-up of a program to prevent foster care.* New York: Child Welfare League of America.

Jones, M. A., & Moses, B. (1984). *West Virginia's former foster children: Their experience in care and their lives as young adults.* New York: Child Welfare League of America.

K. N. v. State, 856 P.2d 468 (Alaska 1993).

Kamphaus, R. W. (1993). *Clinical assessment of children's intelligence.* Boston: Allyn & Bacon.

Kates, W. G., Johnson, R. L., Rader, M. W., & Strieder, F. H.(1991). Whose child is this?: Assessment and treatment of children in foster care. *American Journal of Orthopsychiatry, 61,* 584–591.

Koppitz, E. M. (1964). *The Bender Gestalt Test for young children.* Orlando, FL: Grune & Stratton.

Kotsopoulos, S., Cote, A., Joseph, L., Pentland, M., Chryssoula, S., Sheahan, P., & Oke, L. (1988). Psychiatric disorders in adopted children. *American Journal of Orthopsychiatry, 58,* 608–612.

Kumho Tire v. Carmichael, 97-1709, 131 F.3d 1433, *rev'd*, D. Mar. 23, 1999).

Kusserow, R. (1990, April 5). Testimony of Richard Kusserow, Inspector General of the U.S. Department of Health and Human Services before the Human Resources Subcommittee of the Committee on Ways and Means, House of Representatives.

Lacks, P. (1984). *Bender Gestalt screening for brain dysfunction.* New York: Wiley.

Lauderdale County Department of Human Services v. T. H. G., 90–CA-0713 (Miss. 1992).

Lawrence, N. (1993, October). The untold story of Baby Jessica's heartache. *Midwest Today.*

Lee, J. S., & Twaite, J. A. (1997). Open adoption and adoptive mothers: Attitudes toward birth mothers, adopted children, and parenting. *American Journal of Orthopsychiatry, 67,* 576–584.

LeFreniere, P., & Sroufe, L. A. (1985). Profiles of peer competence in the preschool: Interrelations between measures, influence of social ecology, and relation to attachment history. *Developmental Psychology, 21,* 58–68.

Lincoln, J. H. (1976). Model statute for termination of parental rights. *Juvenile Justice, 27,* 4, 3–8.

Louisiana ex rel. Townzen (La. Ct. App. 1988).

M. v. K., 186 N.J. Super. 363 Ch. Div. (1982).

Mahler, M., Pine, F., & Bergman, A. (1975). *The psychological birth of the human infant: Symbiosis and individuation.* New York: Basic Books.

Main, M., & Hesse, E. (1990). Parents' unresolved traumatic experiences are related to infant disorganized status: Is frightened and/or frightening parental behavior the linking mechanism? In M. T. Greenberg, D. Cicchetti, & E. M. Cummings (Eds.), *Attachment in the preschool years* (pp. 161–184). Chicago: University of Chicago Press.

Marshall, W. L., Hudson, S. M., & Hodkinson, S. (1993). The importance of attachment bonds in the development of juvenile sex offending. In H. E. Barbaree, W. L. Marshall, & S. M. Hudson (Eds.), *The juvenile sex offender* (pp. 164–181). New York: Guilford Press.

Mash, E. J., Johnston, C., & Kovitz, K. (1983). A comparison of the mother–child interactions of physically abused and nonabused children during play and task situations. *Journal of Clinical Child Psychology, 12,* 337–346.

Masten, A. S., & Coatsworth, J. D. (1998). The development of competence in favorable and unfavorable environments: Lessons from research on successful children. *American Psychologist, 53,* 205–220.

Matter of Appeal in Cochise County Juvenile Action, 5666-J 133 Ariz. 157, 650 P.2d 459 (1982).

Matter of Guardianship of J. C., 129 N.J. 1, 29 (1992).

Matter of Loretta Lynn W., 149 A.D.2d 928, 540 N.Y.S. 2d 62 (1989).

McCann, J. T. (1997). *Malingering and deception in adolescents: Assessing credibility in clinical and forensic settings.* Washington, DC: American Psychological Association.

McCann, J. T. (1998). Defending the Rorschach in court: An analysis of admissibility using legal and professional standards. *Journal of Personality Assessment, 70,* 125–144.

McCann, J. T., & Dyer, F. J. (1996). *Forensic asessment with the Millon Inventories.* New York: Guilford Press.

McDermott, P. A., Fantuzzo, J. W., & Glutting, J. J. (1990). Just say no to subtest analysis: A critique on Wechsler theory and practice. *Journal of Psychoeducational Assessment, 8,* 290–302.

Md. Fam. Code 5-313 (1996).

Mech, E. V. (1988). Preparing foster adolescents for self-support: A new challenge for child welfare services. *Child Welfare, 67,* 487–496.

Meloy, J. R. (1992). *Violent attachments.* Northvale, NJ: Jason Aronson.

Melton, G. B., Petrila, J., Poythress, N. G., & Slobogin, C. (1987). *Psychological evaluations for the courts: A handbook for mental health professionals and lawyers.* New York: Guilford Press.

Metro-Dade Department of Youth and Family Development. (1989). *Intensive family services program: Statistical information, 1988–1989.* Miami: Author.

Meyer, G. J. (1997a). Assessing reliability: Critical corrections for a critical examination of the Rorschach Comprehensive System. *Psychological Assessment, 9,* 480–489.

Meyer, G. J. (1997b). Thinking clearly about reliability: More critical corrections regarding the Rorschach Comprehensive System. *Psychological Assessment, 9,* 495–498.

Milchman, M. S. (1996). Breaking bonds to psychological parents in termination of parental rights cases. *New Jersey Lawyer, 175,* 29–32, 44.

Millon, T. (1969). *Modern psychopathology: A biosocial approach to maladaptive learning and functioning.* Philadelphia: Saunders.

Millon, T. (1987). *Manual for the Millon Clinical Multiaxial Inventory–II.* Minneapolis: NCS Assessments.

Millon, T. (1994). *Manual for the Millon Clinical Multiaxial Inventory–III.* Minneapolis: NCS Assessments.

Millon, T., & Davis, R. (1996). *Disorders of personality: DSM-IV and beyond.* New York: Wiley.

Milner, J. S. (1986). *The Child Abuse Potential Inventory Manual* (2nd ed.). DeKalb, IL: Psytec.

Milner, J. S. (1990). *An interpretive manual for the Child Abuse Potential Inventory.* DeKalb, IL: Psytec.

Milner, J. S. (1995). Physical child abuse assessment: Perpetrator evaluation. In J. C. Campbell (Ed.), *Assessing dangerousness.* Thousand Oaks, CA: Sage.

M. L. B. v. S. L. J. (U.S. S. Ct. 1996).

Moore, B. E., & Fine, B. D. (1968). *A glossary of psychoanalytic terms.* New York: American Psychoanalytic Association.

Moore v. Ashland Chemical, Inc., 95-20492, 5th Cir. (Oct. 20, 1997).

Myers, J. E. B. (1992). *Evidence in child abuse and neglect* (2nd ed.). New York: Wiley.

Myers, J. E. B. (1997). *Evidence in child abuse and neglect cases* (3rd ed.). New York: Wiley.

Naglieri, J. A. (1988). *Draw a person: A quantitative scoring system manual.* San Antonio, TX: Psychological Corporation.

National Association of Black Social Workers. (1972). *Position paper developed from workshops concerning transracial adoption.* Unpublished paper distributed at the Third North American Conference on Adoptable Children, St. Louis.

National Association of Black Social Workers. (1994). *Position statement: Preserving African-American families.* Detroit: Author.

Neal, T. (1989). *Termination of parental rights.* State Legislative Report 14, No. 7. Denver, CO: National Conference of State Legislatures.

Nebraska v. D. S. (Neb. Sup. Ct. 1990).

Nebraska v. M. M. (Neb. Sup. Ct. 1988).

Needy who lose parental rights gain in top court. (1996, December 17). *The New York Times,* pp. A1, A22.

New Jersey Board of Psychological Examiners. (1993). *Specialty guidelines for psychologists in custody/visitation evaluations.* Trenton, NJ: Author.

New Jersey Division of Youth and Family Services v. A. W., 103, N.J. 591, 608–12 (1986).

Nitti, T. A. (1994). Stepping back from the psychological parenting theory: A comment on In re J.C. *Rutgers University Law Review, 46,* 1003.

N. J. Assembly (1996a) No. 2336, p. 2 at 47.

N. J. Assembly (1996b) No. 2336, p. 3 at 14.

North American Council on Adoptable Children. (1990). *The adoption assistance and child welfare act of 1980 (Public Law 96-272): The first ten years.* St. Paul, MN: Author.

Ohio Rev. Code Ann., 2151 414 (1996).

Olweus, D. (1980). Bullying among school boys. In R. Barnan (Ed.), *Child and violence.* Stockholm: Academic Literature.

Pancake, V. R. (1985). *Continuity between mother–infant attachment and ongoing dyadic peer relationships in preschool.* Paper presented at the biennial meeting of the Society for Research in Child Development, Toronto.

Parker, G. (1994). Parental bonding and depressive disorders. In M. B. Sperling & W. H. Berman (Eds.), *Attachment in adults* (pp. 299–312). New York: Guilford Press.

Patterson, C. J. (1995). *Summary of research findings in lesbian and gay parenting: A resource for psychologists.* Washington, DC: American Psychological Association.

Patterson, R. J., & Moran, G. (1988). Attachment theory, personality development, and psychotherapy. *Clinical Psychology Review, 8,* 611–636.

Pedder, J. (1976). Attachment and new beginning. *International Review of Psycho-analysis, 3,* 491–497.

People v. Mendible (1992, p. 562).

People v. Stanciel, 153 Ill. 2d 218, 606 N.E.2d 1201 (1992).

People v. Steinberg, 79 N.Y. 2d 673, 681, 595 N.E.2d 845, 847, 584 N.Y.S. 2d, 770, 772 (1992).

Perrin, G. I., & Sales, B. D. (1994). Forensic standards in the American Psychological Association's new ethics code. *Professional Psychology: Research and Practice, 25,* 376–381.

Perry, B. D. (1993). Medicine and psychotherapy: Neurodevelopment and the neurophysiology of trauma. *The Advisor, 6,* 1–18.

Pope, K. S., Butcher, J. M., & Seelen, J. (1993). *The MMPI, MMPI-2, and MMPI-A in court: A practical guide for expert witnesses and attorneys.* Washington, DC: American Psychological Association.

Quinton, D., & Rutter, M. (1985). Parenting behaviour of mothers raised in care. In A. R. Nicol (Ed.), *Longitudinal studies in child psychology and psychiatry: Practical lessons from research experience* (pp. 157–261). New York: Wiley.

Robertson, J., & Robertson, J. (1989). *Separation and the very young.* London: Free Association Books.

Rochlin, G. (1953). Loss and restitution. *Psychoanalytic Study of the Child, 8,* 288–309.

Rodriguez, C. M., & Murphy, L. E. (1997). Parenting stress and abuse potential in mothers of children with developmental disabilities. *Child Maltreatment, 2,* 245–251.

Rosenberg, D. (1984). *The quality and content of preschool fantasy play: Correlates in concurrent social/personality function and early mother–child attachment relationships.* Unpublished doctoral dissertation, University of Minnesota.

Rosenberg, E. B., & Horner, T. M. (1991). Birth parent romances and identity formation in adopted children. *American Journal of Orthopsychiatry, 61,* 70–77.

Rothbard, J. C., & Shaver, P. R. (1994). Continuity of attachment across the life span. In M. B. Sperling & W. H. Berman (Eds.), *Attachment in adults* (pp. 31–71). New York: Guilford Press.

Rubanik v. Witco Chemical Corp., 125 N.J.421, 593 A.2d 733 (1991).

Rutter, M. (1971). Parent–child separation: Psychological effects on the children. *Journal of Child Psychology and Psychiatry, 12,* 233–260.

Rutter, M. (1979). Maternal deprivation, 1972–1978: New findings, new concepts, new approaches. *Child Development, 50,* 283–305.

Rutter, M., Quinton, D., & Liddle, C. (1983). Parenting in two generations: Looking backwards and looking forwards. In N. Madge (Ed.), *Families at risk* (pp. 60–98). London: Heineman.

Sameroff, A. J., & Emde, R. N. (Eds.). (1989). *Relationship disturbances in early childhood: A developmental approach.* New York: Basic Books.

Santosky v. Kramer, 455 U.S. 745 (1982).

Sasserath, V., Witt, P. H., & Weitz, E. (1988). Assessment of parent–child bonding: Legal context. *New Jersey Psychologist, 38,* 13–15.

Saunders, B. E. (1997). Medical and mental health professionals as experts in legal cases. In P. Stern (Ed.), *Preparing and presenting expert testimony in child abuse litigation: A guide for expert witnesses and attorneys.* Thousand Oaks, CA: Sage.

Saunders, E., Awad, G. A., & White, G. (1986). Male adolescent sex offenders: The offenders and the offense. *Canadian Journal of Psychiatry, 31,* 542–549.

Scott, W. J. (1980). Attachment and child abuse: A study of social history indicators among mothers of abused children. In G. J. Williams & J. Money (Eds.), *Traumatic abuse and neglect of children at home.* Baltimore: Johns Hopkins University Press.

Select Committee on Children, Youth, and Families. (1989). *No place to call home: Discarded children in America.* Washington, DC: U.S. House of Representatives.

Shapiro, D. (1984). *Psychological evaluation and expert testimony.* New York: Van Nostrand Reinhold.

Singer, L. M., Brodzinsky, D. M., Ramsay, D., Steir, M., & Waters, E. (1985). Mother–infant attachment in adoptive families. *Child Development, 56,* 1543–1551.

Snyder v. Scheerer (W. Va. 1993).

Sparrow, S. S., Balla, D. A., & Cicchetti, D. V. (1984). *Vineland Adaptive Behav-*

ior Scales: Interview Edition Survey Form Manual. Circle Pines, MN: American Guidance Service.

Sperling, M. B., & Berman, W. H. (1994). The structure and function of adult attachment. In M. B. Sperling & W. H. Berman (Eds.), *Attachment in adults* (pp. 3–28). New York: Guilford Press.

Spitz, R. A. (1945). Hospitalism: An inquiry into the genesis of psychiatric conditions in early childhood. *Psychoanalytic Study of the Child, 1.*

Spitz, R. A. (1946). Anaclitic depression: An inquiry into the genesis of psychiatric conditions in early childhood II. *Psychoanalytic Study of the Child, 2.*

Spitz, R. A. (1965). *The first year of life.* New York: International Universities Press.

Sroufe, L. A. (1983). Infant–caregiver attachment and adaptation in the preschool: The roots of competence and maladaptations. In M. Perlmutter (Ed.), *Development of cognition, affect, and social relations* (pp. 41–81). Hillsdale, NJ: Erlbaum.

Stanley v. State of Illinois, 405 U.S. 645 (1972).

State clears adoption by gay couples. (1997, December 18). *The Star Ledger,* p. 1.

Stern, P. (1997). *Preparing and presenting expert testimony in child abuse litigation: A guide for expert witnesses and attorneys.* Thousand Oaks, CA: Sage.

Stone v. Daviess County Division of Children & Family Services (Ind. Ct. App 1995).

Swan, R. (1998). Religion-based medical neglect and corporal punishment must not be tolerated. *APSAC Advisor, 11,* 2–3.

Tasker, F. L., & Golombok, S. (1995). Adults raised as children in lesbian families. *American Journal of Orthopsychiatry, 65,* 203–215.

Tasker, F. L., & Golombok, S. (1997). *Growing up in a lesbian family: Effects on child development.* New York: Guilford Press.

Tennant, C., Hurry, J., & Bebbington, P. (1982). The relation of childhood separation experiences to adult depressive and anxiety states. *British Journal of Psychiatry, 141,* 475–482.

Tizard, B. (1977). *Adoption: A second chance.* London: Open Books.

Tizard, B., & Hodges, J. (1978). The effect of early institutional rearing on the development of eight-year-old children. *Journal of Child Psychology and Psychiatry, 19,* 99–118.

Tizard, B., & Joseph, A. (1970). Cognitive development of young children in residential care: A study of children aged 24 months. *Journal of Child Psychology and Psychiatry, 11,* 177–186.

Tizard, B., & Rees, J. (1974). A comparison of the effects of adoption, restoration to the natural mother, and continued institutionalization on the cognitive development of four-year-old children. *Journal of Child Psychology and Psychiatry, 16,* 61–73.

Tizard, B., & Rees, J. (1975). The effect of early institutional rearing on the behavior problems and affectional relationships of four-year-old children. *Journal of Child Psychology and Psychiatry, 16,* 61–74.

Tizard, J., & Tizard, B. (1971). The social development of two-year-old children in residential nurseries. In H. E. Schaffer (Ed.), *The origins of human social relations.* London: Academic Press.

Triseliotis, J., & Russell, J. (1984). *Hard to place.* Exeter NH: Heinemann Educational Books.

Troy, M., & Sroufe, L. A. (1987). Victimization among preschoolers: The role of attachment relationships history. *Journal of the American Academy of Child and Adolescent Psychiatry, 26,* 166–172.

U.S. v. Rincon, 28 F.3d 921 (1994).

Vroegh, K. S. (1997). Transracial adoptees: Developmental status after 17 years. *American Journal of Orthopsychiatry, 67,* 568–575.

Wald, M., Carlsmith, C. M., & Leiderman, P. H. (1988). *Protecting abused and neglected children.* Palo Alto, CA: Stanford University Press.

Weber, C. A., Meloy, J. R., & Gacono, C. B. (1992). A Rorschach study of attachment and anxiety in inpatient conduct-disordered and dysthymic adolescents. *Journal of Personality Assessment, 58,* 16–26.

Wechsler, D. (1974). *Manual for the Wechsler Intelligence Scale for Children—Revised.* New York: Psychological Corporation.

Wechsler, D. (1981). *Manual for the Wechsler Adult Intelligence Scale—Revised.* New York: Psychological Corporation.

Weiner, I. B. (1996). Some observations on the validity of the Rorschach inkblot method. *Psychological Assessment, 8,* 206–213.

West, M., & Keller, A. (1994). Psychotherapy strategies for insecure attachment in personality disorders. In M. B. Sperling & W. H. Berman (Eds.), *Attachment in adults* (pp. 313–330). New York: Guilford Press.

West Virginia Department of Health v. Doris S., 475 S.E.2d 865, 878 (W. Va. 1996).

Whitten, M. R. (1994). Assessment of attachment in traumatized children. In B. James (Ed.), *Handbook for treatment of attachment trauma problems in children.* New York: Lexington Books.

Wilkerson, G., & Brown, F. (1998). Robinson puts Texas-sized spin on *Daubert. Testifying Expert, 6,* 6–7.

Williams, G. J. (1980). Editor's introduction. In G. J. Williams & J. Money (Eds.), *Traumatic abuse and neglect of children at home.* Baltimore: Johns Hopkins University Press.

Witt, P. H., & Dyer, F. J. (1997, Winter). Juvenile transfer cases: Risk assessment and risk management. *Journal of Psychiatry and Law,* 581–614.

Wolfenstein, M. (1969). Loss, rage, and repetition. *Psychoanalytic Study of the Child, 24,* 432–460.

Wood, J. M., Nezworski, M. T., & Stejskal, W. J. (1996). The Comprehensive System for the Rorschach: A critical examination. *Psychological Science, 7,* 3–10.

Wood, J. M., Nezworski, M. T., & Stejskal, W. J. (1997). The reliability of the comprehensive system for the Rorschach: A comment in Meyer (1997). *Psychological Assessment, 9,* 490–494.

Woodcock, R., & Johnson, M. B. (1977). *Manual for the Woodcock–Johnson Psycho-Educational Battery.* Allen, TX: DLM Teaching Resources.

Woodcock, R., & Johnson, M. B. (1990). *Manual for the Woodcock–Johnson Psycho-Educational Battery—Revised.* Allen, TX: DLM Teaching Resources.

Wright, J. L. (1980). Sicker or slicker? In G. J. Williams & J. Money (Eds.), *Traumatic abuse and neglect of children at home.* Baltimore: Johns Hopkins University Press.

Wulach, J. (1991). *The law and mental health professionals New Jersey.* Washington, DC: American Psychological Association.

Wulach, J. (1998). *The law and mental health professionals New Jersey* (2nd ed.). Washington, DC: American Psychological Association.

Zachary, R. A. (1990). Wechsler's intelligence scales: Theoretical and practical considerations. *Journal of Psychoeducational Assessment, 8,* 276–289.

Zeanah, C. H., Mammen, O. K., & Lieberman, A. F. (1993). Disorders of attachment. In C. H. Zeanah (Ed.), *Handbook of infant mental health* (pp. 332–349). New York: Guilford Press.

Index